Measuring Self-Concept Across the Life Span

Measurement and Instrumentation in Psychology

Measuring Self-Concept Across the Life Span: Issues and Instrumentation
  Barbara M. Byrne

Psychological Assessment in Medical Rehabilitation
  Laura A. Cushman & Marcia J. Scherer, Editors

Measuring Self-Concept Across the Life Span

Issues and Instrumentation

Barbara M. Byrne

American Psychological Association, Washington DC

First printing April 1996
Second printing September 1996

Published by the
American Psychological Association
750 First Street, NE
Washington, DC 20002

Copies may be ordered from
APA Order Department
P.O. Box 2710
Hyattsville, MD 20784

In the UK and Europe, copies may be ordered from
American Psychological Association
3 Henrietta Street
Covent Garden, London
WC2E 8LU England

This book was typeset in Futura and New Baskerville by Easton Publishing Services, Inc., Easton, MD

Printer: Data Reproductions Corporation, Rochester Hills, MI
Cover designer: Grafik Communications, Ltd., Alexandria, VA
Technical/production editors: Kathryn Lynch and Michele W. Kelliher

Library of Congress Cataloging-in-Publication Data
Byrne, Barbara M.
    Measuring self-concept across the life span : issues and instrumentation / Barbara M. Byrne.
       p.   cm.—(Measurement and instrumentation in psychology)
    Includes bibliographical references and index.
    ISBN 1-55798-332-1 (acid-free paper).—ISBN 1-55798-346-1 (soft cover : acid-free paper)
    1. Self-perception—Testing.   2. Self-perception—Testing—Evaluation.
I. Title. II. Series.
BF697.5.S43B97   1996
155.2'8—dc20

                                    95-45591
                                    CIP

British Library Cataloguing-in-Publication Data
A CIP record is available from the British Library

Printed in the United States of America

To Alex
and to Mom and Dad

Contents

Preface

Twenty years have passed since the two classic reviews by Wylie (1974) and Shavelson, Hubner, and Stanton (1976) first brought to light the growing proliferation of self-concept instruments. Not only did most of these measures lack any firm evidence of the reliability and validity of their scores, but a large percentage of them were developed solely for the purpose of a single study. This imprecision, coupled with the plethora of available instruments, virtually precluded the possibility of any generalization across studies. In an attempt to capture the extreme magnitude of the problem, Shavelson et al. (1976) proclaimed that "the number of different measurement techniques is increasing as rapidly as the number of self-concept studies" (p. 409). Now, two decades later, the proliferation continues. In contrast to the earlier period, however, both the development and testing of self-concept measures tend to be more theoretically and methodologically based, as researchers heed the caveats extended by Wylie and Shavelson et al.

Indeed, it was this ever expanding reservoir of self-concept measures that led me to the writing of this book. For a number of years now, I have had a compelling urge to find out exactly what was out there in the world of self-concept instrumentation. Unfortunately, this desire was always quashed in favor of other commitments demanding more immediate attention; nonetheless, my enthusiasm and motivation for the quest never waned. Finally, no longer able to suppress my intense curiosity, I decided that the time had come—an update of my knowledge of existing self-concept measures was long overdue. So the search and writing began.

Initially, my idea was only to structure a sourcebook of self-concept measures, which I believed would be welcomed by researchers interested in the selection of instruments that were both appropriate and psychometrically sound. However, as is so often the case in ventures of this sort, the project grew like Topsy, gradually taking on increasingly larger proportions. As a consequence, the present book represents a confluence of important theoretical, methodological, and practical considerations in the measurement of self-concept. I am hopeful that researchers and practitioners will find it to be a valuable resource in their search for suitable self-concept measures for use with a diversity of populations across the life span.

From an academic perspective, I wish to thank Richard J. Shavelson, Ruth C. Wylie, and Herbert W. Marsh for their seminal and stimulating works in the area of self-concept; they have been both my inspiration and my mainstay in my own self-concept research.

From a more personal perspective, I wish to thank the many people and organizations who have been instrumental in helping me to complete this book. I am truly grateful to each of them for their various contributions. I wish, first of all, to express my thanks to Richard J. Shavelson (Stanford University) for writing the paper that initially piqued my interest in the area of self-concept research (Shavelson et al., 1976). This paper, together with another (Shavelson & Stuart, 1981), provided the cornerstone for both my doctoral thesis and all subsequent work related to self-concept measurement. I consider myself fortunate, indeed, in having had Rich as a mentor, colleague, and friend over the ensuing years.

I am truly indebted to Darlene Worth Gavin (University of Ottawa) for her invaluable services as my research assistant. Without a doubt, she has to be the crème de la crème of research assistants: superorganized, efficient, thorough, and fast! Without Darlene's assistance, this book would never have seen the light of day! I am also very grateful to Ruth C. Wylie, Walter P. Vispoel (The University of Iowa), and my developmental editor, Peggy Schlegel, for their thorough reading of, and valuable and insightful comments related to, drafts of the manuscript. Finally, I wish to thank Ron Hambleton (University of Massachusetts) for providing feedback regarding my discussion of adequate test translation.

I also wish to thank the many individuals and organization representatives who sent me information and materials pertinent to the various instruments. For forwarding copies of self-concept measures, along with accompanying documentation, my thanks are extended to the following authors: Stephen L. Franzoi (Marquette University), Susan Harter (University of Denver), John Hattie (University of North Carolina), René L'Ecuyer (University of Sherbrooke), Herbert W. Marsh (University of Western Sydney), Neil Oblowitz (chartered psychologist), William M. Reynolds (University of British Columbia), and Walter P. Vispoel (The University of Iowa). Likewise, thanks are extended to the following organizations: American Guidance Service; EDITS Publishers; Office of Health Promotion—Northern Illinois University; PAR Psychological Assessment Resources, Inc.; Pro-Ed Publishers, Inc.; the Stoelting Company; and Western Psychological Services. In addition, I am most grateful for publication reprints and prepublication manuscripts sent to me by the following authors in their efforts to keep me abreast of recent findings from tests of their related instruments: Bruce A. Bracken (University of Memphis), James Chapman (Massey University), Kenneth R. Fox (University of Exeter), Stephen L. Franzoi (Marquette University), Jack Joseph (school psychologist), Herbert W. Marsh (University of Western Sydney), William B. Michael (University of Southern California), and Walter P. Vispoel (The University of Iowa).

Finally, I wish once again to thank my husband, Alex, for his continued support, patience, and understanding—particularly as they relate to my penchant for finding myself involved in yet another seemingly never ending project! Last but not least, I am still happy to have had the company of my yellow Lab, Amy, a constant companion throughout the writing of each of my books. I am certain that her demands for a run from time to time have helped me to maintain at least some modicum of sanity.

Introduction

In their state-of-the-art review of self-concept research, Shavelson, Hubner, and Stanton (1976) reported that most research up to that point had been of a substantive nature, with scant attention paid to methodological issues. Of these issues, two are particularly relevant to self-concept measurement. First, the proliferation of self-concept instruments over the previous decade had, to a large extent, been developed solely to address questions specific to their particular research study; most were poorly described and difficult to obtain, thereby denying any opportunity for replication. Second, most early studies considered the structure of self-concept to be unidimensional and used assessment instruments that were designed to measure general (i.e., global) self-concept. Given that the preponderance of this research addressed substantive issues related to students' perceptions of self within an academic framework, it is not surprising that findings were inconsistent, confounded, and ambiguous (for reviews, see Byrne, 1984; Hansford & Hattie, 1982; Shavelson et al., 1976; West, Fish, & Stevens, 1980; Wylie, 1974).

In response to Shavelson et al.'s (1976) call for critically needed construct validation research in the area of self-concept, there has since been a growing number of studies that have addressed issues related to the structure and measurement of the construct. This work has been fruitful in yielding a literature that is rich in methodological, as well as substantive, information bearing on the study of self-concept. Perhaps the most important finding to emerge from these endeavors is the generally unanimous agreement that self-concept is a multidimensional construct. Furthermore, as researchers delve deeper into the structure of self-concept, it is becoming clear that many of its facets (e.g., academic, physical, and social) are also multifaceted. That the inculcation of this important finding has precipitated other changes in the direction of self-concept research is reflected in the literature in at least two ways: (a) Most, if not all, newly developed self-concept instruments are designed to measure multiple facets of the construct, and (b) increasingly more substantive self-concept research is being designed to take these multiple facets into account.

Purposes and Basic Rationale of the Book

In writing the present book, I was guided by four major aims. The first of these focused on my wish to provide readers with a current source of psychometrically sound self-concept measures applicable to populations across the life span and within the context of particular exceptionalities. As such, this volume addresses several limitations associated with other published summaries of self-concept measures. First, earlier reviews are now seriously out-of-date (e.g., Crandall, 1973; Walker, 1973; Wells & Marwell, 1976; Wylie, 1974, 1979). Second, more recent self-concept volumes have limited their review to only a few instruments (Blascovich & Tomaka, 1991; Wylie, 1989) or limited their selection to a particular population (Breytspraak & George, 1982; Hughes, 1984). Finally, to the best of my knowledge, there is no available reference source that either reviews self-concept measures appropriate for use with specific special populations (e.g., persons with mental or physical handicaps) or documents construct validity research in support of the use of a self-concept measure with particular special populations, albeit the instrument was originally developed for use with a nonspecial population.

Accordingly, the present book includes self-concept instruments designed for use with populations at various stages of the life span, as well as particular special populations. In addition, where construct validity has provided evidence of the valid use of an instrument across populations, including special populations, this has been duly noted. As outlined in the following in more detail, each instrument is fully described in terms of its use, scaling, administration, psychometric properties, and source availability; at least one sample item is illustrated for each.

A second aim of this book was to sketch a comprehensive summary of the present status of empirically testable theories of self-concept. As the reader will readily note, the hierarchical model of self-concept, originally proposed by Shavelson et al. (1976), has stimulated the lion's share of construct validity research bearing on both the structure and measurement of self-concept. As a consequence, the reader may be left with the impression that the Shavelson et al. model has received a disproportionate amount of recognition within the pages of this book. Although, admittedly, this model remains dominant throughout the book, the explanation can be related to three important factors. First, virtually all construct validity research designed to test the hypothesized structure of self-concept has been based either on the original Shavelson et al. model or on its later revisions. Second, the most rigorous and thoroughly conducted construct validity research bearing on tests of the hypothesized structure of a measuring instrument has comprised measures whose structure evolved from the theoretical tenets of the Shavelson et al. model. Finally, many of the recently developed measures of self-concept are theoretically grounded in the Shavelson et al. model.

A third aim of this book was to combine, into a single volume, an information sourcebook of sound self-concept measures appropriate for use across the life span and a summary of basic conceptual and psychometric issues associated with self-concept measurement. To the best of my knowledge, no book of this nature yet exists. Having experienced frustration with the need to consult several sources to formulate a total conceptualization of a particular instrument, I am hopeful that readers will find this information helpful in their own research and practical application.

The final aim of the book was to provide readers with a substantial list of references on construct validity research that is related both to the self-concept measures reviewed and to the theoretical structure of the self-concept construct itself. This information should be helpful in selecting the most appropriate instrument for a particular research or practical application purpose. It can also serve as a valuable springboard from which to build on existing construct validity work.

How the Book Can Be Useful

This book should be useful to a wide variety of readers. Although primarily written to assist researchers and practitioners in the selection and acquisition of psychometrically sound and appropriate self-concept instruments, it can also serve many other beneficial purposes. First, for researchers interested in either substantive or methodological aspects of self-concept, I present a comprehensive and current review of the construct validity literature bearing on seven empirically testable models of self-concept (chapter 1). Second, for practitioners who may not be familiar with the basic concepts of reliability and validity, chapter 2 should be helpful in their evaluation of particular self-concept measures. Third, for researchers and practitioners considering the use of computerized self-concept measures, my review of the various advantages and disadvantages of this approach (chapter 9) may be helpful. This section should also be of interest to those either developing computerized self-concept measures or adapting established measures for computerized administrative use. Finally, for graduate students who have an interest in self-concept research, but who may not as yet have determined an innovative topic on which to build their thesis, my review of three newly constructed instruments, two unique methodological approaches to measuring self-concept, and the notion of possible selves (chapter 9) may provide the stimulus needed to structure important construct validity or substantive work in this area.

Clarification of Concepts and Instrumentation Used in the Book

It is important that the reader be fully informed regarding two notable aspects of this book. One factor relates to my use of the term *general self-concept*; the other relates to the fact that all but one instrument (see chapter 7) described in this volume represents a self-report format. The term *general self-concept,* as used throughout this book, can be regarded as synonymous with the idea of a global sense of self-worth; it is not meant to imply some combination of various components of self-concept.

Relatedly, my discussion of conceptual issues in chapter 1 identifies two basic philosophical approaches to the measurement of general self-concept and illustrates how its scores are determined in both instances; measuring instruments specific to each approach are identified at various points throughout the book. One perspective argues for a general self-concept construct that exists as a separate entity; instruments originating in this approach tap the construct by means of items that constitute a separate general self-concept subscale. The Self-Perception Profile for Children (Harter, 1985b) is one example of an instrument designed around this conceptual perspective. The second perspective supports the notion that general self-concept, albeit a unitary construct, is composed of overlapping facets of information. As such, items on a measuring instrument tap different content areas, each of which is given equal weight; item scores are then summed to yield an overall general self-concept score. The Piers–Harris Children's Self-Concept Scale (Piers, 1984) exemplifies this perspective.

The fact that all but one self-concept measure represent self-report scales also calls for explication. Indeed, it was my original intent to review all self-concept instruments, regardless of their formulation as self-report, interview, rating (by others), projective, or other assessment techniques. However, in my review of both the literature and other referential sources, it soon became clear that this was an overly optimistic goal. For example, even within the parameters of my inclusion/exclusion criteria described in chapter 3, the number of self-concept measures eligible for review was staggering. The fact that a total of 82 self-report measures alone were reviewed for the present volume provides at least a flavor of the massiveness of the entire instrument pool. From my initial review of the literature, in keeping with Wylie's (1989) observation, it also became evident that most published construct validity and other psychometric research had been conducted for self-report measures of self-concept. Because of my resolve to provide readers with a comprehensive review of all selected measures of self-concept, both of these factors, tempered by the reality of space limitations, bore importantly on my decision to limit the present volume to self-report measures. Thus, a comprehensive review of other approaches to self-concept, similar to the one presented here for self-reports, must remain a task for future research.

In the light of the historical and ongoing debate regarding the use of self-reports in tapping perceptions of self (for a review of advantages and disadvantages, see, e.g., Brinthaupt & Erwin, 1992), a note in support of this methodological approach would appear to be in order. Typically, opponents of self-reports have argued for the higher validity of alternative forms of measurement (e.g., teacher ratings and behavioral observations) over self-report measures. However, as Howard (1990) has astutely observed, most researchers interested in comparing the two measurement forms have used a criterion validation, rather than a construct validation approach, in addressing the issue. Implicit in such a strategy, however, is the underlying assumption that the criterion measurements represent perfect estimates of the construct under study. Given that all psychological measurements are imperfect to some extent, Howard concurred with Hogan and Nicholson (1988) that the issue of which measurement scale format is more valid hinges on the relative construct validity of each. In this regard, Howard (1990) noted that on the basis of the rigorous use of multitrait–multimethod (MTMM) analyses within the framework of covariance structure analysis, self-report measures have demonstrated strong evidence of construct validity. Relatedly, Hattie (1992) posited that "there can be no perfectly reliable or valid indicator of an individual's self-concept" (p. 246). Indeed, he argued that self-report measures can often provide more dependable estimates of personality-related constructs than behavioral measures, and Wylie (1989) suggested that "some form of self-report appears to be the most appropriate (perhaps the only) way to try to index self-conceptions" (p. 119).

Organization of the Book

To provide the reader with a more comprehensive framework within which to study the self-concept instruments included in this volume, I considered it important to preface their reviewed features with an overview of both the conceptual (chapter 1) and psychometric (chapter 2) issues related to self-concept research. This preparatory information is followed by chapter 3, in which I outline the reference sources and procedures used to establish the original pool of instruments and I detail the criteria used in selecting the final set of self-concept measures to be included in this volume. Of primary importance in this regard were the frequency of use and adequacy of psychometric properties and evidence of construct validity research. Chapters 4 through 8 are devoted to descriptive and psychometric information bearing on each of the selected 24 instruments. In addition to a general portrayal of the instrument, the descriptive material includes details related to the target population, scale structure, administration and scoring procedures, and instrument development and refinement relative to the normative samples; a sample item for each instrument is also included.[1] Psychometric information comprises reliability and validity findings from research bearing on the normative samples, as well as from research conducted on the same populations by others. However, where additional research has determined the appropriate use of particular instruments with pop-

---

1. For information regarding the source of each sample item, see the Source section at the end of each scale's review.

ulations, other than the one for which the instrument was developed and normed, this information is reported in the chapter pertinent to the nontarget population. Concluding each instrument review, I present an evaluation summary, together with details regarding costs and how interested readers might obtain related materials. Finally, in chapter 9, I evaluate the current status of self-concept measurement, identify particular areas of concern, and suggest possible directions for future research. I turn now to a more detailed breakdown of the content to be addressed in each chapter.

Chapter 1. In this first chapter, I examine widely debated issues associated with the definition and theoretical structure of self-concept. Specifically, I first review difficulties that possibly underlie the definitional confusion. One issue considered, for example, is the semantic ambiguity associated with the constructs of self-concept, self-esteem, and self-efficacy. I next describe seven empirically testable models of self-concept, each of which represents either a unidimensional or multidimensional perspective of theoretical structure. The theoretical model associated with each self-concept measure in the present volume is also identified. Finally, I address the major issues associated with importance-discrepancy ratings of self-concept and identify instruments reviewed in the present volume that embrace this approach to self-concept measurement.

Chapter 2. This chapter addresses recognized problems associated with the measurement of self-concept. The first part of the chapter is devoted to a review of the various forms of reliability and validity. Given the particular importance of construct validity among these psychometric criteria, I discuss its various aspects in more detail than for the other types of validity.[2] As such, I review (a) the concepts of nomological network, within-network and between-network relations, and convergent and discriminant validity; (b) approaches to testing for evidence of construct validity; (c) major limitations inherent in the traditional Campbell–Fiske (1959) MTMM procedure, and the use of covariance structure analysis as the more rigorous approach to MTMM analyses; and (d) the importance of testing for the equivalent factorial structure of self-concept measures across groups. Following this discussion, I next consider measurement issues identified by Wylie (1974, 1979, 1989) and others (e.g., Harter, 1990b; Hughes, 1984; Shavelson et al., 1976) to be

---

2. Indeed, the joint committee charged with the task of revising the guidelines set out in the *Standards for Educational and Psychological Testing* (1985) deemed construct validity to represent the only recognized form of validity (Spielberger, 1995).

the most deleterious in generating the current store of ambiguous and conflicting findings in the self-concept literature. The issues reviewed here are those related to appropriate instrument use, cross-cultural factors, and developmental factors. Finally, I address the issue of response-set bias associated with self-report measures of self-concept.

Chapter 3. Clearly, any review of the self-concept measurement literature, having as its primary intent the selection of an exemplary set of psychometrically favorable instruments, owes its readers a full accounting of the reference sources and the strategy and criteria used in the delineation process. The intent of this chapter, then, is to realize this responsibility. I begin by citing all referential sources used in obtaining the initial pool of self-concept measures and include the list of descriptors and strategy used for an on-line search of both the *PsycLIT* and ERIC databases. I then specify all criteria and the three-step process used in reducing the initial pool of 82 self-concept measures down to the final 24 included in this volume.

Chapter 4. The focus of this chapter is on self-concept measures designed for use with young children, preschool through second grade (ages 3–7 years). All descriptive and psychometric information noted above is presented with respect to two instruments: One considers self-concept as a unidimensional construct, thereby measuring general self-concept (the Joseph Pre-School and Primary Self-Concept Screening Test), and the other considers it as a multidimensional construct (the Pictorial Scale of Perceived Competence and Social Acceptance for Young Children).

Chapter 5. In this chapter, I review six instruments designed to measure multidimensional self-concepts for preadolescents, Grades 3 through 8 (ages 8–12 years). Two assessment scales focus on the more specific facets of academic self-concept (Academic Self Description Questionnaire I and Perception of Ability Scale for Students); the remainder tap multiple self-concept domains (Multidimensional Self Concept Scale, Piers–Harris Children's Self-Concept Scale, Self Description Questionnaire I, and Self-Perception Profile for Children).[3]

Chapter 6. This chapter contains a review of seven self-concept

---

3. One notable exclusion here is the Coopersmith (1967) Self-Esteem Inventory. Despite Wylie's (1974) identification of serious methodological weaknesses associated with the Self-Esteem Inventory over two decades ago, together with her admonition that it not be used in measuring children's self-concepts, its frequency of use is still fairly high. Nonetheless, given replicated findings of an unstable factor structure, high correlations with social desirability, weak evidence of construct validity, and problems with total scale scores, the instrument was not included here (for reviews, see Blascovich & Tomaka, 1991; Chiu, 1988; Hughes, 1984; Wylie, 1974; see also Harter, 1990b; chapter 1 of this volume).

measures developed for use with adolescents, Grades 9 through 12 (ages 13–19 years). Of these instruments, one measures a single facet of general self-concept (Rosenberg Self-Esteem Scale); two measure multiple facets of academic self-concept (Academic Self Description Questionnaire II and Dimensions of Self-Concept [Form S]); one measures multiple facets of physical self-concept (Physical Self-Description Questionnaire); and three measure multiple self-concept domains (Self Description Questionnaire II, Self-Perception Profile for Adolescents, and Tennessee Self-Concept Scale).

Chapter 7. The self-concept measures reviewed in this chapter address three different perspectives of adult life. Four scales are specifically designed for use with college students: One measures multiple facets of academic self-concept (Dimensions of Self-Concept [Form H]), two measure multiple facets of physical self-concept (Body Esteem Scale and Physical Self-Perception Profile), and one measures multiple self-concept domains (Self-Perception Profile for College Students). Although one instrument, the Self Description Questionnaire III, measures multiple self-concept domains and was originally designed for use with late adolescents and college students, findings from substantial construct validity research have shown its various subscales to be useful for other adult populations as well. A second instrument designed to measure multiple self-concept domains (Adult Self-Perception Profile) was designed specifically for use with adults other than college students. Finally, one self-concept measure appropriate for use with seniors (65 years and older) is reviewed. This instrument, the Self-Perception Genesis Method, differs from all others reviewed in this volume in the sense that it uses an open-ended self-report format. The reason for this inconsistency in instrument selection derives from the fact that the literature search yielded no alternative psychometrically adequate self-report measure.

Chapter 8. This chapter reviews measures of self-concept for use with special populations. Although, initially, I hoped to be able to provide readers with several instruments appropriate to a wide variety of exceptionalities, this turned out to be an unrealistic goal. Indeed, there is a very clear need for sound instrumentation in this area of self-concept. The two self-concept measures reviewed here were designed specifically for use with a particular special population: the Self-Perception Profile for Learning Disabled Students and the Self-Concept Scale for the Hearing-Impaired. Another instrument, which is mentioned in this chapter and was reviewed in chapter 5, the Perception of Ability Scale for Students, is a multidimensional scale originally designed to measure facets of academic self-concept for preadolescent children. However, substantial construct validity work over the years has shown it also to be a valid measure of academic self-concept for children with learning disabilities. Finally, I provide a brief summary of research directed toward the development of an adaptation of the Tennessee Self-Concept Scale for use with adolescents and young adults with hearing impairments.

Chapter 9. Finally, in this chapter, I summarize both the positive and negative aspects of the current state of self-concept measurement. Three particular areas of concern are identified and addressed: (a) the use of nonoptimal methodological strategies in testing for the psychometric adequacy of self-concept measures; (b) the absence of self-concept measures appropriate for use with adults engaged in various types of work, as well as for the elderly (over 65 years of age); and (c) the inattention given to cross-cultural factors related to self-concept measurement. Next, I review three recently developed and potentially valuable multidimensional self-report measures (Arts Self-Perception Inventory, Music Self-Perception Inventory, and Reading Self-Concept Scale), as well as three innovative approaches to self-concept measurement (projective, interview, and notion of possible selves). Finally, I describe the basic elements of computerized testing, review and discuss the advantages and perceived disadvantages associated with the computerized administration of psychological measures, and identify known self-concept measures adapted for computerized administration.

Measuring Self-Concept: The Conceptual Issues

The study of self-concept has a long history in the field of social science research (see, e.g., Wells & Marwell, 1976; Wylie, 1974). It is valued as a desirable outcome in many psychological and educational situations and is frequently posited as a mediating variable that facilitates the attainment of other desired outcomes, such as academic performance and social competence (Markus & Wurf, 1987). Despite a wealth of research bearing on substantive issues related to the topic, systematic reviews have revealed inconsistent and indeterminant findings, with methodological weaknesses being cited as the major problems (see, e.g., Byrne, 1984; Hansford & Hattie, 1982; Hughes, 1984; Shavelson et al., 1976; West et al., 1980; Wylie, 1974, 1979).

The intent of this chapter is to examine these shortcomings in self-concept research. In particular, I first review problems of definition, related to the customary use of self terms. I then note how problems of definition at the conceptual level lead ultimately to methodological problems at the measurement level, thereby hindering construct validity research bearing on both the measuring instrument and the theoretical model of self-concept to which it is linked. Next, I describe seven empirically testable theoretical models of self-concept and identify which self-concept measures in the present volume are linked to each. Finally, I address the issue of importance/discrepancy ratings of self-concept. We turn first to the issue of self-concept definition.

Definitional Considerations

Problems of definition related to self-concept research are now widely known. Essentially, these difficulties can be related to five major factors:

1

lack of a universally accepted definition, assumed synonymity of self terms, ambiguous distinction between the terms *self-concept* and *self-efficacy* and between *self-concept* and *self-esteem*, and the tendency to convey informal rather than formal (i.e., systematic) notions of self-concept. Each of these issues is now addressed.

Absence of Universally Accepted Definition

Central to the problem of definition is the lack of any clear, concise, and universally accepted definition of the construct (Byrne, 1984; Wells & Marwell, 1976; Wylie, 1974, 1979, 1989). Indeed, systematic reviews of the literature have yielded a multiplicity of definitions (e.g., Burns, 1979; Byrne, 1984; Hansford & Hattie, 1982; Shavelson et al., 1976; Wells & Marwell, 1976; Zirkel, 1971). Shavelson et al. (1976), for example, determined 17 different conceptual dimensions on which self-concept definitions could be categorized, and Zirkel (1971) identified 15 that were explicitly cited and several more that were implicit in either the selected instrumentation or the study design.

Assumed Synonymity of Self Terms

Adding further to definitional confusion is the tendency by self-concept researchers to interchange, at random, the various self terms (Blascovich & Tomaka, 1991; Hattie, 1992). In an attempt to summarize the most commonly encountered self terms, Hattie categorized them in relation to the two proverbial giants in the area: self-concept and self-esteem (but see below for additional confusion arising from the synonymous use of these two terms). Terms used interchangeably with *self-concept* were identified as *self, self-estimation, self-identity, self-image, self-perception, self-consciousness, self-imagery,* and *self-awareness*; those used interchangeably with *self-esteem* were *self-regard, self-reverence, self-acceptance, self-respect, self-worth, self-feeling,* and *self-evaluation.*

Of course, problems of definition are by no means limited to research concerned only with global conceptions of self. Rather, they apply as well to research that has focused on more specific dimensions bearing on academic, social, and physical attributes (or competence; see, e.g., Byrne, 1984, 1990, 1996). With respect to self-perceptions of academic competence, for example, the terms *academic self-concept, ability self-concept,* and *self-concept of ability* have been used.

Although there is no precise definition of *academic self-concept,* Strein (1993) noted that use of the term could be characterized by two elements common to most research. First, *academic self-concept* reflects descriptive (e.g., "I like most school subjects") as well as evaluative (e.g., "I do well in most school subjects") aspects of self-perception. Clearly, a delineation of the descriptive and evaluative components of self-concept would represent a major contribution to the field. Nonetheless, despite a 20-year hiatus since Shavelson et al. (1976) first noted that a distinction between the description and evaluation had not been clarified, either conceptually or empirically, the feat has not yet been accomplished. (For one attempt to disentangle these two aspects of self-concept measurement, see Shepard, 1979.) Of course, these characteristics (descriptive versus evaluative aspects) apply also to the specific subject-matter (e.g., math, reading, and science) and artistic (e.g., drama, dance, and music) domains of academic self-concept as well as to nonacademic (e.g., physical, social, and emotional) self-concepts.

Strein's (1993) second point is that definitions of academic self-concept tend to focus on self-perceptions of behavior (e.g., "I enjoy most school subjects") rather than on feelings (e.g., "I feel bad about myself in school"). Thus, Strein (1993) contended that "the term academic self-concept is more related to ideas such as self-perceptions of competence (Harter, 1990b) or self-efficacy (Bandura, 1982) than to constructs that might be more accurately labeled self-esteem, self-acceptance, or self-worth" (p. 273; but see the discussion of self-efficacy later).

Self-Concept Versus Self-Efficacy

Because of the increasing pervasiveness of studies in the educational and psychological literatures concerned with links between self-efficacy and various aspects of academic achievement (e.g., Marsh, Walker, & Debus, 1991; Norwich, 1987; Pajares & Miller, 1994; Skaalvik & Rankin, 1995; Zimmerman, Bandura, & Martinez-Pons, 1992) and the fact that their conceptual differences have not always been made clear (for research examples that exemplify such lack of clarity, see Pajares & Miller), I now offer a brief comparison between the terms *self-efficacy* and *self-concept.* Indeed, Bandura (1986) contended that although beliefs of one's confidence are integral to both self-concept and self-efficacy, the two represent different phenomena and thus should not be regarded as synonymous constructs. Rooted in social learning theory (Bandura, 1977)—which emphasizes reciprocal relations among environmental, behavioral, and personal factors—*self-efficacy* represents "people's judgements of their capabilities to organize and execute courses of action required to attain designated types of performances'' (Bandura, 1986, p. 391). Based on inferential processes that bear on prior performance attainment, reflected experiences, verbal persuasion, and emotional arousal, self-efficacy judgments represent the personal aspect of this triumvirate of factors; more specifically, these judgments mediate interplay between the environmental and behavioral factors (Norwich, 1987).

In his earlier writings, Bandura (e.g., 1981 [cited in Norwich, 1987]) contended that the global nature of self-concept not only served to undermine its power to explain behavior in particular situations but also failed to take fully into account the complexity and diversity of self-efficacy judgments across different activities and situations. However, given the wealth of research that has shown self-concept domains, as well as subdomains, to be multidimensionally structured, Norwich argued that this early perspective is less relevant today. Despite this more multifaceted notion of self-concept, Pajares and Miller (1994) maintained that the construct still fails to attain the same level of specificity as self-efficacy. They argued that whereas self-efficacy is ''a context-specific assessment of competence to perform a specific task, a judgement of one's capabilities to execute specific behaviors in specific situations'' (p. 194), self-concept is not measured at the same level of specificity; moreover, self-concept incorporates beliefs of self-worth associated with one's perceived competence (see also Strein, 1993). Within the context of academic endeavors, for example, Pajares and Miller contended that although self-concept judgments may be subject specific (e.g., pertinent to science, history, math, and the like), they are never task specific, in that they represent self-evaluations of perceived competence. In this sense then, self-concept judgments, compared with those of self-efficacy, are more global and less context dependent. For example, whereas a subject-specific self-concept test item might require the respondent to react to the statement ''I am a good science student,'' the self-efficacy item would require reaction to the statement ''I can solve this particular science problem.'' As such, the two items tap different cognitive and affective processes (Pajares & Miller, 1994).

Social comparison and frame-of-reference effects, implicit to the internal/external model proposed by Marsh (1986d; see later in this chapter), are likely to have differential influences on self-concept and self-efficacy responses (Marsh, Walker, & Debus, 1991). For example, in responding to self-concept measures that elicit evaluation of capabilities in relation to a particular school subject, students typically make such judgments by comparing their own performance with that of their classmates (an external comparison), as well as with their own performance in other subject areas (an internal comparison); these dual-comparative processes represent frame-of-reference effects. In contrast, self-efficacy judgments focus on the student's capabilities in relation to the specific criterion items presented; as a consequence, these frame-of-reference effects are minimized.

Although Schunk (1985) suggested that students may use the performance of classmates as a benchmark against which to determine their own likelihood of success (i.e., self-efficacy), Marsh, Walker, and Debus (1991) noted that even this minimal impact of the external comparison process is only likely when the performance being tapped is sufficiently novel or ambiguous that previous experience with a similar task is not possible. Thus, Marsh, Walker, and Debus contended that self-concept responses, compared with self-efficacy responses, are likely to be more influenced by frame-of-reference effects, in particular, the internal comparison process. Marsh, Walker, and Debus pointed to the way in which self-concept and self-efficacy responses are measured as the primary factor contributing to this distinction between the two constructs. (For a further elaboration of conceptual and empirical differences between self-concept and self-efficacy within an academic framework, see Marsh, Walker, & Debus, 1991; Norwich, 1987; Pajares & Miller, 1994.)

Self-Concept Versus Self-Esteem

Perhaps the definitional issue that has generated the most debate in the literature is that bearing on the discrepancy between *self-concept* and *self-esteem*. In general, researchers would seem to agree that conceptually, the two terms represent different aspects of the self system (e.g., Brinthaupt & Erwin, 1992; Hattie, 1992; Juhasz, 1985). Whereas *self-concept* connotes a relatively broad definition of the construct that includes cognitive, affective, and behavioral aspects, *self-esteem* is thought to be a more limited evaluative component of the broader self-concept term (Blascovich & Tomaka, 1991; Wells & Marwell, 1976). Indeed, Brinthaupt and Erwin have likened this distinction to the difference between *self-description* and *self-evaluation.*

For Hattie (1992) and others (e.g., Rosenberg, 1965), however, the key element distinguishing self-concept from self-esteem was the extent to which one considered the attribute under study to be important. For example, a student may describe him- or herself as not being very good at sports and thereby exhibit evidence of low physical self-concept. However, if the student considers sports to be of little importance, his or her self-esteem will be totally unaffected. Hattie therefore considered self-esteem to be closely linked to one's sense of self-worth. Accordingly, he posited that whereas the body (beautiful) was of the highest importance to some, for others it might be more important "to be academically able, to have a happy family life, to gain respect from others, or to have a desirable personality" (Hattie, 1992, p. 55).

Despite conceptual claims supporting the distinctiveness of self-concept and self-esteem, construct validity research to date (e.g., Marsh, 1986b; Shepard, 1979) has been unsuccessful in providing empirical evidence of such discriminability. Brinthaupt and Erwin (1992) and others (e.g., Watkins & Dhawan, 1989) have linked this indeterminacy to the fact that most self-concept research has relied on self-report measurements. Typically, self-report scales comprise items that elicit both descriptive and evaluative aspects of the self, thereby making it difficult, if not impossible, to tease apart the two constructs. As a consequence of the inability to disentangle *self-concept* from *self-esteem,* it is common practice for most researchers to use the two terms interchangeably (Hughes, 1984; Shavelson et al., 1976).

Recent research (Greenwald, Bellezza, & Banaji, 1988; Watkins & Dhawan, 1989) has attempted to gain more insight into this discriminability issue by using open-ended, in lieu of self-report, measures, because they lend themselves to the examination of important aspects of self-concept that may be independent of self-esteem (W. J. McGuire & McGuire, 1982). On the basis of responses from 101 college students, Greenwald et al. (1988) concluded that "self-esteem is a pervasive component of measured self-concept, even for measures that lack manifest esteem-related content" (p. 43).

From a cross-cultural perspective, collective findings reported by Watkins and Dhawan suggest that the degree of discriminability between self-concept and self-esteem may be a function of the extent to which particular societal values have been internalized. Summarizing findings from a comparison of American and Indian undergraduate students (Dhawan & Roseman, 1988), New Zealand (Watkins, Alabaster, & Freemantle, 1988), and Filipino (Watkins, 1988) high school students, Watkins and Dhawan contended that although the descriptive and evaluative aspects of self were strongly intertwined, they were definitely not synonymous; the distinction was more evident for the Asian (Indian and Filipino) than for the Western samples. This clearer distinction for the non-Western samples was attributed to the cultural emphasis on group, rather than on individual, success. Encouraged by these findings, and in keeping with the argument that any construct loses its scientific utility if it is defined too broadly (see Fleming & Courtney, 1984), Watkins and Dhawan argued for a clear need to distinguish between the terms *self-concept* and *self-esteem*. Construct validity research concerned with the discriminability of these two self terms is clearly in the embryonic stage; as such, it provides a rich source of challenges to be met through future studies of self-concept measurement.

Prevalence of Informal Notions of Self-Concept

A final definitional problem bearing on self-concept measurement is the tendency by researchers to substitute "common-language notions" (Blascovich & Tomaka, 1991, p. 116) of the construct for more precise, academic connotations. Echoing this lament, Marsh (in press-a) very aptly stated that "self-concept, like many other psychological constructs, suffers in that 'everyone knows what it is,' so that many researchers do not feel compelled to provide any theoretical definition of what they are measuring." Given that self-concept is a hypothetical construct and therefore not directly measurable, it is critical that its meaningfulness and legitimacy be established through tests of its construct validity (a topic to be described in chapter 2).

Problems of definition at the conceptual level, of course, lead ultimately to methodological difficulties at the measurement level. Indeed, definitional imprecision leads inevitably to at least three deficiencies in the conduct of self-concept research: (a) It retards scientific progress by making the task of replication difficult, if not impossible; (b) it severely hinders the selection of appropriately valid self-concept instruments; and (c) it obscures the conceptual framework of the study, thereby making it difficult to link the research hypotheses and the interpretation of findings to a particular self-concept theoretical model. Each of these factors bears importantly on the construct validity related to both the measuring instrument and the theoretical model. We turn our attention now to a review of postulated theoretical frameworks of self-concept that can be tested empirically.

Theoretical Considerations

In any discussion of self-concept measurement, it is worthwhile to first reflect on Harter's (1990b) cogent caveat that we take care not to put "the methodological cart before the conceptual horse" (p. 292). Because there are many definitions of self-concept, as noted earlier, it is critical that the researcher first clarify the particular theoretical framework he or she wishes to adopt and then select the most appropriate self-concept measures accordingly. Perhaps as an offshoot of the increasing use of structural equation modeling in tests of construct validity (see, e.g., Bentler, 1978; Byrne, 1994), it has now become common practice to refer to such conceptual frameworks as *theoretical models* (but see Hattie, 1992, for a discussion of differentiation between the two terms). Essentially, the term *theoretical model* conveys the notion that relations among the constructs embodying a particular theory (i.e., its nomological network [Cronbach & Meehl, 1955]) can be modeled pictorially, thereby providing a clearer conceptualization of the theory under study.

Although numerous theories of self-concept abound (for a comprehensive review, see Hattie, 1992), the term *theoretical model* is typically reserved for those theories that have undergone empirical scrutiny. More specifically, the construct validity of the theory has been evaluated statistically by testing hypotheses that bear either on its postulated nomological network or on the factorial structure of a measuring instrument developed within the framework of that particular theory. Before 1980, very few self-concept instruments could be linked to any concrete theory. Furthermore, of the self-concept instruments that were theoretically conceived, most were grounded in the notion that self-concept is unidimensionally structured (although see Sears, 1966, for an example of a multidimensional instrument: the Sears Self-Concept Inventory). As a consequence, most instruments were designed to measure only a global aspect of the construct (Harter, 1990b).

After 1980, however, and perhaps in answer to urgent pleas (Shavelson et al., 1976; Wylie, 1974, 1979) for a cessation of substantive research albeit implementation of construct validity research in the area of self-concept, there is now a wealth of evidence that substantiates the multidimensional nature of self-concept (e.g., Hattie, 1992; Marsh, 1990b). In keeping with these findings, most measuring instruments developed since 1980 are multidimensionally structured, and many are closely tied to a particular theoretical model.

In general, theoretical models of self-concept can be polarized into two broad perspectives: those supporting the unidimensionality of the construct versus those supporting multidimensionality. Within these two broad categories, and despite some inconsistency with respect to nomenclature, it seems safe to suggest that there are basically seven theoretical models of self-concept (Byrne, 1984; Harter, 1990b; Hattie, 1992; Marsh & Hattie, 1996; Strein, 1993); each, in turn, dictates a related measurement strategy.

To facilitate a clearer conceptualization of these models, a schematic representation of those embracing a unidimensional perspective is shown in Figure 1.1 and of those embracing a multidimensional perspective in Figure 1.2. Before turning to a descriptive review of each of these self-concept models, a brief explanation of the symbolism used in both figures is perhaps in order. In keeping with convention associated with covariance structure modeling, the ovals represent latent constructs, whereas the boxes represent observed scores. Thus, in Figure 1.1a, for example, GSC depicts the latent construct of general self-concept, and the indexed letters (A_1, A_2, A_3, and A_4) represent observed scores on Items 1, 2, 3, and 4, respectively, of the academic self-concept subscale. The single-headed arrows represent the influence of the underlying latent construct on the observed scores. In Figure 1.1a, then, the first arrow on the left represents the prediction of the observed score on A_1 from general self-concept. The two-headed curved arrows in Figure 1.1c, for example, represent correlations among the latent self-concept constructs. Finally, because the prediction of observed scores by underlying latent constructs is not without error, these residual terms are typically indicated schematically by short, single-headed arrows pointing toward the related observed score. However, for sake of simplicity and clarity in the present instance, these symbols have been omitted in Figures 1.1 and 1.2. We turn first to a discussion of the models that represent a unidimensional self-concept structure.

Unidimensional Perspectives

Nomothetic Model

The nomothetic model (Figure 1.1a) represents the oldest and most traditional view of self-concept, and was first labeled as such by L. M. Soares and Soares (1983). Perhaps because the term *nomothetic* implies generality or universality, Marsh and Hattie (1996) have chosen instead to reference it as the "unidimensional, general-factor model." Al-

Figure 1.1

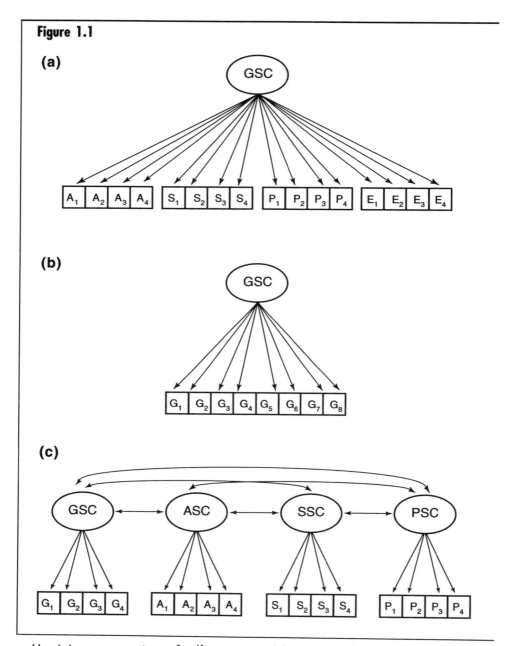

Heuristic representations of self-concept models that embrace a unidimensional perspective. GSC = general self-concept, ASC = academic self-concept, SSC = social self-concept, PSC = physical self-concept, $A_1 - A_4$ = Items 1 to 4 on an academic self-concept scale, $S_1 - S_4$ = Items 1 to 4 on a social self-concept scale, $P_1 - P_4$ = Items 1 to 4 on a physical self-concept scale, $G_1 - G_8$ = Items 1 to 8 on a general self-concept scale.

Figure 1.2

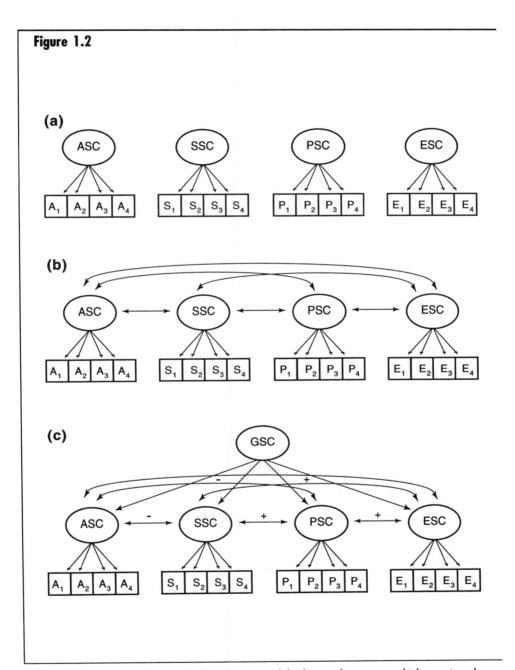

Heuristic representations of self-concept models that embrace a multidimensional perspective. GSC = general self-concept, ASC = academic self-concept, SSC = social self-concept, PSC = physical self-concept, ESC = emotional self-concept, A_1–A_4 = Items 1 to 4 on an academic self-concept scale, S_1–S_4 = Items 1 to 4 on a social self-concept scale, P_1–P_4 = Items 1 to 4 on a physical self-concept scale, E_1–E_4 = Items 1 to 4 on an emotional self-concept scale.

Figure 1.2, continued

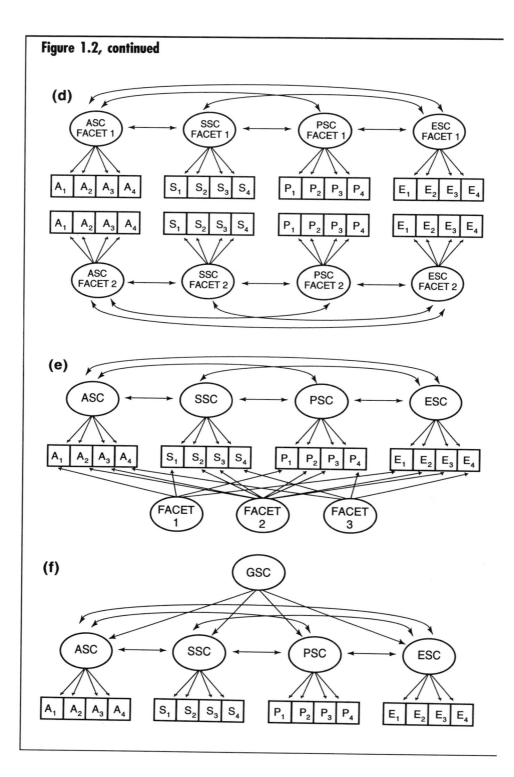

though the nomothetic model considers self-concept to be unidimensional, it argues for a unitary construct that is made up of overlapping facets of information. In other words, this model dictates that items on a measuring instrument tap different content areas and that each be given equal weight; item scores are then summed to yield one overall self-concept score. In Figure 1.1a, for example, general self-concept is shown to be a summative representation of academic, social, physical, and emotional self-concepts. The nomothetic model thus makes the assumption that the single score derived from this additive combination represents an accurate unidimensional reflection of an individual's sense of self as it relates to the various facets of his or her life (Harter, 1990b). Proponents of this perspective (e.g., Coopersmith, 1967; Marx & Winne, 1978; Piers & Harris, 1964) have argued that given the heavy dominance of an overall, global self-concept factor, it is virtually impossible to differentiate among its subcomponents.

Since the early 1980s, the validity of the nomothetic model has been challenged and severely criticized by researchers who support the opposing view that self-concept is a multidimensional construct. Their contention is that by simply combining all item scores together, one masks important distinctions that individuals make in their self-perceptions of adequacy related to various aspects of their lives (Harter, 1990b). Over the past decade, a substantial amount of construct validity research, most of which has been spearheaded by Marsh and colleagues (see Marsh & Hattie, 1996), has shown no support whatsoever for the nomothetic model. In contrast, these studies have demonstrated quite clearly not only that self-concept is a multidimensional construct but also that it cannot be adequately understood unless this multidimensional structure is taken into account. Indeed, Marsh and Hattie have suggested that conclusions drawn by supporters of the nomothetic model regarding the unidimensionality of self-concept are rendered dubious as a consequence of problematic measurement and statistical analyses.

In the light of a plethora of evidence that argues against the validity of the nomothetic model, it seems curious that this perspective should have weathered the tests of time for so long. Strein (1993) has attributed the longevity to "its conceptual simplicity, its historical predominance in the field, and its support for the 'magic bullet' view, that changes in self-concept will alter a variety of situation-specific behaviors without having to intervene in each specific situation" (p. 274). In addition, the answer may lie with methodological factors that too are bound by the constraints of time. For example, it is only since the early 1980s that applications of highly sophisticated statistical procedures such as confirmatory factor analyses have been used to test hypothesized factorial structures of measuring instruments.

Self-concept instruments in this volume that are rooted in the nomothetic model are the following: the Joseph Pre-School and Primary Self-Concept Screening Test (Joseph, 1979, see chapter 4); the Piers–Harris Children's Self-Concept Scale (Piers & Harris, 1964; chapter 5); the Dimensions of Self-Concept scales (Form S: Michael & Smith, 1976, chapter 6; Form H: Michael, Denny, Knapp-Lee, & Michael, 1984, chapter 7); and the Self-Concept Scale for the Hearing Impaired (Oblowitz, Green, & Heyns, 1991, chapter 8).

"True" Unidimensional Model

To distinguish the unidimensional view of self-concept found in the work of Rosenberg (1979) from that associated with the nomothetic model, I have termed the Rosenberg perspective as the *true* unidimensional model. Two schematic representations of this model are depicted here. The first, Figure 1.1b, represents a unidimensional structure as tapped by items constituting a scale designed to measure only general self-concept (e.g., the Rosenberg Self-Esteem Scale, 1965). The second illustration (Figure 1.1c) reflects the true unidimensional model within the context of a multidimensional scale (Harter's, 1985b, Self-Perception Profile for Children); in contrast to the nomothetic model depicted in Figure 1.1a, general self-concept is tapped by items comprising its own subscale. Although Rosenberg acknowledged that individuals form self-evaluations of their adequacy in other areas of their life, in addition to possessing a general sense of worth as a person, he chose to focus solely on the latter. The Self-Esteem Scale (Rosenberg, 1965) was developed within the framework of the true unidimensional model (see chapter 6, this volume). As such, the instrument yields a single score that represents only the level of an individual's overall (i.e., global) self-esteem (or general self-concept); it does not measure the extent to which other dimensions of the construct filter into this global sense of well-being. Thus, as shown in Figure 1.1b, each item (G_1–G_8) is designed to measure general self-concept.

As noted by Harter (1990b), it is critical to distinguish between the two unidimensional perspectives of self-concept as operationalized by, for example, Coopersmith (1967) and Rosenberg (1965) in the development of their measuring instruments. Whereas the Coopersmith measure (the Coopersmith Self-Esteem Inventory)[1] assumes that one's sense of global self-worth is a simple additive combination of item responses that tap attributes or competencies representing content-specific domains, the Rosenberg scale makes no such assumption. Rather, it measures global self-esteem directly and makes no attempt to tap the more specific self-perceptions, which, for Rosenberg, are quite likely combined in a very complex and obscure manner of which the individual is unaware. The Rosenberg Self-Esteem Scale is the only measuring instrument in the present volume that is linked to the true unidimensional model.

We turn now to self-concept models representative of a multidimensional perspective, as schematically portrayed in Figure 1.2.

Multidimensional Perspectives

Independent-Factor Model

The theoretical perspective underpinning this model (see Figure 1.2a) was first proposed by A. T. Soares and Soares (1980); to date, these researchers appear to be its only supporters. Although they originally tagged it the *taxonomic model*, this label runs counter to a taxonomic model as interpreted by Marsh and Hattie (1996) on the basis of theories of intelligence. The major thesis of the A. T. Soares and Soares (1980) research was that the self-concept is composed of multiple facets, each of which is independent of all other dimensions; at worst, they should be only weakly correlated. According to A. T. Soares and Soares, multiple self-concepts develop independently as a consequence of one's daily experiences, capabilities, and interaction with significant others. Furthermore, they (L. M. Soares & Soares, 1986) argued against the existence of both a global (i.e., general) self-concept and a correlated hierarchical structure, as proposed by Shavelson et al. (1976), which is described later.

The independent-factor model of self-concept was derived as a theoretical framework within which to develop the Affective Perception Inventory (API; A. T. Soares & Soares, 1979), a 9-point semantic differential scale designed to measure perceptions of self as a person, a student, and with respect to competency in English, math, science, social sciences, the arts (i.e., music and art), and physical education. A ninth subscale tapped perceptions of school, and it could be de-

---

1. The Coopersmith Self-Esteem Inventory is currently published by Consulting Psychologists Press.

scribed more as a measure of attitudes toward school than perceptions of self within the school environment. Interestingly, little if any justification of a strong independent-factor model can be found in the self-concept literature; rather, recent research has provided ample evidence to dispute all claims in its support. For example, not only have substantial correlations been identified among the API subscales (Byrne & Shavelson, 1986; Hattie, 1992; Marsh & Hattie, 1996), but a secondary analysis of the correlation matrix reported by L. M. Soares and Soares (1983) yielded a hierarchical factor structure comprising two higher order factors (Hattie, 1992). These findings, together with strong criticism of the statistical analyses used in the Soares and Soares research (Hattie, 1992; Marsh & Hattie, 1996), argue strongly against the validity of the independent model of self-concept. Indeed, Marsh and Hattie (1996) concluded that there was "little or no support for the strong version of the multidimensional, independent model." No self-concept measure in the present volume is grounded in the independent-factor model.

Correlated-Factor Model

In direct contrast to the independent-factor model, this theoretical structure allows the multiple, domain-specific self-concepts to be correlated both among themselves (as shown in Figure 1.2b) and with a separate facet of global self-concept (as indicated in Figure 1.1c). On the basis of developmental theory and findings from empirical research (see, e.g., Harter, 1983, 1990c; Marsh, 1989, 1990b), the postulated specificity of self-concept facets will vary with age. The Self-Perception Profile for Children (as well as the other Harter instruments, some of which are described in chapters 4–8) exemplifies an assessment instrument developed within the framework of the correlated-factor model.

Harter (1990b) argued that an important aspect of the conceptual and empirical separation of domain-specific facets of self-perceived competence from a global self-worth construct is that it enables the determination of relations that the specific competencies bear to global self-worth. In other words, it allows one to specify the manner by which the various dimensions are weighted and combined in yielding an overall sense of self-worth (i.e., general self-concept). Within the framework of the correlated-factor model, then, self-concept is conceptualized along a continuum of very specific to very global perceptions of one's competency, and these approaches are not necessarily mutually exclusive (Harter, 1990b).

To the best of my knowlege, no construct validity research has endeavored to test hypotheses *directly* bearing on the structure of the correlated-factor model. Nonetheless, findings from some validity studies of the Shavelson et al. (1976) hierarchical model (e.g., Marsh, 1990c; Marsh, Byrne, & Shavelson, 1988; Marsh & Shavelson, 1985), as well as extended versions of that model (see Vispoel, 1995c), demonstrated weak evidence of hierarchical structure, thereby offering indirect support for the correlated model. Furthermore, substantial construct validity research abounds that has indirectly tested its postulated network through the validation of assessment measures developed from this model. Research bearing on the self-concept instruments developed by Harter and colleagues, for example, are a case in point.

Instruments in the present volume that are based on the correlated-factor model comprise the self-perception profiles developed by Harter and colleagues for preschool children (Harter & Pike, 1983; chapter 4); preadolescents (Harter, 1985b; chapter 5); adolescents (Harter, 1988d; chapter 6); college students (Neemann & Harter, 1986; chapter 7); adults (Messer & Harter, 1986; chapter 7); and children with learning disabilities (Renick & Harter, 1988; chapter 8); as well as the Body Esteem Scale (Franzoi & Shields, 1984; chapter 7).

Compensatory Model

This model (Figure 1.2c), initially proposed by Marx and Winne (1980), argues that once a global self-concept has been accounted for, remaining variation is explained by multiple bipolar facets (e.g., academic, social, and physical) that are inversely rather than proportionally related; that is to say, these domain-specific facets can be negatively rather than positively correlated. For example, in Figure 1.2c, the correlations of social and physical self-concepts with academic self-concept are negative, whereas all other correlations are positive. These negative correlations indicate either that low scores on academic self-concept are associated with high scores on social and physical self-concepts (typically the case in research bearing on low academically tracked students) or that high scores on academic self-concept are associated with low scores on social and physical self-concepts (often found in research related to academically gifted students).

The major thrust of the compensatory model is that in the unconscious attempt to maintain one's sense of well-being, self-perceptions of low status in one domain will be compensated by self-perceptions of high status in other domains. With respect to low-ability students, for example, it would be argued that whereas they are likely to perceive themselves as less capable academically, their perceptions of social competence are likely to be high, thereby balancing out their overall perceptions of self.

Although the basic rationale underlying the compensatory model seems intuitively sound, research in support of this model (Marx & Winne, 1978, 1980; Winne & Marx, 1981; Winne, Marx, & Taylor, 1977) has been strongly challenged. Some researchers (Hattie, 1992; Shavelson, Bolus, & Keesling, 1983) have severely criticized their statistical analyses; others (e.g., Marsh & Hattie, 1996) have denounced their use of the same data to support both unidimensional and compensatory models of self-concept. Taken together, Marsh and Hattie concluded that support for the compensatory model, as claimed by Marx, Winne, and colleagues, was more an artifact of the use of ipsative rating (i.e., rank order) scales than a compensatory process underlying self-concept structure. As these authors (Marsh & Hattie) noted, ipsative scores are necessarily negatively correlated because ranking yourself more highly on one scale inevitably means that rankings on the other scales must be lower.

Research bearing on Marsh's (1986d) "internal/external frame of reference (I/E) model" appears to provide substantially stronger and more rigorous support for the compensatory model. This model supports the notion that in addition to a natural inclination to compare their academic abilities with those of their peers in the same school environment, students also compare their own ability in one academic subject with that in other school subjects. The model was originally derived from construct validation of the Shavelson et al. (1976) model of self-concept, wherein Marsh (1986d; Marsh et al., 1988) uncovered intriguing relations between English and math self-concepts and between English and math academic achievement. Specifically, English and math achievement correlated at approximately .5 to .8, whereas the correlations between respective self-concepts were near zero. The I/E model was designed specifically to explain why English and math self-concepts are so distinct.

According to the I/E frame-of-reference perspective, the formation of students' perceptions of their own academic competence is based on two sets of comparisons: an external comparison by which students compare their abilities in particular subjects with the abilities of other students in their classroom or school and an internal (ipsative-like) comparison by which students compare their own abilities in one subject in relation to their ability in another subject. (Development of the I/E model, however, grew out of research related only to the areas of math and English.)

For example (see Marsh, 1993a), suppose a student accurately perceives him- or herself as performing below average in both math and English but is better at math than English. Although her or his math skills are below average in relation to those of other students (external comparison), but higher than average in relation to her or his own English (internal comparison), the student may exhibit an average or above-average math self-concept, depending on how these two factors are weighted. Because math and English achievement test scores are substantially correlated, the external comparison should yield a positive correlation between their matching self-concepts. In contrast, because math and English achievements are compared with each other and it is the differential between these two scores that results in a higher self-concept in one area or another, the internal comparison should lead to a negative correlation. Depending on the relative strength of each, then, the joint operation of both sets of comparisons will lead to a near-zero correlation between English and math self-concepts.[2]

A second aspect of the I/E model argues that the impact of math achievement on English self-concept should be negative, and vice versa. That is to say, a high math self-concept is expected when a student's math skills are good compared with those of other students (external) and high compared with one's own English skills (internal). Holding math achievement constant, then, it is the difference between math and English achievement that is predictive of math self-concept; high English achievement serves only to weaken a high math self-concept (Marsh, 1993a).

Marsh and colleagues have empirically tested the basic tenets of the I/E model with data from Australian (Marsh, Richards, & Barnes, 1986b), American (Marsh, 1990a), and Canadian (Marsh et al., 1988) students at various levels of the educative system; near-zero correlations between math and English self-concepts were reported in all studies, thereby providing ample evidence in support of the I/E model. Although the consistently small correlation between math and English self-concepts is inconsistent with the original Shavelson model, it is nonetheless consonant with the revised Marsh/Shavelson model (Marsh, 1993a). (For a more extended discussion of the I/E model,

---

2. The I/E model does not require that the correlation between math and English self-concepts be zero; however, the correlation must be substantially less than the math–English achievement correlation (Marsh, 1993a).

see Byrne, 1996; Marsh, 1990a, 1990b, 1993a.) Thus far, however, research bearing on the I/E model has been limited to relations between academic self-concepts and academic achievement. Although this body of research holds great promise as a replacement for the earlier work of Marx and Winne (1978, 1980; Winne & Marx, 1981; Winne et al., 1977) in support of the compensatory model, substantially more research that incorporates nonacademic facets of self-concept is needed.

Taxonomic Model

This paradigm of self-concept structure was inspired by Guilford's (1969) model of intelligence. A unique aspect of this model is that the components of intellect reflect the intersection of two or more facets, each of which has at least two levels (Marsh & Hattie, 1996). Given the complexity of theoretical structures that can result as a consequence of the variant number of self-concept dimensions, facets, and facetal levels, two possible formulations of the taxonomic model are illustrated (see Figure 1.2d and e).

Although the term *taxonomic* was first used by A. T. Soares and Soares (1980) in labeling their proposed model of self-concept, it seems clear that their description of self-concept structure matched the independent-factor model rather than the taxonomic model that derived from Guilford's (1969) work. In sharp contrast to A. T. Soares and Soares's (1980) description of the taxonomic model, Guilford (1985) recently noted that factors constituting his proposed structure of intelligence are postulated to be correlated and hierarchically ordered. Marsh and Hattie (1996), in a review of self-concept models, concluded that the A. T. Soares and Soares (1980) interpretation of the taxonomic model was inappropriate.

Before trying to either explain or comprehend the structure of the taxonomic model, I will highlight a critical distinction between the usual meaning of the term *multifaceted* and its meaning in relation to this particular model. Using terminology associated with an analysis of variance (ANOVA) design, Marsh and Hattie (1996) likened this distinction to the difference between a one-way design (which reflects most self-concept models) and a factorial design (which reflects the taxonomic model). Within the context of the one-way design, there would be one facet (e.g., general self-concept) that has several levels (i.e., multiple self-concept facets such as academic, social, and physical). In a factorial design, on the other hand, there would be at least two self-concept facets, each of which would have two or more levels.

Two self-concept instruments that can be linked to the taxonomic model are the Tennessee Self-Concept Scale (TSCS; Roid & Fitts, 1988/1994) and the Multidimensional Self Concept Scale (MSCS; Bracken, 1992); the TSCS is described in chapter 6, and the MSCS in chapter 5, of this volume. Turning first to the TSCS, we find an underlying structure that reflects a taxonomic model having three facets. Applied to the Clinical and Research Form of the scale (see chapter 6), these facets can be further described as embracing a 5 (external frame of reference) × 3 (internal frame of reference) × 2 (positively/negatively worded items) design. The five levels of the external frame-of-reference facet are physical, moral, personal, family, and social self-concepts. Each of these traits is hypothesized as being manifested in relation to three internal frames of reference (the second facet): identity (e.g., "what I am"), satisfaction (e.g., "how I feel about myself"), and behavior (e.g., "what I do, or how I act"). Identity represents the private internal self; satisfaction reflects a discrepancy between the actual and the ideal; and behavior represents the external, observable self. The third facet represents the wording of the items, thereby providing a mechanism for controlling various response biases; it may or may not be substantively important.

The MSCS is also structured on a three-facet taxonomic model. The domain facet, reflecting context-specific self-concepts, has six levels: social, competence, affect, academic, family, and physical. The second facet, evaluative perspectives, has two levels: a personal perspective (acquired directly through an individual's evaluations of his or her own behavior) and a significant-other perspective (acquired indirectly through inferences about evaluations by others). The third facet, evaluative standards performance, has four levels: absolute, ipsative, comparative, and ideal standards. Additionally, the MSCS contains both positively and negatively worded items that could be used to reflect a fourth facet. Thus, in ANOVA terms, the MSCS exemplifies a 6 × 2 × 4 taxonomic design.

Marsh and Hattie (1996) noted that scores that are based on the taxonomic model are not always consistent with the design of the instrument. The TSCS and MSCS serve to exemplify this point. For example, the design of the TSCS allows for three manifestations of social self-concept (identity, satisfaction, and behavior). However, because the combining of these three scores into a single social self-concept score results in a confounding of the three manifestations, this mode of scoring may be inappropriate (Marsh & Hattie, 1996; Marsh & Richards, 1988b). In contrast, Marsh and Hattie (1996) noted that although Bracken (1992) discusses all eight multiplicative combinations of the two perspectives and four standards, and despite the theoretical importance of the perspectives and standards facets in the design of the MSCS, these facets are ignored in scoring the instrument; only six scores reflecting the domain facet are used.

On the basis of their evaluation of the TSCS and MSCS, then, Marsh and Hattie (1996) concluded that although the taxonomic model may be consistent with the underlying structure of some multidimensional self-concept measures, it may be quite inconsistent with their yielded scores. Nonetheless, because the taxonomic model appears promising as a potentially fruitful means to combining structural (i.e., domain) and process components of self-concept, Marsh and Hattie have called for future construct validity research that identifies ways by which to determine: (a) the most appropriate structure, (b) corresponding scores related to this structure, and (c) the manner in which scores reflecting various combinations of the facets are differentially related to external criteria.

Hierarchical Model

The theoretical notion underpinning this model is that general self-concept is a higher order factor that comprises multiple, domain-specific self-concepts, which, although correlated, can be interpreted as separate constructs. As such, general self-concept and each of its related domain-specific facets are tapped by items constituting each of their separate subscales. The heuristic representation of the hierarchical model is shown in Figure 1.2f.

Although the conceptualization of self-concept as a hierarchically ordered structure has been implicit in the writings of several theorists (e.g., S. Epstein, 1973; Kelly, 1955; L'Ecuyer, 1981; for a review, see Harter, 1985a), Shavelson et al. (1976) were the first to propose a model of self-concept that could be tested empirically. This model (commonly cited as the Shavelson model) portrayed a multidimensional and hierarchically ordered structure, with global perceptions of self as a person (i.e., general self-concept) at the apex and actual behavior at the base; moving from the top to the bottom of the hierarchy, the structure became increasingly differentiated. More specifically, global self-concept was shown to split into two branches: academic and nonacademic self-concepts. The nonacademic branch comprised three facets: social, physical, and emotional self-concepts. Each of these four facets, in turn, was shown to branch into separate and more specific self-concepts (e.g., math, peers, and physical appearance). A schematic representation of Shavelson et al.'s originally hypothesized hierarchical model is shown in Figure 1.3. However, because (a) the Shavelson model is the most extensively validated model of self-concept to date and (b) the development of many recent measures of self-concept is theoretically linked to this hierarchical model, I consider it important that readers be informed (as much as is possible at this time) regarding the current status of construct validity research related to this model. Accordingly, several additional schematic figures representing proposed adaptations of this model accompany this discussion.

Since its inception, the Shavelson model has undergone extensive construct validation. However, until recent tests of the social (Byrne & Shavelson, 1996) and physical (Fox & Corbin, 1989; Marsh & Redmayne, 1994) self-concept components of the model, virtually all construct validity research designed to directly test its theoretical structure has focused on the academic branch of the model. In contrast, many construct validity studies have indirectly tested hypotheses related to the Shavelson model. These have included tests for the validity of (a) measuring instruments theoretically linked to the Shavelson model (e.g., Bracken & Howell, 1991; Marsh & O'Neill, 1984) and (b) multidimensional and hierarchical structure relevant to an extension of the model that included visual arts and music self-concepts (Vispoel, 1995c).

Because construct validation of the Shavelson model has been approached from different perspectives, particularly with respect to the testing of hierarchical structure, it is important to clarify Shavelson et al.'s (1976) intended meaning in their postulation of a multidimensional and hierarchically ordered self-concept structure. Accordingly, *multidimensionality* implies that self-concept facets, although intercorrelated, can be interpreted as separate constructs. For example, with reference to the academic portion of the model (see Figure 1.3), although general self-concept is expected to correlate with academic self-concept, academic self-concept with subject-specific self-concepts, and general self-concept with subject-specific self-concepts, each of these dimensions operates as a separately interpretable entity. Hierarchical structure, on the other hand, suggests that the strength of correlations between self-concept facets varies in a systematic pattern so that (a) general self-concept correlates highest with academic self-concept, next highest with subject-specific self-concepts, and lowest with academic achievement

Figure 1.3

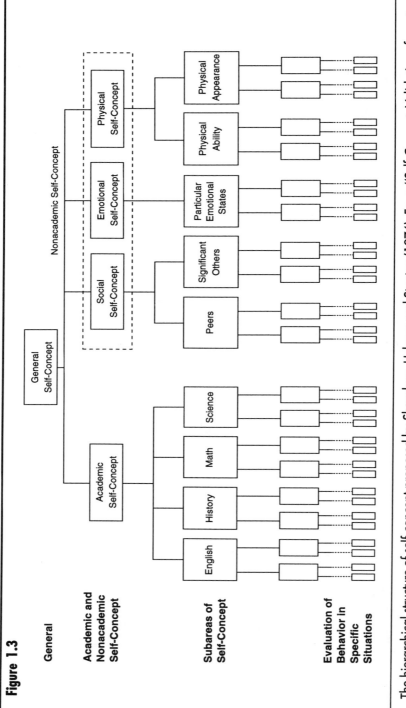

The hierarchical structure of self-concept proposed by Shavelson, Hubner, and Stanton (1976). From "Self-Concept: Validation of construct interpretations," by R. J. Shavelson, J. J. Hubner, and G. C. Stanton, 1976, *Review of Educational Research, 46*, 413. Copyright 1976 by the American Educational Research Association. Reprinted with permission.

(i.e., actual behavior); (b) academic self-concept correlates higher with subject-specific self-concepts than with academic achievement; and (c) subject-specific self-concepts (e.g., math self-concept) correlate higher with their matching academic achievement scores (e.g., math) than with nonmatching academic achievement scores (e.g., history).

In testing for the hierarchical ordering of academic self-concept structure, researchers have examined the pattern of latent factor correlations among self-concept facets (Byrne, 1986; Byrne & Shavelson, 1986; Byrne & Worth Gavin, in press; Shavelson & Bolus, 1982) and have compared the fit of differently specified higher order factor structures (e.g., Marsh, 1990c; Marsh et al., 1988; Marsh & Shavelson, 1985). With respect to these two different approaches to testing for hierarchical structure, note that the use of higher order factor analyses is only statistically possible when there are multiple first-order factors, as in the case of self-concepts in relation to several academic subject areas (see, e.g., Marsh, 1990c). This contingency is directly related to the issue of statistical identification in the analyses of covariance structures (for an elaboration of this topic, see Bollen, 1989; Byrne, 1994). Because statistical identification must be satisfied at each level of higher order model specification, third-order models are rare.[3]

Four primary conclusions from this validation work of academic self-concept are of particular import here. First, on the basis of an abundance of evidence across various populations, it seems clear that academic self-concept is multidimensionally structured. One interesting complication, however, is the replicated finding of a negligible correlation between math and English self-concepts, albeit both facets are presumed to be explained by the higher order factor of academic self-concept (which, by definition, assumes their substantial correlation). Paradoxically, whereas the correlation between math and English self-concepts has been found to be close to zero, the correlation between math and English achievement has been relatively high. These findings have been consistent across all three Self Description Questionnaire instruments (Marsh, 1990b) as well as across other self-concept measures (Byrne & Shavelson, 1986; Marsh et al., 1988). In search of answers to this conundrum, Marsh proposed (a) a revised academic struc-

---

3. To evaluate the appropriateness of a third-order model and, thus, the validity of interpretations that are based on its structure, readers need to familiarize themselves with at least the basic elements of statistical identification. For a nonmathematical and simplified introduction to the topic, and for an application of the basic assessment criteria to a second-order model, see Byrne (1994).

ture for the Shavelson model, which he labeled the *Marsh/Shavelson model* (Marsh & Shavelson, 1985), and (b) the I/E frame-of-reference model (Marsh, 1986d), which was described earlier.

Second, although the hierarchical structure of academic self-concept, as originally postulated by Shavelson et al. (1976) and noted earlier, has been shown to basically hold across age when the pattern of latent correlations among self-concept facets has been examined (e.g., Byrne & Shavelson, 1986; Byrne & Worth Gavin, in press; Shavelson & Bolus, 1982), this structure has been shown to differ slightly when multiple academic subjects are included in the model and it is tested as a higher order structure (see Marsh, 1990c; Marsh et al., 1988; Marsh & Shavelson, 1985). This revised structure was incorporated into the Marsh/Shavelson model. For the sake of clarification, both the orginal (Shavelson et al., 1976) and modified (Marsh & Shavelson, 1985) academic components of the hierarchical model are portrayed in Figure 1.4.

Third, substantial research has demonstrated that although academic self-concept becomes increasingly differentiated during preadolescence (Grades 2–5), these facets tend not to become more so in the adolescent years (e.g., Byrne & Worth Gavin, in press; Marsh, 1989, 1990b).

Finally, findings related to developmental changes in the hierarchical structure of academic self-concept are somewhat mixed. Whereas Marsh has reported this pattern to be relatively clear for preadolescents, albeit to gradually weaken with age (Marsh, 1990b), findings reported by Byrne and Worth Gavin showed only minor deterioration in fit. However, these differences are quite likely a function of the two different approaches taken in analyzing hierarchical structure, as noted earlier. Given multiple subject-specific self-concepts at the first-order level, the most rigorous test of hierarchical structure is to use higher order factor analysis. Typically, findings from these analyses will render intercorrelations among self-concept facets to be smaller, hence the findings of a weaker pattern of hierarchical structure in the Marsh studies.

Construct validity research bearing on the nonacademic branch of the Shavelson et al. (1976) hierarchical model is only now beginning to appear in the literature. Focusing only on social self-concept, Byrne and Shavelson (1996) recently tested the validity of a multidimensional and hierarchical structure for pre-, early, and late adolescents. Because social self-concept structure, as originally depicted by Shavelson et al. (see Figure 1.3), was intended only as a general representation of dimensional structure, it was necessary to modify this portion of the

Figure 1.4

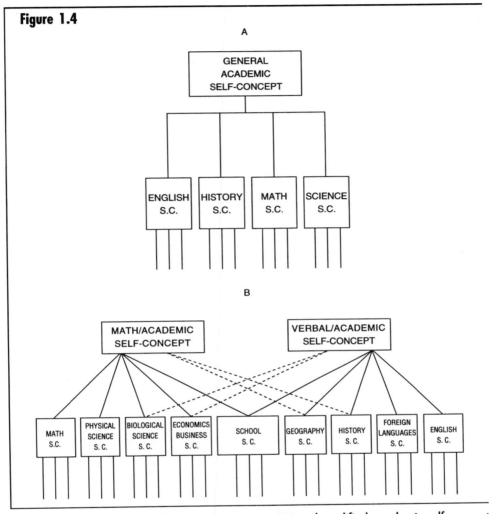

The original academic self-concept component (A) and modified academic self-concept component (B) of the Shavelson, Hubner, and Stanton (1976) hierarchical model (Marsh, Byrne, & Shavelson, 1988). Reprinted from *Journal of Educational Psychology, 80,* 378. Copyright 1988 by the American Psychological Association. (S.C. = self-concept.)

model to enable the testing of conceptually viable hypotheses. As such, global social self-concept occupied the apex of the pyramid; it then branched into two subcomponents: social self-concept (school) and social self-concept (family). The third tier of the hierarchy comprised the more specific facets of social self-concept; these were classmate and teacher social self-concepts and sibling and parent social self-concepts as subcomponents of the higher order facets of school and family, re-

Figure 1.5

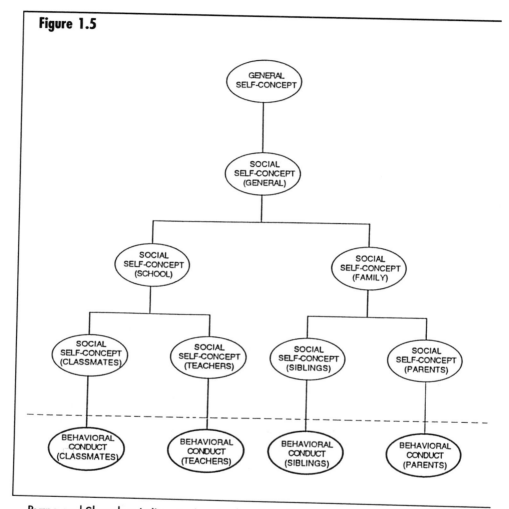

Byrne and Shavelson's (in press) revised social self-concept component of the Shavelson, Hubner, and Stanton (1976) hierarchical model. Reprinted from *Journal of Personality and Social Psychology* (in press). Copyright 1996 by the American Psychological Association.

spectively. A pictorial display of this revised social self-concept portion of the hierarchical model is shown in Figure 1.5.

On the basis of self, peer, teacher, and parent ratings of perceived social competence for each of three age groups—preadolescents (Grade 3), early adolescents (Grade 7), and late adolescents (Grade 11)—findings from this initial study of the social self-concept component of the Shavelson model revealed a multidimensional social self-concept structure that becomes increasingly differentiated and a hierarchical ordering that becomes better defined with age. Overall, findings were in keeping with both the Shavelson et al. (1976) conceptualization of self-concept structure and developmental processes that underlie self-concept formation (see, e.g., Harter, 1983, 1988a, 1990b).

Recently, Marsh and Redmayne have begun a series of construct validity studies bearing on the physical self-concept portion of the Shavelson hierarchical model (Marsh, 1994a, in press-a; Marsh & Redmayne, 1994). Of importance in this research is Fox's (1990; Fox & Corbin, 1989) postulated hierarchical model of physical self-concept, which incorporates aspects of the Shavelson et al. (1976) model. In keeping with all applications of the latter, Fox (1990; Fox & Corbin, 1989) proposed a hierarchical structure composed of general self-concept at the apex and global physical self-concept at the next level, with specific facets of physical self-concept on the lower tier. Formal testing of this hypothesized structure is an important component in the present construct validity work being conducted by Marsh and Redmayne.

From studies of Australian boys and girls age 9–15 years (Marsh, 1993c), adolescent girls age 13–14 years (Marsh & Redmayne, 1994), and high school students age 12–18 years (Marsh, 1994a), Marsh and Redmayne reported findings that supported the hierarchical model of self-concept. That is, they validated that global physical self-concept could be subdivided into components analogous to the subdivision of global academic self-concept into specific school subjects (see Figure 1.3); the specfic physical self-concept components related to endurance, balance, flexibility, strength, and appearance.

Although another revision of the Shavelson model that involved both the academic and nonacademic branches of the model was originally proposed by Song and Hattie (1984), it has only recently been tested by Hattie (1992).[4] Song and Hattie made two major modifications to the Shavelson model; these involved the division of (a) academic self-concept into achievement self-concept (perceived actual achievement), ability self-concept (perceived capabilities for achievement), and classroom self-concept (confidence in classroom activities); and (b) nonacademic self-concept into social self-concept and self-presentation (self-regard) self-concept; these, in turn, branched into family and peer self-

---

4. The focus of Song and Hattie's study was to investigate relations among home environment, self-concept, and academic achievement, within the framework of a structural equation model. More specifically, they tested the impact of family structure and socioeconomic status on social self-concept, academic self-concept, presentation of self, and academic achievement, mediated through a composite variable termed *psychological characteristics.*

concepts and confidence in self and physical self-concepts, respectively. In describing the Song and Hattie revision, Marsh and Hattie (1996) underscored two important differences from the original Shavelson et al. (1976) formulation. First, physical self-concept is intended to emphasize physical appearance. Second, confidence, although related to emotional self-concept, overlaps with general self-esteem. A schematic presentation of the Song and Hattie (1984) model is shown in Figure 1.6.

On the basis of self-concept responses from Korean and Australian adolescents and of a comparison of several second-order factor models, Hattie (1992) reported strong support for the postulated seven first-order factors; his findings therefore further substantiate the multidimensionality of self-concept. Furthermore, although his analyses yielded support for three second-order self-concept facets, this structure differed from the one originally postulated. As such, classroom self-concept related more to the second-order social, rather than the academic, self-concept facet. In keeping with the original Shavelson model, however, Hattie found that the ability and achievement facets could be extended to include specific subject matter self-concepts; in addition, the physical domain was found to represent both appearance and ability components (Hattie, 1992; Marsh & Hattie, 1996). (For an extended discussion of each of the theoretical models discussed in this section, readers are referred to Marsh & Hattie, 1996).

Finally, interesting research has recently begun in which the Shavelson model is extended to incorporate self-concepts bearing on artistic areas such as dance, dramatic art, visual art, and music skills (see, e.g., Vispoel, 1995c). Vispoel compared several alternatively specified models, with the initial intents (a) to determine the model that most optimally allowed for the integration of the artistic domains into the Shavelson hierarchy and (b) to assess relations between artistic and other self-concept facets. On the basis of work with self-concept responses for 831 college students, he reported that dance, dramatic art, visual art, and music skills were best integrated into the hierarchy as components of a higher order artistic self-concept factor that was distinct from academic (math and verbal) and other nonacademic (physical, social, and moral) higher order factors. Overall, findings from this research substantiated the multidimensionality of self-concept structure but provided only a modicum of support for a hierarchical ordering of self-concept facets.

As a follow-up to this important research, Vispoel (1995b) concen-

Figure 1.6

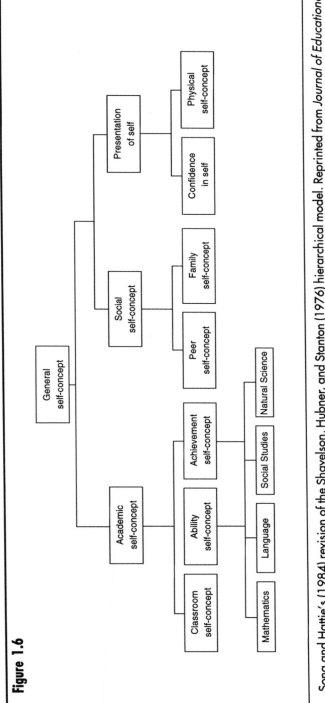

Song and Hattie's (1984) revision of the Shavelson, Hubner, and Stanton (1976) hierarchical model. Reprinted from *Journal of Educational Psychology, 76,* 1270. Copyright 1984 by the American Psychological Association.

trated on the music component of his initial model and subsequently proposed a theoretical model of music self-concept that could be used to guide future investigative inquiry related to this aspect of the fine arts. With this postulated model, Vispoel hypothesized that music self-concept was organized, multifaceted, and hierarchically ordered and that relations between music and higher order facets of self-concept were mediated to some degree by domain importance. As such, Vispoel's music self-concept model embraces the features of the Shavelson model as well as the notions of domain importance advocated by Harter (1985b).

Although the Shavelson hierarchical model remains the most empirically tested and validated of all self-concept models, it nonetheless has not been without some modicum of criticism (see, e.g., Harter, 1983, 1985a, 1986; Hattie, 1992). Hattie suggested that the form of the hierarchical model was still equivocal and suggested two directions that future research should undertake. The first of these relates to the match between homogeneity of sample and appropriateness of theoretical model. He argued, for example, that although a multidimensional, hierarchical structure of self-concept might be optimal for one group of individuals, a unidimensional structure might better represent another group. Hattie's second concern represented an extension of his first one but related more directly to developmental considerations. For example, arguing that self-concept was "more unitary before the child reaches adolescence," Hattie (1992, p. 87) called for research that predicted, from theoretical concerns, which persons were likely to have self-concepts that were multidimensional and hierarchical and which ones were likely to have self-concepts that were unitary. In the light of the substantial volume of research that has addressed such developmental concerns in relation to the hierarchical model, however, the latter call seems rather curious. Finally, Harter's (1983, 1985a, 1986, 1990c) concerns would appear to echo those of Hattie, that the hierarchical model cannot be generalized to all. Arguing that individuals differ in the extent to which a particular structure of self-concept is optimal, she supports the incorporation of information that reflects the perceived importance of domains being targeted by the researcher.

In summary, the hierarchical model, to some extent, can incorporate one of four models described earlier as a special case (Marsh, in press-a). For example, in keeping with the true unidimensional model, it hypothesizes a global self-concept at the apex of the hierarchy. Thus, Marsh (in press-a) argued that support for the true unidimensional model can also reflect concomitant support for the hierarchical model when the hierarchical structure is very strong. Conversely, support for a weak version of the independent model could be interpreted as support for the hierarchical model when the hierarchy is very weak. In fact, Marsh (in press-a) stated that "only in extreme cases in which correlations among the self-concept factors approach the reliabilities of the factors, or are consistently close to zero, would support for the hierarchical model be dubious." Relatedly, support for the correlated-factor model, by implication (in terms of higher order factoring), means support for the hierarchical model. Finally, given the possibility of a hierarchical ordering of levels in one or more facets (Marsh & Hattie, 1996), support for the taxonomic model implies support for the hierarchical model. As noted by Marsh (in press-a), however, this versatility of the hierarchical model is both its strength and its weakness. It is a strength in the sense that it provides a broad framework within which to study the structure of self-concept; it is a weakness because it may not be falsifiable. It is critically important, therefore, that any hypothesized hierarchical model of self-concept be specified in sufficient detail to allow for a rigorous testing of its postulated structure (Marsh, in press-a). Because (a) the Shavelson et al. (1976) model, together with all its later revisions (e.g., Byrne & Shavelson, in press; Marsh & Shavelson, 1985; Marsh et al., 1988; Song & Hattie, 1984), has met these demands of specification and (b) virtually all construct validity research has directly tested its theoretical structure using statistically sophisticated and rigorous methodological strategies, one can feel confident in construct interpretations arising from this research.

Self-concept instruments in the present volume that have been developed from the Shavelson hierarchical model comprise the following: all Self Description Questionnaires (Marsh, 1990c, 1992b; chapter 5; Marsh, 1990c, 1992c; Marsh, Richards, Johnson, Roche, & Tremayne, 1994; chapter 6; Marsh, 1992d; chapter 7); the Perception of Ability Scale for Students (Boersma & Chapman, 1992; chapter 5), and the Physical Self-Perception Profile (Fox & Corbin, 1989).

Importance-Discrepancy Ratings of Self-Concept

Harter has been steadfast in her contention that any model of self-concept should incorporate the importance (or salience), as well as the valence and strength of the domains, about which the individual is asked to make a self-judgment. Thus, in the development of their series of self-concept measures, Harter (1985b, 1988c) and colleagues (Harter & Pike, 1984; Messer & Harter, 1986; Neemann & Harter, 1986; Renick & Harter, 1988) addressed this concern through the introduction of importance ratings and the actual/importance discrepancy approach to self-concept scoring. Although this aspect of self-concept measurement certainly has its proponents (e.g., Vispoel, 1992, 1993b, 1995a), it also has its critics (e.g., Cronbach & Furby, 1970; Marsh, 1986b; Wylie, 1974, 1979, 1989). In the light of substantial debate on the topic over at least the past two decades, we turn now to a brief review of the issues, as they relate to this particular approach to self-concept measurement. However, for a more extended discussion of the actual/importance discrepancy, as well as other approaches to the formulation of self-concept scores, see Marsh (1986b, 1993e), Marsh and Hattie (1996), and Wells and Marwell (1976); for a summary of empirical research designed to test these approaches, see Harter (1988a, 1988b, 1990a), Hattie (1992), and Marsh (1986b, 1993e).

The notion of importance ratings and discrepancy scores is rooted in James's (1890/1963) contention that domain-specific self-evaluations, as the building blocks of global self-esteem, are integrated according to their perceived importance, salience, certainty, and relations to ideals. On the basis of this theoretical perspective, one could conclude that relations between general and domain-specific self-concepts (e.g., math self-concept) should be a function of (a) the importance that an individual associates with each domain, (b) the standard of excellence (or ideal) that the individual sets for each domain, and (c) the certainty with which the individual views each domain. Researchers who endorse this view typically have respondents complete a global self-concept (i.e., self-esteem) scale (e.g., Rosenberg's [1965] Self-Esteem Scale) or subscale (e.g., Global Worth subscale of Harter's [1985b] Self-Perception Profile for Children [SPPC]); a multidimensional, domain-specific scale (e.g., Harter's SPPC); and a rating scale designed to tap the perceived importance of each domain (e.g., the Importance Rating Form accompanying Harter's SPPC).

Taken together, the essence of James's perspective is that for individuals who perceive themselves as competent in areas that they deem to be important, general self-concept will be high; for those perceiving themselves as incompetent in these same areas, general self-concept will be low. Thus, for domains regarded as unimportant, it makes little difference whether perceptions of competence are high or low (Harter, 1990a). To tap the ratio between perceptions of competence and their related importance for particular content domains, Harter (1988b) proposed the idea of subtracting the importance score from the competence score; this differential has been labeled the "actual/importance discrepancy score" (see Marsh & Hattie, 1996).

Although the idea of discrepancy scores seems intuitively reasonable, at least three important criticisms are noted here. First, in the same way that gain scores are considered to be unreliable (see, e.g., Thorndike, Cunningham, Thorndike, & Hagen, 1991), so too are discrepancy scores. As such, because the magnitude of reliability is typically inversely related to the correlation between two measures (Hattie, 1992) and the correlation between one's perceived importance and perceived competence for a particular domain is expected to be high, the reliability will necessarily be low. Consequently, variables having high correlations with discrepancy scores are scarce. Second, because the variance of a discrepancy score represents the arithmetic combination of two variables, the variances of which are conceptually meaningful when considered separately, there is the question of the extent to which its correspondence with the construct of interest is of a similar magnitude. The problem relates to validity and raises the question of how to interpret "variance that is common to both single measures and that which is specific to each" (Wells & Marwell, 1976, p. 97). Finally, there is the question of metric with respect to discrepancy scores. Because these scores result from the subtraction of one score from another, it seems unlikely that they manifest the properties of an interval scale. As a consequence, discrepancy scores cannot be meaningfully interpreted (Hattie, 1992; Wylie, 1974, 1979, 1989). In summary, these major problems associated with discrepancy scores led Cronbach and Furby (1970) to posit that they "are rarely useful, no matter how they may be adjusted or refined" (p. 68) and Wylie (1989) to state that their use "cannot be recommended" (p. 115).

Instruments in the present volume that are accompanied by importance-rating scales comprise all Self-Perception Profiles developed by Harter and colleagues (chapters 4–8); the Physical Self-Perception Profile (Fox & Corbin, 1989; chapter 7); and the Arts and Music Self-Perception Profiles developed by Vispoel (1992, 1993b, 1995a; chapter 9).

Measuring Self-Concept: The Psychometric Issues

2

The classic reviews of self-concept research by Shavelson et al. (1976) and Wylie (1974, 1979) were instrumental in heightening awareness of methodological problems that permeated the growing number of confusing and conflicting findings in the area. These researchers identified several areas of psychometric concern. In addition to the conceptual problems noted in chapter 1, they cited psychometric weaknesses associated with the development, testing, and use of most self-concept measures. These deficiencies related to the paucity of reported reliability and validity data, the disregard of normative information, and the lack of concern for cross-cultural and developmental factors. Over the years, there has also been mounting concern regarding the widespread use of self-report inventories and their reputed proneness to various types of response-set bias.

This chapter contains a brief discussion pertinent to each of these psychometric issues. More specifically, I begin with a description of the basic elements of *reliability* and *validity*. Readers who are familiar with the basic principles of reliability and validity may wish to circumvent this initial section and advance, instead, to the next section, which addresses the issue of appropriate instrument use in accordance with available normative data. I then discuss issues related to cross-cultural and developmental factors in measuring self-concept. Finally, I review different types of response bias typically associated with the self-report approach to self-concept measurement.

The Issue of Reliability and Validity

Although the reliability and validity of measuring instruments are inseparably intertwined, they effectively represent two sides of the same coin; the estimation of one requires certain presumptions about the other (Wells & Marwell, 1976). In essence, reliability serves as the upper bound for validity in the sense that it delimits the magnitude of the validity coefficient, a statistic representing the extent to which test scores may be interpreted as valid.[1] For example, even in the unlikely event that all score variance of a particular measure were considered to be valid, its validity at best could only equal the square root of its reliability (e.g., Cohen, Montague, Nathanson, & Swerdlik, 1988; Wells & Marwell, 1976). In relation to psychological measurement in general, and self-concept measurement in particular, several forms of reliability and validity are of concern. Each of these is now reviewed.

Reliability

The concept of *reliability* refers to the extent to which measurements (or scores) on an assessment instrument are consistent. The indicator of such consistency is the reliability coefficient, which is often reported and interpreted as a Pearson *r* statistic; the closer this value is to 1.00, the higher the reliability. The lower the reliability of a measuring instrument, the less consistent will be any scores resulting from its use.

Basically, examination of a measure's reliability centers on the estimate of error variance associated with its scores. According to Anastasi (1988), this error variance can derive from *content sampling, time sampling,* or *interscorer differences.* (For a more detailed breakdown of major categories, see Nunnally, 1978.) Typically, content-sampling error focuses on the extent to which items measuring the same construct (i.e., items in the same subscale) are homogeneous and is represented by *internal consistency reliability.*[2] Time-sampling error focuses on the stability of measurements over time and is represented by *stability reliability,* based on a suitable intervening time interval. Finally, interscorer-differences error is concerned with the extent to which independent observers or

---

1. *Validity,* in this sense, refers to criterion-related validity because it is possible that a test can yield weak evidence of criterion-related validity, albeit strong evidence of other types of validity (e.g., content-related validity).

2. Although item homogeneity can also be evaluated by means of parallel forms of reliability (equivalent forms of a test that have been built from the same set of test specifications), this procedure engenders a number of practical problems, especially as they relate to self-concept measurement.

examiners of the same phenomena are consistent in their scores; it is represented by *interrater reliability*. Because this type of reliability is typically associated with measures that require subjective judgments regarding the interpretation of scores, they are not of interest in the present volume, in which only self-report measures using specific scale formats are evaluated. Internal consistency reliability is typically estimated by means of one of three procedures: the *split-half method*, the *coefficient alpha formula*, or the *Kuder–Richardson (K–R 20) formula*. The split-half method involves administering a questionnaire once to a group of subjects, splitting the items into equivalent halves using some logical procedure (e.g., odd/even numbers), scoring and summing the scores for each half, and computing the correlation between the two summative scores. This correlation then represents the internal consistency reliability coefficient. Calculation of the coefficient alpha is based on a formula developed by Cronbach (1951) and can be conceptualized as the mean of all possible split-half correlations that have been calculated by means of the Rulon (or Guttman) method (Crocker & Algina, 1986); it is most appropriately used on tests that comprise polychotomous items. Finally, the K–R 20 formula yields a reliability coefficient that is a special case of coefficient alpha when the items of the test are dichotomously scored (Thorndike et al., 1991).

Stability reliability is most commonly represented by the test–retest reliability coefficient, which is computed through the correlation of scores on the same subjects obtained from an administration of the same test on two different occasions. Ideally, the pair of scores should be the same or, at least, highly similar. Although the time delay between tests can vary from a few days to several months, 2 weeks has been found to be the most common practice (Hammill, Brown, & Bryant, 1992). Nonetheless, there is no absolute criterion regarding this issue of time. Clearly, the time span between testing depends both on the purpose of testing and on the hypothesized stability of the construct being measured. However, the time period should be long enough to allow the effects of memory or practice to dissipate but short enough to ensure that test scores are not adversely affected by developmental or historical changes (Crocker & Algina, 1986).

The question of how large a reliability coefficient should be before it can be considered adequate is not easily answered. This value will depend on a number of factors, such as purpose of testing, decisions to be made, and the like. As a result, opinions bearing on recommended criterion values have ranged from .70 to .98 over the years.

However, in establishing a standard against which to evaluate tests for inclusion in *A Consumer's Guide to Tests in Print,* Hammill et al. (1992) chose .80 as the minimally acceptable level of reliability, with a value of .90 being preferred. For an excellent discussion of the issue of minimum reliability level, see Thorndike et al. (1991).

In her review, Wylie (1974, 1979) noted that despite the ease with which reliability coefficients can be computed, such information was sadly lacking for the majority of measures used in self-concept research. As a consequence, she strongly advocated that reliability indexes be routinely reported in all substantive research. Indeed, the *Standards for Educational and Psychological Testing* (1985) states that "test developers and publishers have primary responsibility for obtaining and reporting evidence concerning reliability and errors of measurement adequate for intended purposes" (p. 19). Furthermore, it is suggested that users also have a responsibility to ensure that the available information regarding reliability is relevant to their intended uses and interpretation (*Standards,* 1985). For a more detailed discussion of the many aspects of reliability, see Crocker and Algina (1986), Nunnally (1978), Thorndike et al. (1991), and the *Standards* (1985).

Validity

It is customary to regard *validity* as the extent to which an assessment instrument measures that which it was designed to measure. However, the more precise definition presented in the *Standards* (1985) makes clear the fact that it is not the instrument per se that is valid, but rather, the scores that derive from the administered and completed instrument. As defined in this document, "the concept [of validity] refers to the appropriateness, meaningfulness, and usefulness of the specific inferences made from test scores" (p. 9). Test validation, then, involves the gathering of evidence in support of these inferences. Thus, "inferences regarding specific uses of a test are validated, not the test itself" (*Standards,* 1985, p. 9).

Historically, evidence in support of validity can be categorized as content related, criterion related, and construct related. Although the *Standards* (1985) advises that, ideally, validation should embrace all three categories, it concludes that it is the quality rather than the quantity of evidence that is of primary importance. We turn now to a brief description of these three strategies for obtaining evidence in support of validity.

Content validity refers to the extent to which the sample of items on a measuring instrument adequately represents some defined universe or domain of content (*Standards*, 1985). Typically, content-related validity is sought in support of achievement measures. Nonetheless, Wells and Marwell (1976) argued that such validity is also important with respect to attitude and psychological measures, contending "to the extent that the items of a measure have meaning and content, they will be limited and specific to some degree" (p. 153). Clearly, then, evidence in support of content-related validity is just as critical to the development of self-concept measures as it is to that of achievement measures. In other words, if a measure's scores are to be valid, it is essential that the content of its items be interpreted in exactly the same way by all respondents. This, of course, would be the concern, for example, in administering a self-concept measure across ability levels of schoolchildren (e.g., low track/high track; Byrne, 1988a). Indeed, substantive researchers interested in testing for mean group differences on some variable(s) typically assume that the measuring instrument is factorially invariant across groups. Although this assumption is rarely, if ever, tested within the context of a substantive study, methodological self-concept research has demonstrated that there can be differences in terms of both the item measurements (i.e., factor loadings) and the structural relations among the underlying latent constructs (see, e.g., Byrne & Schneider, 1988; Byrne & Shavelson, 1987).

Criterion validity examines the correlation between a score on a particular instrument with some criterion (or standard of judgment) such as a test, diagnostic classification, or performance of a specific task (Hammill et al., 1992). There are two types of criterion-related validity: *predictive validity* and *concurrent validity*. In seeking evidence of predictive validity, a researcher examines the correlation between scores on the measure of interest, and performance (or other) scores on some related criterion, at some later time. Although typically associated with aptitude and achievement tests as predictors of job performance and academic success, respectively, a hypothetical case could be made for the search for predictive validity in relation to self-concept. For example, given that (a) there is a sufficiently strong relation between math self-concept and grades in math (which there is [e.g., Byrne, 1996; Marsh, 1993a]) and (b) self-concept causes achievement (rather than the reverse), which, to date, remains unresolved (e.g., Byrne, 1990, 1996), predictive validity might be determined by correlating scores on a measure of math self-concept with scores on a math achievement test, administered after the completion of a remedial math intervention program perhaps 6 months later.

In seeking evidence of concurrent validity, the researcher typically correlates scores on the instrument of interest with those on some well-established instrument designed to measure the same construct (or constructs, in the case of subscales). In contrast to predictive validity procedures, however, the scores used in testing for concurrent validity derive from measures that were administered at the same point in time. In contrast to Wells and Marwell's (1976) observation 20 years ago that criterion validity had shown little application in the area of self-concept, there are now numerous examples of this type of validity work bearing on self-concept measures. For example, in seeking evidence of concurrent validity related to the newly developed Physical Self-Description Questionnaire (Marsh & Redmayne, 1994), Marsh, Richards, Johnson, Roche, and Tremayne (1994) correlated scores from this instrument with those from two other more established instruments—the Physical Self-Perception Profile (Fox, 1990) and Physical Self-Concept Scale (Richards, 1988)—and then examined the correlations within the framework of a multitrait–multimethod (MTMM) matrix.

Another approach to seeking evidence of concurrent validity is to correlate scores on particular domain-specific subscales of an instrument with the criterion variable that each is designed to measure. For example, in testing for the validity of subscale scores on the Self Description Questionnaire III, Marsh and O'Neill (1984) hypothesized that math achievement would correlate most highly with math self-concept (as represented by its subscale score), less highly with other academic achievement areas, and not at all with nonacademic factors (such as social behavior). Although this important type of concurrent validity is not often found in self-concept research, Marsh made it a standard practice in the development and testing of his series of self-concept measures.

Construct validity encompasses two modes of inquiry: (a) the validation of a theory and (b) the validation of a measuring instrument. In validating a theory, a researcher seeks empirical evidence in support of hypothesized construct relations both among facets of the same construct (within-network relations) and among different constructs (between-networks relations). These theoretical linkages represent the nomological network of the hypothesized construct (Cronbach & Meehl, 1955).

Validation of a measuring instrument entails the testing of construct interpretations of scores derived from the instrument. Accordingly, the researcher seeks empirical evidence that the constructs purportedly measured by the instrument are, in fact, the ones being measured. In the case of an instrument comprising several subscales, evidence of construct validity is demonstrated if the scales exhibit a well-defined factor structure that is consistent with the underlying theory.

Because construct validation involves the interplay of theory construction and test development (Anastasi, 1986), the two processes are complementary rather than concurrent. Thus, a researcher either validates a theory by ensuring sound instrumentation or validates a measuring instrument by ensuring the soundness of the theory within which it was developed. In this regard, the *Standards* (1985) states that constructs inherent to any measure should be embedded in a conceptual framework, "no matter how imperfect that framework might be" (p. 9). Given the focus of the present volume on the measurement of self-concept, the following discussion of construct validity issues is limited to measuring instruments only.

In seeking evidence of construct validity related to a measuring instrument, the researcher tests hypotheses bearing on the underlying theoretical framework.[3] Such hypotheses can test many aspects of construct validity. For example, given that an instrument purports to measure multidimensional facets of self-concept (e.g., academic, social, and physical), one can test for the validity of its underlying factorial structure; either exploratory or confirmatory factor analytic procedures would be used, depending on the development status of the instrument. If an instrument is in the embryonic stage of development, then exploratory procedures would be most appropriate; if, on the other hand, its development has been completed and, thus, it purports to measure one or more constructs, then confirmatory factor analyses would be most appropriate. For a nonmathematical and paradigmatic introduction, see Byrne (1989, 1994); for two examples of comprehensive descriptions of these procedures applied to self-concept measures, see Byrne (1988b) and Marsh and Richards (1988b).

Other aspects of construct validity, such as evidence of convergent and discriminant validity related to particular self-concept facets, may also be of interest. Most typically, these questions are addressed using

---

3. Construct validity bearing on the conceptual framework itself also can be tested. However, hypotheses related to both the theoretical structure and the measuring instrument cannot be tested simultaneously; the testing of one necessarily presumes the validity of the other (Byrne, 1984; Wells & Marwell, 1976).

MTMM analyses—a technique introduced by Campbell and Fiske (1959), whereby multiple traits (e.g., self-concept facets) are measured by multiple methods and all trait–method correlations are arranged in an MTMM matrix. (For an excellent discussion and paradigmatic application of MTMM analysis using the Campbell–Fiske methodology, see Rogers, 1995.)

Construct validity research conducted within the framework of an MTMM design focuses on three issues: (a) evidence of convergent validity, the extent to which different assessment methods concur in their measurement of the same trait (or construct)—ideally, these values should be moderately high; (b) evidence of discriminant validity, the extent to which independent assessment methods diverge in their measurement of different traits—ideally, these values should demonstrate minimal convergence; (c) evidence of method effects, an extension of the discriminant validity issue. Method effects represent bias that can derive from use of the same method in the assessment of different traits; correlations among these traits are typically higher than correlations among those measured by different methods.

Although Campbell and Fiske's (1959) approach to MTMM analyses has made substantial contribution to the psychometric literature over the years, numerous limitations in its basic methodology are now widely known (for reviews, see Byrne & Goffin, 1993; Schmitt & Stults, 1986; Widaman, 1985). First, the Campbell–Fiske criteria function as rules of thumb rather than as precise quantitative measurements of construct validity. Second, with each addition of traits or methods to the model, the number of nonindependent comparisons increases dramatically; this factor, coupled with the subjectivity of the evaluative criteria, makes it difficult, if not impossible, to determine the extent to which convergent and discriminant validity have been attained. Third, despite criteria based on only visible inspection of observed correlations, inferences are made regarding the underlying (i.e., latent) traits and methods. Fourth, the provision of separate estimates of variance due to traits, methods, and error and estimated relations among the latent trait and method factors is not possible. Finally, hypotheses related to construct validity issues cannot be tested statistically.

In the light of these weaknesses in the Campbell–Fiske design, increasingly more MTMM studies are being based on the analysis of covariance structures within the framework of a confirmatory factor analytic model that can address these issues. Indeed, following Widaman's (1985) seminal paper, in which he proposed a taxonomy of nested model comparisons, use of the general confirmatory factor analytic model to test various aspects of construct validity escalated substantially. For a nonmathematical introduction to, and application of, this approach to MTMM analyses based on Widaman's taxonomy, see Byrne (1994) and Byrne and Bazana (in press).

Although construct validity research related to self-concept is still sparse compared with substantive research on the topic, the years after the Shavelson et al. (1976) and Wylie (1974, 1979) critiques have demonstrated substantial increase in this regard. Of vital importance in the selection of a measuring instrument is the extent to which it demonstrates evidence of construct validity. Furthermore, because the focus of most substantive research is concerned with testing for mean group differences, it is critically important for the researcher to know that the instrument is functioning in exactly the same way across groups. That is to say, for each group under study, the interpretation of item content, the subscale clustering of items, and the subscale correlations are the same. Thus, in evaluating the construct validity of a particular measure, I strongly urge researchers to seek evidence from multiple-group as well as single-group analyses. The most rigorous approach to multiple-group construct validity entails the analysis of covariance structures wherein the equivalency of the instrument's factorial structure is tested statistically. As such, the researcher tests for the invariance across groups of factor loading weights and pattern, as well as relations among the underlying constructs (i.e., multidimensional structure of the construct being measured).

For comprehensive reviews of construct validity research, readers are referred to other sources with respect to each of the following topics: (a) diverse self-concept instruments, see Byrne (1984, 1990); (b) a particular family of instruments (e.g., Self Description Questionnaires I, II, and III), see Marsh (1990a); and (c) tests for factorial invariance across populations, see Byrne (1988a, 1988b), Byrne and Schneider (1988), and Marsh (1987b). For more comprehensive discussions of validity issues in general, see Crocker and Algina (1986), Nunnally (1978), Thorndike et al. (1991), and the *Standards* (1985).

The Issue of Appropriate Instrument Use

A second difficulty in self-concept research noted by Wylie (1974, 1979) was the clear misuse of established measuring instruments. In particular, she noted that although many scales were developed and normed for one population, they were often used with samples representative of another population. Such use of a measuring instrument makes the very strong assumption that the interpretation of all questionnaire items and the conceptual structure of the underlying construct are equivalent across the two populations. However, the probability of this being so is quite likely scant. Indeed, the extent to which they are not equivalent reflects on their content validity, the interpretability of the test scores, and, ultimately, on the construct validity of the instrument. Thus, it is critically important that researchers be fully cognizant of all normative information related to a particular measuring instrument before finalizing any decision regarding its use. In particular, researchers need to evaluate the relevancy, recency, and representativeness of the normative data in selecting the instrument for their own use.

The previous caveat notwithstanding, it is often of interest to examine the validity of scores from a particular measure for a population that differs from the one on which the instrument was normed. Indeed, such applications are likely to be welcomed by the test developer (and publisher). However, use of the instrument in this way carries with it psychometric and ethical responsibilities that bear on the construct validity of the test. Indeed, the onus is on the researcher to provide evidence in support of both the reliability and validity of an instrument's scores in relation to the newly tested population. In this regard, the *Standards* (1985) advises that test users "verify periodically that changes in populations of test takers, objectives of the testing process, or changes in available techniques have not made their current procedures inappropriate" (p. 42).

The Issue of Cross-Cultural Factors

Although, substantively, mean differences in self-concept across culturally diverse groups have been of interest for many years, the methodological focus on the extent to which self-concept measures are equivalent across culture is relatively recent. Indeed, construct validity research in this area has revealed a number of ways in which differential psychometric properties of an instrument and differential response reactions to an assessment procedure can lead to statistically significant differences in self-concept across cultural groups representing clinical (e.g., Jewell, 1989) as well as nonclinical (Watkins & Akande, 1992) populations.

Before I review issues related to these findings, note that much of the literature advanced as cross-cultural research has, in essence, addressed questions of ethnicity or race. Thus, it seems appropriate at the outset to clarify the distinguishing features of these somewhat ambiguous terms. The term *culture* is a much broader concept than are the other two and refers to the total way of life of a particular social group: its customs, values, beliefs, patterns of behavior, and the like; some definitions also include material artifacts such as crafts, tools, and so on (Theodorson & Theodorson, 1969). The term *ethnicity*, although encompassing some of the same features as culture, has a more limited context. *Ethnicity* refers to a common cultural tradition and sense of identity that defines a subgroup of individuals within a larger society; typically, the term is used in reference to visible minority groups. As such, members of a particular ethnic group exhibit cultural characteristics (e.g., language and dress customs) that differ from those of other members of their society. Common to members of an ethnic group is a sense of identification and distinctiveness that sets them apart from the larger society. Finally, although the term *race* is technically an anthropological classification of mankind that is based on particular physical characteristics, it is most commonly used in reference to any group that is visibly different from the larger society (Theodorson & Theodorson, 1969). Thus, the terms *ethnic* and *racial* tend to be used synonymously with respect to a minority group. Typically, cross-cultural research embraces one of two perspectives in measuring a construct of interest: (a) use of the same measuring instrument in its original linguistic form across ethnic/racial (i.e., minority) groups or across ethnic/racial and dominant cultural groups and (b) use of a translated version of an instrument for populations whose culture differs from the one for which the instrument was originally developed and normed. In both instances, researchers and clinicians have no grounds for assuming either that the instrument operates equivalently or that the norms are equally applicable across groups. Although most research concerned with these methodological issues has focused on achievement tests, the issues are particularly potent for psychological assessment, in general, and self-concept measurement, in particular. For, as Oyserman and Markus (1993) aptly noted, "though individuals worldwide all appear to have a sense of self, its content, processes, and structures are bound to socio-cultural context and thus are likely to differ" (p. 212). While recognition of this cultural factor is often exalted by reviewers and theorists, its presence is rarely realized in empirical investigation (Hart & Edelstein, 1992). In general, problems indigenous to cross-cultural comparisons of self-concept relate to two primary issues: instrument equivalence and adequate test translation. I turn now to a review of each of these topics.

Instrument Equivalence

As noted earlier, a common, albeit incorrect, assumption in research that tests for mean differences across groups is that the measuring instrument is operating in exactly the same way for each group under study. Such assumptions imply equivalence across populations with respect to (a) the factor pattern and weighting of loadings (i.e., group-equivalent interpretation of item content); (b) the factorial structure of the instrument (i.e., group-equivalent correlations among multidimensional facets of the underlying construct); and (c) errors of measurement (i.e., group-equivalent reliability of the instrument). Of additional concern in cross-cultural research, however, is the presence of systematic error in the form of response-set bias for one group but not for the other, or, in the event that it exists for both groups, that it is of an equivalent form (Van de Vijver, 1995). To the extent that the instrument of measurement is not equivalent, any comparison of test and normative scores will be impaired. Thus, it is imperative that the researcher test for the construct validity of his or her measuring instrument for the group whose cultural heritage differs from that used in the instrument development.

Differential interpretations of item content and interconstruct relations by members of culturally different groups derive largely from a diversity of sociocultural contexts that include the family, the school, the peer group, and society at large. For example, Oyserman and Markus (1993) noted that whereas American families urge children to stand up for themselves and not be pushed around, Japanese families stress the value of working in cooperation with others; in contrast to Americans, they do not perceive the yielding of personal autonomy as a depression of one's self-esteem. In another illustration of sociocultural differences, Kitayama and Markus (1992, cited in Oyserman & Markus, 1993) pointed to the positive emphasis placed by American parents on their children's uniqueness and distinctiveness, in contrast to the focus of Japanese parents on determining ways in which their children's behavior is inconsistent with group norms and how such behavior can be corrected. Thus, from these two examples specific to the family context, it seems evident that differential socialization practices cannot help but lead to different sets of criteria against which to judge one's perception of self (for other examples involving family socialization factors, see Hart & Edelstein, 1992).

These family-oriented examples epitomize the contrasting values and philosophical tenets held by individualistic Western societies versus collectivist Eastern societies. Whereas Western societies place high value on independence and individual freedom, Eastern societies neither assume nor value such individualism; in contrast, these societies seek to maintain interdependence among individuals (Markus & Kitayama, 1991). This basic principle of individualistic versus collectivist thought can lead to differential assessments of self in at least two other ways. First, response to self-concept items often involves the process of social comparison. However, because perspectives of others are rooted in widely discrepant philosophies within Western and Eastern societies, this comparative process will be influenced by a cultural bias that ultimately leads to differential perceptions of self. For example, Oyserman and Markus (1993) noted that whereas Japanese, Korean, and Thai respondents tend to view others as better, smarter, more sociable, and more in control than themselves, Americans tend to perceive themselves as better than others in a number of different domains. This perception of others on the part of these Eastern respondents has been termed the *self-efficacy bias,* which is consistent with the tendency to be other-serving, rather than self-serving, in the attempt to submerge the self (Oyserman & Markus, 1993). Second, response to self-concept items will also be governed by the importance of one's self-representations in relation to other society members. For example, in Western societies, these representations tend to be located within the individual and are tied to particular desires, preferences, and attributes (Markus & Kitayama, 1991). As a consequence, they stimulate concerns with self-actualization, developing one's potential, and the like. Thus, although others in society are important to the individual, they are only so in the sense of providing a benchmark against which to evaluate one's own inner attributes of self (Markus & Kitayama, 1991). In contrast, for individuals from Eastern societies, self-representations are determined by perceptions of the self in relation to others. Thus, the emphasis is placed on the individual's connectedness or interdependence to others (Markus & Kitayama, 1991). As a consequence, self-evaluations by these individuals are based on their relationships with others rather than on their own unique attributes.

From these examples, it seems clear that one's self-perceptions are very closely linked to the cultural context within which he or she is socialized. For more detailed discussions of contrasts between Eastern and Western cultures and their related impact on the structure of self-concept, readers are referred to Markus and Kitayama (1991) and Oyserman and Markus (1993).

Adequate Test Translation

Needless to say, the rigor with which an instrument is translated into another language bears critically on its construct validity. In this regard, Spielberger (1992) argued not only that it is not sufficient merely to demonstrate the adequacy of translation and back translation, but also that the psychometric properties of the test in the second language are as adequate as those in the original language. Indeed, in a recent study of cultural differences in item functioning for translated American and German intelligence tests, Ellis (1989) concluded that "even the most meticulous and painstaking translation and back-translation will not ensure measurement equivalence" (p. 919). Thus, in adapting a measuring instrument to another language, it is essential to test the extent to which the factorial measurements (i.e., factor loadings) as well as the factorial structure (i.e., relations among the underlying constructs or factors) of the instrument are consistent with the original instrument (Ellis, 1989; Van de Vijver & Poortinga, 1992). Because the conversion of a measuring instrument from one language to another involves more than just linguistic translation, then, these modified instruments are more appropriately termed *adapted* rather than *translated* tests.

One of the major difficulties in translating psychological measures is the accurate transmission of meaning associated with idioms that may be unique to a particular culture (Spielberger, 1992). For example, the expression "I am usually calm, cool, and collected," which is often used in item content related to emotional self-concept, is an American colloquialism that does not translate smoothly into other languages. Thus, in adapting any instrument into another language, it is important to seek out metaphors in the target language that most closely tap the essence of the construct being measured. For items containing culture-specific content, which cannot be translated, Poortinga (1995) suggested that they be either modified before being translated or removed entirely.

Because cultural and linguistic differences are a function of traditional customs, norms, and values, it is possible for a construct to be interpreted and conceptualized within a completely different framework by two culturally different groups. For example, Hambleton (1994) noted that in most Western cultures, a mark of one's intelligence is associated with the quick production of responses; in many Eastern societies, on the other hand, intelligence is associated with slow thoughtfulness, reflection, and the making of appropriate statements. In another example that involved a translated version of the How I See Myself Questionnaire (Juhasz, 1985), Watkins and Regmi (1993) found the appropriateness of self-concept dimensions related to friends, family, and physical appearance to be somewhat dubious for Nepalese adolescents; in sharp contrast, these dimensions are highly salient for adolescents in Western societies. Thus, these examples serve to illustrate the importance in determining the extent to which a construct is meaningful in a particular culture before translating an instrument into the language of the target culture.

In summary, it is evident that the use of adapted tests is a complex process that encompasses a number of underlying assumptions concerning the equivalency of the original and adapted versions of a measuring instrument. Given the rapid growth of cross-cultural research in recent years, together with the resulting translation of many psychological tests into other languages, the International Test Commission (ITC) recognized the need for a standardized set of guidelines regarding the development and use of translated tests. Thus, in 1993, the ITC established a 13-person committee of international experts in the area of psychological assessment, under the direction of R. K. Hambleton, to study the issue and produce such guidelines. The resulting document, entitled "Guidelines for Adapting Educational and Psychological Tests," comprises 22 guidelines that are organized into four categories: context, instrument development and adaptation, administration, and documentation/score interpretations. In turn, each guideline is described by a rationale for inclusion, steps to its achievement, a list of common errors, and references for follow-up research. This document is now in the final stages of production; a brief description can be found in Hambleton (1994).[4]

Having emphasized the importance of testing for the equivalency

---

4. These guidelines will be available in early 1996. Readers interested in obtaining a copy may write to Ronald K. Hambleton, School of Education, University of Massachusetts, Amherst, Massachusetts 01003–4140.

of an adapted version of an instrument with its original scale, the question thus arises as to how one should proceed, given findings of non-equivalent factorial measurement and structures. Such findings need not be the cause of any despair. Rather, researchers are advised to identify the theoretical elements or processes that possibly account for the cultural differences (Ellis, 1989; Markus & Kitayama, 1991); these, in themselves, can provide insight into important cultural differences related to psychometric phenomena. In this regard, Van de Vijver and Poortinga (1992) recommend that researchers further validate particular interpretations of observed intergroup differences. For an example of differential factorial structure related to a self-concept instrument, see Watkins, Hattie, and Regmi (1994).

The Issue of Developmental Factors

The research and writings of Harter and colleagues over this past decade have been exemplary in highlighting the need to consider developmental factors in the assessment of self-concept; in particular, these relate largely to changes in cognitive ability. Although most of Harter's work to date has focused on children and adolescents, sensitivity to these developmental issues, of course, applies to populations across the life span, as well as to special populations with cognitive deficits. Developmental factors that need to be addressed in any meaningful construction and selection of appropriate self-concept instruments are the cognitive abilities, language skills, and attention spans of the respondents (Hughes, 1984; Stone & Lemanek, 1990). These factors bear importantly on the measurement of self-concept with respect to (a) the dimensionality of self-concept, (b) the salience of self-concept dimensions, and (c) the appropriateness of item structure and administrative instructions (Harter, 1990b; Hughes, 1984; Stone & Lemanek, 1990). We turn now to a brief discussion of how each of these factors bears on the structure of a self-concept measure.

Dimensionality of Self-Concept

There is now substantial empirical evidence that documents the increasing differentiation of self-concept structure with age (e.g., Byrne & Shavelson, in press; Harter, 1983, 1990a, 1990b; L'Ecuyer, 1981; but see Byrne & Worth Gavin, in press; Marsh, 1989, 1990b). On the basis of research related to the Pictorial Scale of Perceived Competence and Social Acceptance for Young Children, for example, Harter and Pike (1984) found that young children (4–7 years of age) are able to make reliable judgments of their own academic competence, physical competence, social acceptance, and behavioral conduct, but only if these domains are depicted as concrete, observable behaviors (see also Stone & Lemanek, 1990). Nonetheless, they noted that children at this early age were unable to clearly differentiate among these four facets. An additional limitation of young children is that although they possess a sense of global self-concept, they are incapable of communicating any judgments related to it (Harter, 1990b). On the basis of Harter's empirical research with young children, and of developmental principles, it seems evident that the most appropriate measures of self-concept for this age group are those that tap a minimal number of dimensions, that comprise items that elicit self-descriptive responses related to concrete behaviors, and that do not contain items that tap a global self-concept.

During middle childhood (8–12 years of age), a child's self-concept structure undergoes several important changes. First, the dimensionality of self-concept not only increases, but also children are now capable of distinguishing among the various facets (Byrne & Shavelson, in press; Harter, 1990b; L'Ecuyer, 1981; Marsh, 1990b; Stone & Lemanek, 1990). Second, children are able to make meaningful and reliable judgments related to their global self-concepts (Harter, 1988b, 1990b). Third, self-conceptions gradually shift from being concrete descriptions to being more traitlike (Harter, 1988b; L'Ecuyer, 1981; Stone & Lemanek, 1990); whereas trait descriptions in early preadolescence focus on qualities of character or ability (e.g., *smart* or *honest*), they tend to reflect interpersonal traits (e.g., *friendly* or *shy*) during later preadolescence (Harter, 1990c).[5] Finally, children begin to use social comparison processes in their judgments of self (Harter, 1988b, 1990c; Stone & Lemanek, 1990). Nonetheless, there is indication that during the early period of this developmental stage, at least, they tend to be relatively indiscriminate in their choice of comparative others, using both those similar and dissimilar as referents. The use of similar others, however, tends to increase and stabilize with age—at least until middle age (Suls & Mullen, 1982). In the light of these developmental factors, it is apparent that measures of self-concept for children 8 to 12 years of age

---

5. The term *trait* is used here in the cognitive–developmental sense as a higher order generalization about the self, as opposed to the personality sense of connoting stability or consistency (Harter, 1990b).

can reliably tap multiple perceptions of self related to specific competencies, as well as perceptions of global self-worth, using a questioning
approach that may call for social comparison with others.

During adolescence, further differentiation and articulation of self-
conceptions have been noted (e.g., Byrne & Shavelson, in press; Harter,
1988b, 1990b, 1990c; L'Ecuyer, 1981; Stone & Lemanek, 1990). However, there is some evidence that this is not true of academic self-concept. For example, empirical findings from the developmental work of
Marsh (1989, 1990a, 1990b) and Byrne and Worth Gavin (in press) have
indicated that although academic self-concept becomes increasingly differentiated during preadolescence, it does not become more so during
adolescence. By this time, also, the use of social comparison processes
based on similar, rather than dissimilar, others is fairly well established
(Suls & Mullen, 1982).

One major change during the adolescent years, however, is the
increasing use of abstract concepts in making reference to the self.
Whereas preadolescent children were able to combine only particular
behaviors into traitlike constructs, adolescents can infer their latent
characteristics by integrating selected traits into general abstractions
(Harter, 1988b). For example, to describe oneself as *sensitive,* the child
needs to combine such traits as *friendly, helpful, caring,* and *good listener.*
Thus, many perceptions of self during adolescence can focus on social
attitudes, personal choice, and moral issues (Harter, 1990c; L'Ecuyer,
1981). Finally, adolescents possess the ability to describe themselves in
terms of "multiple selves" that reflect perceptions of self with respect
to specific roles or social contexts (Hart, 1988; Harter, 1988b). In other
words, the adolescent may convey one perception of self in relation to
interaction with peers, but yet another in relation to interaction with
parents. Overall, then, instruments designed to measure adolescent self-
concept should contain several subscales, each of which taps a particular
domain; items can assess latent as well as concrete behavioral aspects of
self and can require the use of social comparison processes.

Although self-concept structure throughout the adult years remains both multidimensional and active up to at least 100 years of age
(L'Ecuyer, 1981), both the saliency and distinctiveness of these facets
necessarily change (Harter, 1990a; Mueller, Johnson, Dandoy, & Keller,
1992). For college students, for example, academic self-concept is more
appropriately measured as three facets: academic performance, intellectual potential, and creativity (Harter, 1990a). Once a person gradu-
ates from college, perceptions of scholastic competence will quite likely

become less important than, say, perceptions of performance in the workplace or adequacy as a provider (Harter, 1990a). Although social comparison processes are still used in the formation of self-conceptions, Suls and Mullen (1982) suggested that as a consequence of needing to feel somewhat unique, there is a gradual shift from the use of similar others to the use of dissimilar others after age 40. Finally, in formulating self-conceptions during the latter years of one's life (65+ years), individuals come to rely increasingly less on interpersonal and more on temporal comparisons. That is to say, they tend to evaluate their present performance compared with their past performance (Suls & Mullen, 1982).

Saliency of Self-Concept Dimensions

Discussion in the previous section flowed from the widely held contention that the dimensionality of self-concept structure increases with age. Harter (1990a) noted, however, that these distinctive components derive not only from developmental advances in cognitive abilities but also from shifts that reflect salient concerns indigenous to particular stages in the life cycle. Accordingly, Damon and Hart (1982) reported a gradual shift in salience from a focus on the physical and active self in early childhood to a focus on the social and psychological self in adolescence (see also Harter, 1988b, 1990c); research by others (Harter, 1990a; L'Ecuyer, 1981) has shown saliency of the latter perspective to remain throughout adulthood.

Broadly speaking, it would appear that the import of saliency in the expansion of self-concept dimensionality is most influential during the preadolescent and adolescent periods. For example, researchers have shown that physical appearance and sexual orientation (L'Ecuyer, 1981; Marsh, 1989, 1990b) gradually take on more importance across the late preadolescent and adolescent periods. As such, Marsh (1992c, 1992d), in developing the Self Description Questionnaires II and III, respectively, considered it more meaningful to measure perceptions of social competence with peers of the same, as well as the opposite, sex rather than perceptions in relation to peers in general. Analogously, in later adolescence and continuing into young adulthood, saliency in perceived social competence can shift to perceptions of one's ability to establish close friendships or to possess romantic appeal (Harter, 1990a).

During adulthood, however, it would seem to be not so much that the number of dimensions continues to increase as one grows older, but rather, that there are shifts in the saliency of the existent dimensions at particular developmental stages. This notion is in keeping with that of Markus and associates (Markus & Nurius, 1986, 1987; Markus & Wurf, 1987), who contend that not all self-knowledge is available for use at any point in time, but rather, there is a set of self-conceptions that is presently active in thought and memory, and these operate as the "working" self-concept. As such, the working multidimensionality of the adult self-concept would seem to be dictated by an individual's roles in his or her daily life. Concerns related to these roles may reflect competencies bearing on social relations (e.g., with coworkers, friends, and family), performance at work, parental responsibilities and nurturance, and so on. It is critical that items constituting a self-concept instrument should tap salient dimensions of the self during the selected developmental period of interest.

Appropriateness of Instrument Format and Item Structure

Although there are several means by which researchers and clinicians can obtain information on the self (e.g., rating scales, behavioral observations, and projective techniques), self-report methodology is by far the most frequently used (Blascovich & Tomaka, 1991; Brinthaupt & Erwin, 1992; Wells & Marwell, 1976). Within this classification, self-report information is most commonly determined through the completion of either dichotomous or polychotomous questionnaires that ask respondents to indicate their level of agreement or disagreement with a series of statements. This is usually accomplished by having the respondent circle, or identify in some other way, one of the two (in the case of dichotomous items) or multiple (in the case of polychotomous items) answers provided.

In the two previous sections, we examined how developmental changes in cognitive ability bore on the dimensionality of self-concept and, thus, on the content validity of self-concept measures. We consider now several technical issues associated with the items used in eliciting information about the self by means of a self-report assessment.

The first developmental issue to consider in the use of a self-report measure is the ability of the respondent to comprehend and react appropriately to the questions asked. Thus, language and reading skills are essential to the validity of any interpretation of self-concept scores. This concern is particularly critical when assessments involve young children (Flanery, 1990; Harrington & Follett, 1984; Hughes, 1984; Stone & Lemanek, 1990); individuals with learning disabilities and emotional disturbances; and individuals from ethnic minority and low socioeconomic groups because they tend to have lower reading abilities than their same-age peers (Harrington & Follett, 1984). For these populations, then, one of the most important requisites is that the self-concept items use language suitable to the vocabulary and reading skills of the respondents. Unfortunately, an all-too-common occurrence is that groups of individuals are subjected to the same set of items because their age or school level is consistent with the age/grade norms provided in the test manual. More appropriately, however, individuals whose language/reading skills are dubious should have these skills evaluated before completing any self-report measure. To assist clinicians and researchers in determining this information, Stone and Lemanek (1990) have recommended using the readability formulas reported by Prout and Chizik (1988). Harrington and Follett, on the other hand, outlined a brief screening procedure, which they consider to have merit.

The second developmental factor having an important influence on item construction is that of attention span (Hughes, 1984). This factor is particularly relevant to young children, elderly adults, and individuals with cognitive deficiencies, because failure to take it into account can lead to one type of response-set bias, thereby reducing the validity of the test scores.[6] For example, Stone and Lemanek (1990) noted that preschoolers presented with a yes/no question format tend to respond in the affirmative and that preschoolers presented with a forced-choice format tended to endorse the last of the alternatives. To offset the tendency of response sets with this age group, test developers have used a number of different strategies: reading each response alternative twice and reversing the order on the second reading (Mischel, Zeiss, & Zeiss, 1974); providing picture cues (Harter & Pike, 1984); and having children choose first, the extent to which an alternative is true for them instead of forcing a choice between true and false (Harter, 1985a). Although many test developers have elected to reverse the keying of some items to deter the incidence of response sets (see, e.g., Moskowitz, 1986), Marsh (1986a) reported the use of negatively worded items to be inappropriate with young children.

---

6. Although there are other types of response-set bias, they are not particularly sensitive to developmental factors and, thus, are discussed in text as a more general psychometric issue.

As a final guard against this type of response-set bias arising from short attention spans, researchers and clinicians should be cognizant of the number of items constituting the self-report inventory and the amount of time required to complete the task. Clearly, use of an excessive number of items, which exceeds the attention-span boundaries of respondents, will serve to precipitate this problem. Furthermore, for elderly respondents in particular, the physiological effects of fatigue, cautiousness, and psychomotor speed should be taken into account (Lawton & Storandt, 1984). Thus, for this population, it might be pertinent to extend the amount of time allotted for completion of the self-report questionnaire.

A final developmental factor to consider in the structure of items is that of memory capacity. As might be expected, this concern is perhaps most relevant to young children and the elderly. For example, Mueller et al. (1992) reported decreased efficiency of memory accessibility and information processing for elderly adults, compared with young and middle-aged adults. Thus, memory has an important influence on what information an individual may report about him- or herself. Because recent experiences will quite likely be more readily accessible than those in the past, reported perceptions of self run the risk of being biased (Brinthaupt & Erwin, 1992).

Although self-report interview procedures have been used for many years with elderly adults (see, e.g., Breytspraak & George, 1982; L'Ecuyer, 1981, 1992), only recently did their use with children become of interest (see, e.g., Brinthaupt & Erwin, 1992; La Greca, 1990). As a consequence, research related to children is still relatively sparse (Flanery, 1990; Stone & Lemanek, 1990). However, Stone and Lemanek noted that in contrast to their interviewing techniques with adults, clinicians and researchers use substantially different strategies with children. In particular, they take a more active role in structuring the interview, are careful to use age-appropriate vocabulary and sentence structures, and use a variety of means to establish and maintain a good rapport with the child. (For an excellent paradigmatic application of these points, see Boggs & Eyberg, 1990.)

The Issue of Response Bias in Self-Reports

Historically, the validity of self-report measurements of self-concept has been the subject of considerable debate. The primary issue arising out of these deliberations has been the tendency for their test scores to be contaminated with response bias, a systematic tendency to respond to questionnaire items in a way that is unrelated to the item content (Paulhus, 1991). Paulhus distinguished between two types of response bias: *response set* and *response style*. Typically, a response set is triggered by context effects such as item format or the substantive content of previous items in the questionnaire. Response style is evidenced by a display of the same response set across time and situations. One type of response-set bias, particularly prone to developmental factors, was noted earlier. Here, we note three additionally common types of response-set bias: *acquiescence, social desirability,* and *extremity bias* (see Moskowitz, 1986; Paulhus, 1991; Wells & Marwell, 1976).

Acquiescence (sometimes referred to as *yea-saying*) is the tendency for respondents, despite what they actually believe to be true, to be agreeable out of politeness by agreeing with all statements in a questionnaire or interview (Vogt, 1993). One ploy to offset this tendency in the completion of self-concept measures is to reverse the keying of high-score answers (but see Marsh, 1986c, discussed earlier, regarding the use of this strategy with children). Typically, half the items are keyed positively (a high score indicates strong evidence of the construct being measured), and half are scored negatively (a low score indicates strong possession of the construct being measured). In other words, for an individual to exhibit a high level of self-concept, some items would require that he or she respond in the opposite direction. Take, for example, the statement "I'm pretty good at math." Given a scaling format ranging from *disagree* (1) to *agree* (4), a score of 4 would be indicative of high math self-concept. The same statement reformulated as a reverse-keyed item would be "I'm not very good at math." To project the same high-level self-concept score, the respondent would have to disagree with the statement, thereby selecting the 1 alternative.

However, although many developers of self-concept measures have used the reversal strategy described, Paulhus (1991) noted that the simple addition of a negation (e.g., *not good*) to an item, originally worded as an assertion, is not sufficient. He contended that the researcher must add conceptual opposites that are also worded as assertions. In this way, then, we can refine the negative item above as "I'm very bad at math." Paulhus further noted, however, that the use of a forced-choice format that combined matched options would be an even better choice.

Overall, reviewers of this literature concur that acquiescent responding has gradually declined in recent years. If this is so, it would seem that this positive trend quite likely stems from a more heightened awareness of psychometric issues in the construction of self-report measures.

Social desirability is the tendency for subjects to respond in a socially approved (i.e., acceptable) manner; that is, to respond in the "right" way, regardless of what they believe to be true (Thorndike et al., 1991). Typically, the selected response is one that makes the respondent look good. In this regard, Paulhus (1991) distinguished between two dimensions of socially desirable responding: (a) *impression management,* which he referred to as self-presentation tailored for an audience and (b) *self-deception,* which is self-presentation that, although honest, is overly positive. This form of response set has long been linked to self-reported perceptions of the self. Indeed, Wylie (1989), in her most recent review of self-concept measures, reported a consistent tendency for scores to be negatively skewed. For items keyed in a positive direction, these findings reflect a disproportionate number of subjects rating themselves at the self-favorable end of the scale and strongly suggest the influence of a social desirability bias.

Although one way of counteracting this influence is the direct assessment of social desirability using one of the established measures of the construct (see Paulhus, 1991), this strategy has not been a common occurrence. More typically, opponents of the self-report methodology have lauded the use of more objective measurement strategies; the two most common to self-concept research are ratings by significant others and behavioral observations. Ratings data represent scores that derive from a questionnaire in which the significant other (e.g., parent, teacher, peer, or clinician) evaluates some specified behavior of the individual. In self-concept research, for example, teachers are often asked to rate the academic competence of their students. Behavioral observation data are collected by specially trained observers in artificially constructed laboratory settings or in naturally occurring settings (Moskowitz, 1986). For example, in a study of play behavior among 3-year-old children, an observer may be required to code the number of times, and in what manner, a particular child interacts with his or her peers in a daycare setting.

Other methods of controlling social desirability bias are varied and often complex. One relatively straightforward procedure that can be implemented in the development of an instrument, however, is the use of a forced-choice format in which the two statements are equated for social desirability (Paulhus, 1991). A good example of this mechanism would be the self-report scales developed by Harter and colleagues; each is based on a forced-choice structured-alternative format (see, for example, chapter 5).[7]

Finally, extremity bias represents the tendency to select extreme choices on a measurement scale. For example, given an 8-point Likert-type scale, the respondent would consistently choose either 1 or 8. As Paulhus (1991) noted, this type of bias is problematic in at least two ways. First, because it is not possible to determine whether an extreme score is truly indicative of a strong opinion or, rather, a reflected tendency to use extremities in rating scales, any comparability of scores across individuals is necessarily precluded. Second, extremity bias induces spurious correlations among variables that would otherwise be unrelated. Although extremity bias can be controlled by using a multiple-choice format, it cannot be corrected simply by balancing positively and negatively keyed items, because both ends of the scale-point range are affected. For a more extensive discussion of response bias and for a review of the related literature, see Paulhus (1991).

Typically, in self-concept research where self-reported and other-reported perceptions of some behavior have been measured, interest focuses on the "accuracy" of the self-reported assessment. The term *accuracy* is placed in quotation marks here because many authors use this term in describing their research on the topic. I must admit, however, that I have great difficulty legitimizing its use in this sense. Is it ever possible to determine the true value of any perceived construct? Whose perception of an adolescent's social competence, for example, is correct: the adolescent's, the parent's, the teacher's, his or her peers? In my view, it is more correct to describe the research in terms of the extent to which the multiple measures are in agreement (i.e., provide evidence of convergent validity). Another dubious practice that is prevalent in this area of research is to use teacher- and parent-rating instruments to measure what is commonly termed *inferred self-concept.* However, Marsh (1990b) argued that unless the external observer knows the person well, observes a wide range of behaviors, and is able to make skillful perception, his or her responses will tend not to agree with those derived from self-reports. In particular, Marsh contended that the only way one can measure inferred self-concept is to have the significant

---

7. For a description of other methods of controlling social desirability, see Paulhus (1991).

other respond to the self-concept measure as if he or she were the actual targeted subject.

Although these objective (or inferential) techniques admittedly offset some difficulties, they too are not without their limitations (for an extensive review, see Moskowitz, 1986). Furthermore, reviews of research focusing on the degree of agreement across various combinations of self-reports and ratings by significant others have resulted in equivocal results (Stone & Lemanek, 1990). In fact, some argue that there is little evidence supporting the clear superiority of these inferential methods in overcoming the weaknesses of self-reports (La Greca, 1990; L'Ecuyer, 1992; Moskowitz, 1986; Wylie, 1974). In summing up his view of the issue, L'Ecuyer argued that reports by others are incapable of tapping the same aspects of the self-concept as self-reports because the latter involves the individual's self-perceptions, what he or she perceives and thinks about him- or herself, regardless of the impression presented to others.

All self-concept instruments reviewed in the present volume, with the exception of L'Ecuyer's, represent self-report measures. However, note that this circumstance arose purely as a function of space limitations and is in no way associated with the research results that have just been reported.

Search for and Selection of Self-Concept Measures

Location of Measures

The initial pool of self-report self-concept measures from which the final set of instruments discussed in this volume were drawn was determined from a diversity of sources, as summarized below:

1. Formal reviews of self-concept measures (Blascovich & Tomaka, 1991; Breytspraak & George, 1982; Chiu, 1988; Cowan, Altmann, & Pysh, 1978; Hughes, 1984; Wylie, 1974, 1979, 1989)
2. My own knowledge of both well-established and newly developed measures in the area (Byrne, 1984, 1990, 1996)
3. Known psychometric articles in scholarly journals that described potentially valuable measures
4. Published lists of measuring instruments, including the following:

   - *Tests in Print III* (Mitchell, 1983)
   - *Seventh, Eighth, Ninth, Tenth,* and *Eleventh Mental Measurement Yearbooks* (and supplements; Buros, 1972, 1978; Mitchell, 1985; Conoley & Kramer, 1989; Kramer & Conoley, 1992; respectively)
   - *Test Critiques* (Vol. 9; Keyser & Sweetland, 1992)
   - *Tests: A Comprehensive Reference for Assessments in Psychology, Education, and Business* (Sweetland & Keyser, 1986)
   - *A Consumer's Guide to Tests in Print* (Hammill et al., 1992)

- *Directory of Unpublished Experimental Mental Measures* (Vol. 4; Goldman & Osborne, 1985)
- *The ETS Test Collection Catalog (Vol. 5): Attitude Tests* (Educational Testing Service, 1991)
- *The ETS Test Collection Catalog (Vol. 6): Affective Measures and Personality Tests* (Educational Testing Service, 1992)
- commercial test publishers' catalogues

In addition to these sources, an on-line search was conducted by means of the *PsycLIT* database relevant to the years 1980 or later. The search strategy followed a three-step process. First, in searching the title, abstract, key phrases, and descriptors of articles, I used the following terms: *self-concept, self-esteem, self-perception,* and *self-image.* Second, I invoked the psychometrics classification code; as such, articles could be classified in one of three categories: "psychometrics," "test construction and validation," and "statistics and mathematics." Finally, as a further delimiter of methodological rather than substantive articles on self measures (see, e.g., Blascovich & Tomaka, 1991; Wylie, 1989), the following terms were added to the search of key phrases and descriptors: *validity, reliability, discriminant validity, divergent validity, convergent validity, construct validity, face validity, test reliability, test item analysis, internal consistency, factor analysis,* and *multitrait–multimethod.* This on-line search yielded 463 abstracts.

Each of these sources was thoroughly reviewed in the initial process of identifying potentially valuable self-concept instruments. For purposes of the present volume, only self-report measures were considered.[1] This screening process identified *82* self-concept measures, which thus constituted the original instrument pool.

Criteria Underlying Instrument Selection

The reduction process to select psychometrically sound self-concept measures for inclusion in the present volume was carried out in three stages. First, for all instruments developed before 1990, a search was conducted to determine the number of citations each had received in scholarly journal articles; the citation-exclusion criteria are described

---

1. As noted in the Introduction of this volume, although it was my original intent to include a cross-section of self-concept measures based on a variety of formats, the sheer volume of existing instrumentation made this goal highly unrealistic.

below. Second, the remaining instruments (72) were subjected to a second search to identify articles that reported results from psychometric studies pertinent to each.[2] Finally, on the basis of a review of these articles and conclusions from the formal reviews noted in the beginning of this chapter, a second elimination of measures was carried out on the basis of psychometric inadequacy.

For all instruments developed in 1990 or later, I requested psychometric data directly from the authors or commercial publishers. After a critical review of psychometric properties reported in these materials and in related journal articles, I made a final selection from this set of recently developed instruments. Consequent to this screening strategy, I selected 24 self-concept measures for inclusion in the present volume. I now outline details related to each of these selection stages.

Stage 1

An initial attempt to determine the number of citations associated with each instrument was made by means of the *Social Science Citations Index* (*SSCI*) as the source database. This citation information was used as a basis for including each instrument in the present volume. The list of self-concept measures was divided into three temporal segments and the deletion criteria were established for each. Accordingly, instruments were eliminated from the pool if they were

- developed before 1980 and had fewer than five citations
- developed between 1980 and 1984 and had fewer than four citations
- developed between 1985 and 1990 and had fewer than three citations

One major limitation in using the *SSCI* database was the manner by which this information must be retrieved. Because volumes are published annually with no provision of cumulative listings, each volume must be checked for each instrument in question. Needless to say, this approach, in addition to being extremely cumbersome, is very time-consuming and thus represents a substantial monetary consideration.

Owing to economic constraints in the present case, then, an alternative strategy was taken, using the on-line *PsycLIT* and ERIC databases; accordingly, the number of abstracts that mentioned a particular mea-

---

2. Where reported psychometric data were relatively scant, such information was sought directly from the author or the commercial publisher of the instrument.

suring instrument was tabulated. However, in using this approach, two problems became evident. First, authors may not cite an instrument's name completely and correctly. For example, reference may be made to "Harter's self-concept scale" rather than Harter's (1985b) Self-Perception Profile for Children. This omission was most common when several measuring instruments were used in the same study. The second problem arose if a string of words used in the abstract coincided with the name of a particular instrument. For example, the text "several dimensions of self-concept were found to be related" coincides with the actual name of an existing instrument (Dimensions of Self-Concept [DOSC]). Yet the DOSC may not have been the instrument used in the study. Consequently, a search strategy that addressed these difficulties was established in an effort to keep them at a minimum. The *PsycLIT* and ERIC databases were each searched separately as follows:

PsycLIT

For each instrument, the following search terms were used: *self concept* or *self-concept*, or *self esteem* or *self-esteem*, or *self perception* or *self-perception*, or *self concepts* or *self-concepts*, or *self image* or *self-image*, AND "test name" (in title or abstract), as well as key words from the test name AND Publication Year >19*xx*, where *xx* was the year of interest.

ERIC

For each instrument, the following search terms were used: *self concept* or *self-concept*, or *self esteem* or *self-esteem*, or *self perception* or *self-perception*, or *self concepts* or *self-concepts*, or *self image* or *self-image*, or *self evaluation* or *self-evaluation*, or *self concept measures* or *self-concept measures*, or *self concept tests* or *self-concept tests*, AND "test name" (in title, abstract, or descriptor), as well as key words from the test name AND Publication Year >19*xx*, where *xx* was the year of interest.[3]

Once this search was completed, all abstracts were read for accuracy and compared, to eliminate the risk of possible duplication across the two on-line databases. This initial process to identify self-concept measures that had been used seldom over the past decade resulted in the deletion of 10 instruments, thereby reducing the original pool to 72.

---

3. Test names were found most often in the descriptors in ERIC; this field is not available in *PsycLIT*.

Stage 2

The second stage in screening instruments to be included in this volume involved a review of the psychometric literature pertinent to each of these 72 self-concept measures. Judgment of psychometric adequacy was based on the extent and quality of the methodological research conducted in testing for evidence of construct validity and reliability related to each instrument. This evaluation process resulted in further reducing the original instrument pool to 24. Specifically, 48 instruments were eliminated because (a) the psychometrically related literature was either nonexistent or minimal and inadequate or (b) the studies described were methodologically weak or flawed.

As a consequence of this thorough screening process, 24 self-concept measures have been selected for inclusion in the present volume. Although some are old and well-established instruments, others are relatively new and thus would benefit from further construct validity research. However, given the inevitability of social change, testing for construct validity must be an ongoing process with respect to any measuring instrument, regardless of its age and establishment status. These newly developed instruments are included here because they have already undergone extensive psychometric testing, have a strong theoretical base, and fulfill an important need to measure particular facets of self-concept (e.g., physical self-concept). It is my hope that the 24 measures described in this book not only will provide researchers with an adequate selection from which to choose but also will offer some assurance that their selected instrument is psychometrically sound.

Organization of Content Related to Self-Concept Measures

Chapters 4 through 8 are devoted to a review of the 24 self-concept measures selected as a consequence of the screening process just described. Accordingly, I summarize descriptive and psychometric information related to each of the selected measures; this material is pertinent only to the age group or population for which the measure was initially developed. More specifically, chapters 4 through 7 address the developmental stages of the life span; chapter 8 addresses particular exceptionalities. Each instrument is fully described with respect to preschool and early school age (chapter 4), preadolescence (chapter 5), adolescence (chapter 6), adulthood (chapter 7), and special populations (chapter 8).

In many cases, the validity of using particular instruments across populations has been tested and reported to be psychometrically sound. Where this is so, details related to the administration, structure, and psychometric properties of the instrument, with information concerning its availability source and cost, are presented only in the chapter bearing on its original target population; psychometric findings related to additional nontarget populations are presented in the chapter devoted to these other populations. With particular reference to chapters 4 through 7, note that the instruments are presented and reviewed in alphabetical order and not in any ranked order of preference on my part.

For each self-concept measure, I included the following information:

- Description of target population and details related to scale structure, theoretical underpinning, length, format, and administration
- Scale construction and psychometric properties based on the normative data
- Related psychometric and construct validity research
- Overall evaluation summary
- Source

4

Measures of Self-Concept for Young Children (Preschool–Grade 2; Ages 3–7 Years)

Although there is consensus that young children, even as early as 3 years of age, possess at least some descriptive self-conceptions (Harter, 1988b; Wylie, 1989), measuring instruments appropriate for use with this population are relatively few. Problems associated with both the cognitive development and self-reporting of young children place additional demands on the test developer, and this factor may be the underlying reason for their scarcity. In particular, the instrument must be designed so that it (a) maintains the interest of the child, (b) provides very concrete and specific descriptions of the question being asked, (c) uses a simple and straightforward method of response, and (d) offsets the tendency toward socially desirable responding. Of the 15 preschool measures found through the literature search, the Joseph Pre-School and Primary Self-Concept Screening Test (JPPSST; Joseph, 1979) and the Pictorial Scale of Perceived Competence and Social Acceptance (PSPCSA; Harter & Pike, 1983) were considered to be the most psychometrically adequate for use with this young population. Both instruments use a pictorial format that is accompanied by an oral clarification of item content and method of response by the examiner. Whereas the JPPSST measures multiple facets of general self-concept, the PSPCSA measures multiple domain-specific facets of perceived competence. Information related to these two measures is now summarized.

Measurement of Single Self-Concept Domains

Joseph Pre-School and Primary Self-Concept Screening Test

Description

The JPPSST is designed to measure global self-concept and is based on the theoretical notion that self-concepts represent the way individuals perceive themselves, their behaviors, and how others view them; it also embraces the feelings of personal worth and satisfaction that accompany these perceptions (Joseph, 1979). In particular, this perspective argues that self-concept is the key element in determining the extent to which a child copes with both the cognitive and social demands of school. In keeping with this view, the JPPSST was developed as an objective tool for use in screening and identifying children at the preschool and primary school levels who may be at risk for developing learning problems or other adjustment difficulties as a consequence of negative appraisals.

Joseph (1979) contended that the JPPSST is unique in that "it is able to assess the perceptions that an individual holds toward himself as well as his level of satisfaction with these currently held perceptions" (p. 8). As such, the measurement of global self-concept is based on a two-tiered composite of five dimensions. Of primary importance are the dimensions of Significance (the extent to which individuals perceive themselves as being valued by others) and Competence (the perceived ability to successfully perform and master environmental demands). Three secondary dimensions of self-concept tapped by the JPPSST are Power (the perceived ability to influence, manipulate, and control others), General Evaluative Contentment (feelings of satisfaction with one's present life circumstance), and Virtue (perceived adherence to moral standards). Taken together, the three secondary dimensions are considered to be derivatives (or indirect expressions) of the two primary dimensions of Significance and Competence (Joseph, 1979). To date, the JPPSST has been translated into Chinese, Indian (Urdu), Spanish, and Hebrew (J. Joseph, personal communication, October 11, 1994).

Although the manual does not explicitly link the JPPSST to a particular theoretical model, I suggest that it is most closely affiliated with the nomothetic model of self-concept described in chapter 1.

Target Population

The JPPSST is suitable for use with both boys and girls at the preschool and primary school levels; appropriate ages range from 3-1/2 to 9 years.

Scale Structure

The JPPSST is based on a pictorial format and is composed of two parts: an Identity Reference Drawing (IRD) form and a set of 15 self-concept situation items. The IRD form represents a line drawing of a figure with a blank face; separate gender-specific figures are available for boys and girls. The 15 scale items are based on a forced-choice self-report format, 12 of which are illustrated with dichotomous pairs of gender-appropriate pictures; one picture represents a negative self-concept situation, and the other represents a positive self-concept situation. Of the remaining 3 items, 1 uses three pictures (Item 11), and 2 use no pictures at all (Items 9 and 15).

To compensate for the effects of socially desirable responding, Joseph (1979) suggested and allowed for the adjustment of high-risk cut-off scores at the upper age levels (5–9 years). To offset acquiescence response sets, approximately half the items begin with a positively scored option, and the remaining half begin with a negatively scored option. Relatedly, the paired picture cards are presented to the child in standardized positions.

Joseph (1979) emphasized that each item on the JPPSST taps one or more dimensions of self-concept. As a consequence, an item-response analysis can yield several aspects of a child's overall perception of self in need of remediation. Furthermore, if a child is unable to correctly distinguish a stimulus-picture situation, a value termed a *confusion score* is assigned for that entry. Joseph (1979) suggested that high confusion scores might be indicative of cognitive deficits or other difficulties. In addition, features of the child's completed IRD can also be evaluated qualitatively. Readers interested in using the JPPSST for remedial screening, however, are encouraged to examine reviews of the instrument by Gerken (1985) and Gray (1986), in which they noted several limitations associated with these scoring procedures.

A sample item of a dichotomous picture pair is shown in Figure 4.1; one that requires no use of pictures is shown in Figure 4.2.

Administration and Scoring

The JPPSST is administered individually and is estimated to take approximately 5–7 min. Before proceeding to the self-concept items, the child is first presented with the IRD figure and asked to draw his or her face in the blank. This initial step is meant to impress on the child that the figure represents him or her; it subsequently serves as a tangible reminder that he or she is being asked to describe himself or

Figure 4.1

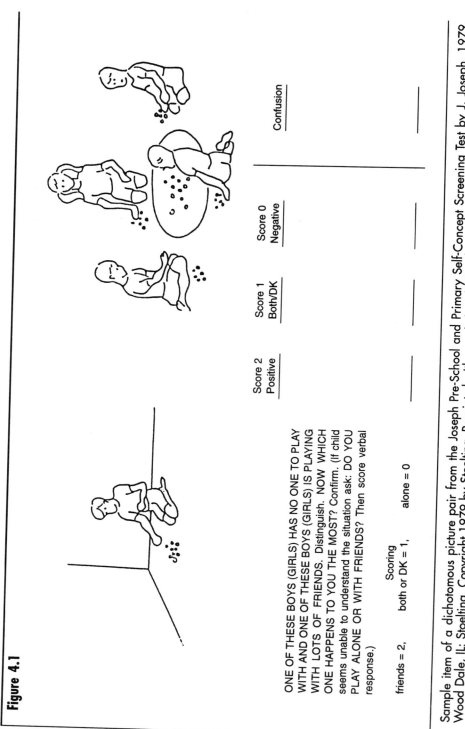

ONE OF THESE BOYS (GIRLS) HAS NO ONE TO PLAY
WITH AND ONE OF THESE BOYS (GIRLS) IS PLAYING
WITH LOTS OF FRIENDS. Distinguish. NOW WHICH
ONE HAPPENS TO YOU THE MOST? Confirm. (If child
seems unable to understand the situation ask: DO YOU
PLAY ALONE OR WITH FRIENDS? Then score verbal
response.)

Scoring

friends = 2,   both or DK = 1,   alone = 0

Score 2   Score 1   Score 0
Positive   Both/DK   Negative   Confusion

Sample item of a dichotomous picture pair from the Joseph Pre-School and Primary Self-Concept Screening Test by J. Joseph, 1979, Wood Dale, IL: Stoelting. Copyright 1979 by Stoelting. Reprinted with permission. (DK = don't know.)

Figure 4.2

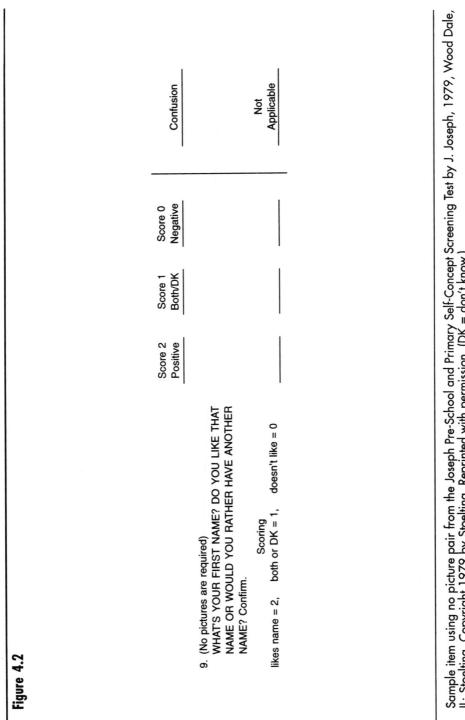

9. (No pictures are required)
WHAT'S YOUR FIRST NAME? DO YOU LIKE THAT
NAME OR WOULD YOU RATHER HAVE ANOTHER
NAME? Confirm.

Scoring
likes name = 2,   both or DK = 1,   doesn't like = 0

Score 2 Positive	Score 1 Both/DK	Score 0 Negative	Confusion
			Not Applicable

Sample item using no picture pair from the Joseph Pre-School and Primary Self-Concept Screening Test by J. Joseph, 1979, Wood Dale, IL: Stoelting. Copyright 1979 by Stoelting. Reprinted with permission. (DK = don't know.)

herself. Once the child has completed the IRD form, the examiner proceeds to ask the child to respond to the self-concept items. For each item, the child must first correctly distinguish each picture in the pair and then indicate (by pointing) which one (of the two pictures) most resembles him or her. The pictures used in the JPPSST are simple black-and-white line sketches that were simulated from those drawn by children during the initial development of the instrument; they are presented on plasticized 5″ × 8″ cards. The primary use of these stimulus drawings is to ensure that the child has a clear understanding of each question before making a response, a factor that is particularly relevant to the testing of very young children.

A general self-concept score is computed by adding the child's scores across the 15 items. Interpretation of scores is based on five levels of classification: high positive, moderate positive, watch list, poor, and high-risk negative. Score distributions across the five categories vary according to three age groups: 3.6 to 4.6 years, 4.7 to 5.11 years, and 6.0 to 9.11 years; cutpoint scores relative to each group are provided on the scoring sheet. For children whose responses place them in the poor or high-risk negative categories, further diagnostic information may be obtained from an Item Dimensional Chart provided on the scoring sheet. As such, each item is linked to the five dimensions of self-concept noted earlier as follows: Significance and its derivative, Virtue; Competence and its derivative, Power; and General Evaluative Contentment.

Normative Data

Samples. Initial testing and standardization of the JPPSST was conducted with 1,245 children residing in rural, suburban, and urban areas of Illinois. Subjects were drawn from 5 public and 4 private preschool programs, 28 public school classes that ranged from kindergarten to fourth grade, and 4 special education classes (2 preschool and 2 kindergarten); they represented diverse socioeconomic strata, and most (91%) were White (Joseph, 1979). Normative data were categorized according to three age groups: 3.6 to 4.6 years ($n = 285$), 4.7 to 5.11 years ($n = 328$), and 6.0 to 9.11 years ($n = 632$).

Selection and Refinement of Items. In deciding how best to elicit responses reflective of a child's self-concept, Joseph (1979) first identified several situations that he, in his experience as a school psychologist, believed could be used to evoke self-reports from children. In an effort to glean some idea of how children might pictorially represent these situations, he elicited 1,120 drawings from first and second graders, along with teachers' transcripts of the children's interpretations. These were subsequently reduced and grouped into the present 15 item situations constituting the JPPSST.

Psychometric Properties. Reliability. Based on a sample of 18 preschoolers over a 4-week interval, Joseph (1979, p. 56) reported a test–retest reliability coefficient of .89. Although he also reported K–R 20 internal consistency reliability coefficients ranging from .59 to .81 (*Md* = .73) and item-discrimination coefficients ranging from .30 to .70, Joseph failed to identify the population to which these findings may be generalized. No other reliability is presented in the manual.

Validity. Although Joseph (1979) argued for evidence of construct validity bearing on the JPPSST, such claims were based on very limited and statistically weak analyses. For example, correlations between JPPSST global self-concept scores and two teacher-rating scales of self-concept—the Inferred Self-Concept Judgment Scale and the Behavior Rating Form (Coopersmith, 1967), both based on a sample of 25 preschoolers (median age = 4.10 years)—were reported to be .51 and .65, respectively. Other similarly correlated results are reported for other age groups. However, given that (a) these rating scales can at best measure only inferred self-concept and (b) there is considerable debate in the literature regarding the measurement of inferred self-concept, these findings offer weak, if any, testimony for construct validity.

Joseph (1979) contended that the JPPSST may be used as a predictor of academic success. In substantiation of this claim, he reported correlations between scores from the Competence dimension of the JPPSST with scores from cognitive-related measures for 27 preschoolers (median age = 4.11 years). Results yielded validity coefficients of .66 with the Slosson Intelligence Test (Slosson, 1963), .63 with the Preschool Language Scale, and .69 with the Developmental Test of Visual–Motor Integration (cited in Joseph, 1979).

Related Psychometric Research

On the basis of a longitudinal study of 45 preschool children (median age = 4.3 years) and 125 kindergarten children (median age = 5.4 years), Joseph (1986) reported that after 4 years, 83% of preschoolers and 70% of kindergarteners who were currently receiving special education services had originally attained JPPSST scores (in Year 1) that fell into the poor or high-risk negative category. He argued in support of further evidence of the predictive validity of the JPPSST. Additionally, in a recent study of 422 first-grade children (median age = 6.4 years),

Joseph (personal communication, October 11, 1994) reported a test–retest reliability coefficient of .69, albeit no time interval was indicated.

Evaluation Summary

In general, reviewers (Gerken, 1985; Gray, 1986; Telzrow, 1985) have agreed that the JPPSST is a reasonably sound measure of global self-concept for young children. Additionally, the instrument has a number of other excellent features that make it particularly appealing for use with this age range. Of primary note has been the ease and speed with which the JPPSST can be administered, the suitability of both the procedure and pictorial materials used to elicit responses from preschool children, and the clearly described directions related to its use and scoring procedure.

Limitations associated with the JPPSST lie with the paucity of psychometric findings reported. Although Joseph (1979) reported some evidence of both reliability and validity, there is consensus among the reviewers (Gerken, 1985; Gray, 1986; Telzrow, 1985; Wylie, 1989) that substantially more information is needed in this regard. In particular, there is a critical need for both exploratory and confirmatory factor analytic research to clarify the five-factor structure underpinning the diagnostic dimensional evaluation. Additional construct validity research that tests for evidence of convergent and discriminant validities related to this structure is also needed. Finally, further literature and psychometric documentation is needed to support use of the JPPSST as a diagnostic and screening tool (see Gerken, 1985; Gray, 1986).

Joseph advised me (personal communication, October 11, 1994) that he has recently "undertaken an extensive concurrent validity study of the JPPSST related to children's stress exposure, developed an improved administration format, compiled additional norming information related to non-disabled and disabled populations, and created three additional test items for inclusion in a future revision of the scale." Given the many positive features associated with the JPPSST, it is hoped that the psychometric limitations noted will be addressed and reported in subsequent editions of the manual. The instrument is included in this volume because of its strong potential as a sound measure of general self-concept for young children. The development of a unique adaptation of the JPPSST for use with adolescent and adult populations is currently in progress (J. Joseph, personal communication, October 11, 1994).

Source

Location: Stoelting Company, 620 Wheat Lane, Wood Dale, Illinois
              60191

Cost: Manual: $25.00
              Kit: $150.00 (includes manual, set of 56 stimulus cards, 50
              boy and 50 girl identity drawings, and 100 record forms)

Measurement of Multiple Self-Concept Domains

Pictorial Scale of Perceived Competence and Social Acceptance for Young Children

Description

The PSPCSA (Harter & Pike, 1983) was designed as a downward extension of the Self-Perception Profile for Children (Harter, 1985a,b). As
such, it is based on a domain-specific approach to the measurement of
self-perceived competence.[1] However, although the instrument comprises four separate subscales—Cognitive Competence, Physical Competence, Peer Acceptance, and Maternal Acceptance—Harter and Pike
(1983) noted that scores should be interpreted within the framework
of a two-factor structure that represents General Competence and Social
Acceptance.[2] This structure is based on factor analyses that have shown
a clustering of the cognitive and physical scores, and the peer and maternal acceptance scores, respectively. Despite findings of a two-factor
structure, Harter and Pike argued that by retaining the four separate
scales, important information would be gained in the study of an individual child's self-perception profile. The PSPCSA is theoretically linked
to the correlated-factor model of self-concept described in chapter 1.

Target Population

Separate versions of the PSPCSA are available for use with preschool
and kindergarten children and with first- and second-grade children.

---

1. Because certain self-judgments of cognitive or physical competence or certain behaviors
   may reflect perceptions of one's capabilities, Harter and Pike (1984) urged that this scale
   be used as a measure of perceived competence rather than self-concept or self-esteem.
2. I was recently advised that two additional sources of social acceptance (Dad and teacher)
   and two additional self-concept domains (conduct and appearance) will be added to an
   upcoming revision of the PSPCSA (S. Harter, personal communication, October 27, 1994).

Scale Structure

Each of the four subscales comprises 6 items, making a total of 24 items for the entire scale. Although all 6 items in the Cognitive Competence subscale differ across the two versions of the instrument, 4 of the 6 items in the Physical Competence, Peer Acceptance, and Maternal Acceptance subscales are common to each.

The PSPCSA uses a pictorial format that allows for the concrete depiction of specific skills and activities. In addition to a separately bound set of pictures for preschool and kindergarten and for Grade 1 and Grade 2 children, there is a separately bound set for boys and girls relevant to each age group. Although the activities depicted in each item are identical for both sexes, the gender of the target child is different; reactions to the illustrated competencies should be based on the same-sex child.

Each scale item is designed as a structured response format to offset the tendency toward social desirability response bias (Harter, 1990b) and is scored on a 4-point scale. For each item, the child is presented with two contrasting pictures, one depicting a competent child and the other depicting an incompetent child. After first being read a statement describing the child in the picture, the respondent is asked to identify which of the two (competent vs. incompetent) child is most like him or her. Once this choice has been made, the respondent is then asked to indicate, by pointing to the appropriate circle, whether the pictured child is a lot like him or her (big circle) or just a little like him or her (small circle). Within each subscale, three items depict the competent child on the left, and three items depict the competent child on the right.

A sample item from the Cognitive Competence subscale of the Preschool/Kindergarten version (for girls) is shown in Figure 4.3, a sample item from the Maternal Acceptance subscale of the First- and Second-Grade version (for boys) is shown in Figure 4.4, and a sample item from the Physical Competence subscale common to both versions (for girls) is shown in Figure 4.5.

Administration and Scoring

The PSPCSA is administered individually. Each set of picture plates is constructed of a heavy, cardboardlike material held together in a spiral binder, thus enabling it to sit in an upright position on a desk between the examiner and the child being tested; the side facing the child presents the pictures, each with its accompanying large and small circles.

Figure 4.3

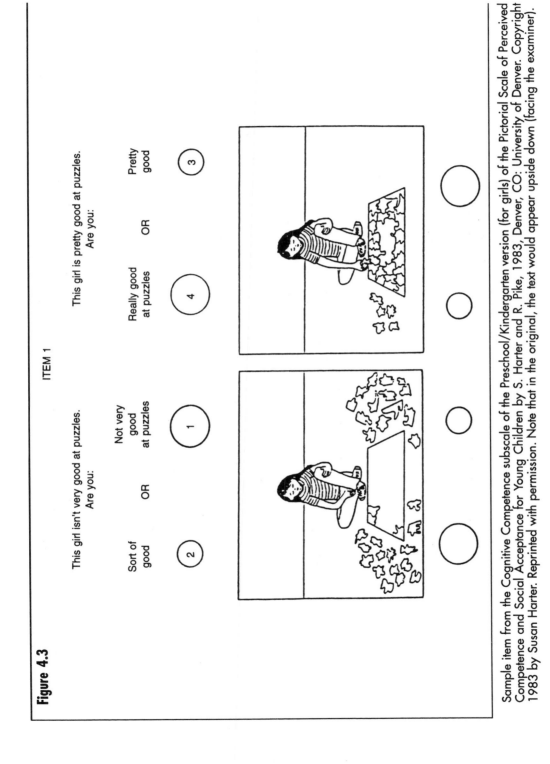

ITEM 1

This girl isn't very good at puzzles.
Are you:

This girl is pretty good at puzzles.
Are you:

Sort of good   OR   Not very good at puzzles

Really good at puzzles   OR   Pretty good

②   ①   ④   ③

Sample item from the Cognitive Competence subscale of the Preschool/Kindergarten version (for girls) of the Pictorial Scale of Perceived Competence and Social Acceptance for Young Children by S. Harter and R. Pike, 1983, Denver, CO: University of Denver. Copyright 1983 by Susan Harter. Reprinted with permission. Note that in the original, the text would appear upside down (facing the examiner).

Figure 4.4

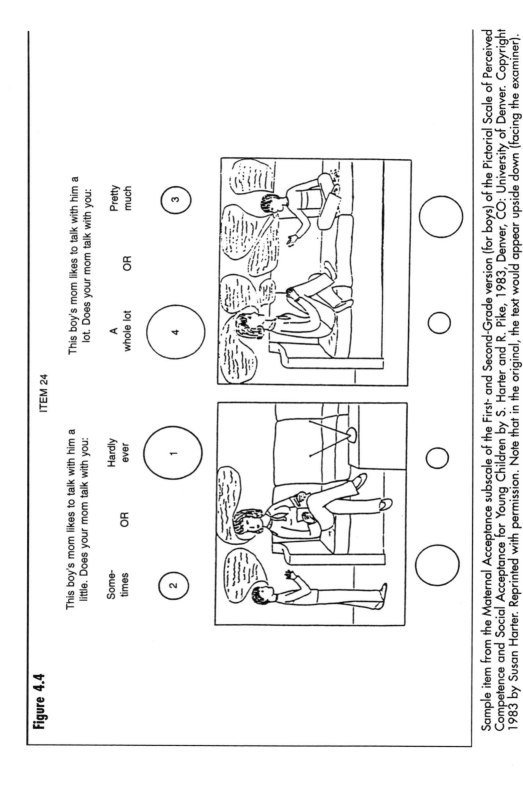

ITEM 24

This boy's mom likes to talk with him a little. Does your mom talk with you:

Some-
times   OR   Hardly
ever

This boy's mom likes to talk with him a lot. Does your mom talk with you:

A
whole lot   OR   Pretty
much

Sample item from the Maternal Acceptance subscale of the First- and Second-Grade version (for boys) of the Pictorial Scale of Perceived Competence and Social Acceptance for Young Children by S. Harter and R. Pike, 1983, Denver, CO: University of Denver. Copyright 1983 by Susan Harter. Reprinted with permission. Note that in the original, the text would appear upside down (facing the examiner).

Figure 4.5

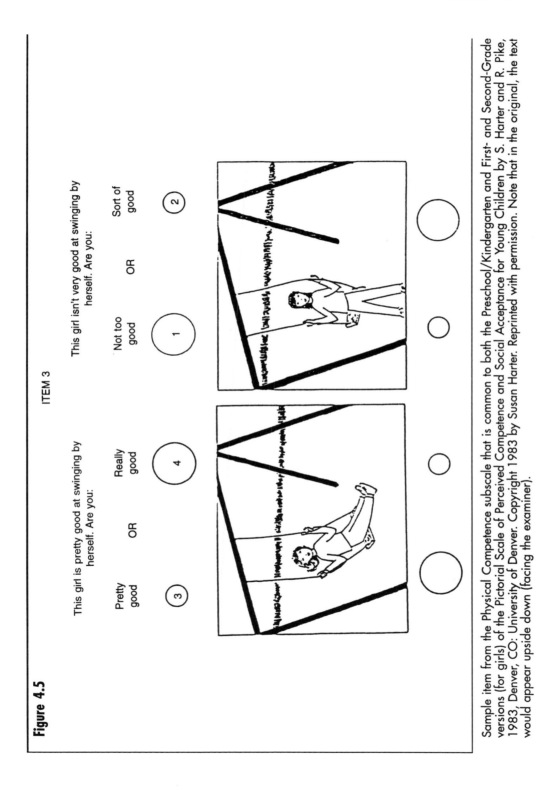

ITEM 3

This girl is pretty good at swinging by herself. Are you:

Pretty good   OR   Really good

③   ④

This girl isn't very good at swinging by herself. Are you:

Not too good   OR   Sort of good

①   ②

Sample item from the Physical Competence subscale that is common to both the Preschool/Kindergarten and First- and Second-Grade versions (for girls) of the Pictorial Scale of Perceived Competence and Social Acceptance for Young Children by S. Harter and R. Pike, 1983, Denver, CO: University of Denver. Copyright 1983 by Susan Harter. Reprinted with permission. Note that in the original, the text would appear upside down (facing the examiner).

The side facing the examiner presents the statements to be read aloud, as well as the score point associated with each circle. Once the respondent points to his or circle of choice, the examiner records the value on a separately provided score sheet.

Scoring of the PSPCSA is simply a matter of adding the scores obtained from the six items constituting each subscale. The numerical value of each subscale will then range from a value of 6 (if the child has been given a 1 for each response) to a value of 24 (if the child has been given a 4 for each response).

Normative Data

Samples. Initial testing of the PSPCSA was conducted with 90 preschool (mean age = 4.45), 56 kindergarten (mean age = 5.54), 65 first-grade (mean age = 6.32), and 44 second-grade (mean age = 7.41) children; these samples provided the primary data on which the reported psychometric properties were based; subjects were from middle-class neighborhoods, and most were white. Harter and Pike (1984) reported that additional data were subsequently obtained from samples of 77 preschool, 28 kindergarten, and 38 first- and second-grade children.

Selection and Refinement of Items. Harter and Pike stated that the PSPCSA underwent numerous revisions with respect to its scale structure, item content, and question format, on the basis of extensive pilot testing with a large number of subjects (see Harter & Pike, 1984). However, specifics related to these preliminary analyses have not been provided.

Psychometric Properties. *Reliability.* Based on the Preschool/Kindergarten version of the PSPCSA, Harter and Pike (1984) reported internal consistency reliability coefficients for the Competence subscales to range from .52 to .71 (mean α = .63) for the Cognitive Competence scale, from .55 to .66 (mean α = .61) for the Physical Competence scale, and from .66 to .79 (mean α = .74) for a single testing of the two competence subscales combined.[3] Coefficient alpha values for the Acceptance subscales ranged from .74 to .75 (mean α = .74) for the Peer Acceptance scale, from .81 to .85 (mean α = .83) for the Maternal Acceptance scale, and from .86 to .87 (mean α = .87) for the two scales combined.

Based on the First- and Second-Grade version of the PSPCSA, co-

---

3. Recall the two-factor structure representing General Competence and Social Acceptance, noted earlier.

efficient alpha values ranged from .71 to .79 (mean α = .75) for the Cognitive Competence scale, from .50 to .62 (mean α = .55) for the Physical Competence scale, and from .75 to .80 (mean α = .77) for the two scales combined. For the Acceptance subscales, the values ranged from .78 to .83 (mean α = .80) for the Peer Acceptance scale, from .72 to .78 (mean α = .75) for the Maternal Acceptance scale, and from .85 to .87 (mean α = .86) for both scales combined.

No other reliability information was reported either in the manual or in the major article describing the PSPCSA (Harter & Pike, 1984).

Validity. For both preschool and kindergarten and first- and second-grade children, factor analyses of the PSPCSA revealed a clear two-factor solution. The first factor, representing general competence, was defined by the Cognitive Competence and Physical Competence subscales; the second factor, representing social acceptance, comprised loadings from the Peer Acceptance and Maternal Acceptance subscales. Harter and Pike (1984) reported factor loadings ranging from .19 to .70 (*Md* = .44 for preschool and kindergarten children and from .22 to .72 (*Md* = .51) for Grade 1 and Grade 2 children (no loadings < .19 were reported).

Although Harter and Pike (1984) argued for evidence of convergent, discriminant, and predictive validity in relation to the PSPCSA, this information was based on very limited data. That is to say, in addition to the samples being very small, they varied across tests for each type of validity; likewise, the subscales tested also varied across testing procedures. Of the three types of validity tested for, evidence related to convergent validity was perhaps the strongest.

Evidence of convergent validity was tested by asking children (after the PSPCSA had been administered) to explain why they responded as they did to the two competence subscales. For example, children were asked, "How do you know you are good at/not good at (depending on the child's initial response) this (activity specified)? How can you tell?" (Harter & Pike, 1984, pp. 1976–1977). On the basis of findings that most children were able to provide specific reasons in support of their responses, thereby yielding an overall pattern of convergence between initial perceived-competence judgments and the related underlying rationales, the authors concluded that evidence of convergent validity is adequate.

Related Psychometric Research

At this time, I am aware of no additional psychometric studies of the PSPCSA. However, one study (Ulrich & Collier, 1990) tested the validity of test scores based on a modification of the Physical Competence sub-scale for use with 7- to 12-year-old children with mild mental retardation.

Evaluation Summary

The PSPCSA has many attractive features that make it a potentially valuable measure for use with young children. The pictorial format of the items, the tailoring of the items to make them developmentally appropriate for preschool and kindergarten and first- and second-grade children, and the availability of gender-specific plates are definite assets. Additionally, the instrument is easily administered and scored.

Although the internal consistency reliability of the General Competence and Social Acceptance subscales is generally adequate, reviewers (Michael, 1992; Sheridan, 1992) have called for substantially more psychometric research to be conducted. In particular, construct validity studies of the instrument are urgently needed before the psychometric soundness of its structure and use with the intended populations can be judged appropriately. Despite these limitations, however, the PSPCSA is included here because (a) its basic factorial structure and scale format are theoretically reasonable and (b) there are few established measures available for use with children in the early age range of 4 to 7 years.

Source

Location: Susan Harter, University of Denver, Department of Psychology, 2155 South Race Street, Denver, Colorado 80208-0204

Cost: Manual: $15.00
            Preschool/Kindergarten plates for girls (or boys): $25.00
            First and Second Grades plates for girls (or boys): $25.00

5 Measures of Self-Concept for Preadolescents (Grades 3–8; Ages 8–12 Years)

At this stage of the life cycle, children's self-descriptions take on characteristics that are different in a number of ways from those of early childhood. Primary among these is the ability to describe their own behavior in relation to the varied domains of their life. Thus, the multidimensionality of preadolescent self-concept is more clearly defined than it is for preschool children. Furthermore, preadolescents are able to define themselves in terms of trait labels such as *smart, popular, helpful,* and the like (Harter, 1988b). Other features of self-descriptions at this age include a sensitivity to the opinions of others and the use of social comparison in making these evaluations.

Perhaps as a consequence of these improved self-descriptive skills, the number of preadolescent self-concept measures is substantially larger than for young children. Unfortunately, however, many of these instruments are still in dire need of sound construct validity research. Of the 29 preadolescent self-concept instruments reviewed, only 6 were considered to be worthy of inclusion in this volume. In keeping with the preadolescent's ability to describe himself or herself in relation to different life domains, all instruments were designed to measure multiple dimensions of the self-concept; in addition, 2 instruments were designed to measure general (i.e., global) self-concept as a separate facet (Self-Perception Profile for Children and Self Description Questionnaire I). Note, however, that although 2 instruments are specific to the measurement of multiple academic self-concepts, none of the others are specific to the measurement of either physical or social self-concept; these remaining scales all tap multiple self-concept domains.

Measurement of Single Self-Concept Domains

ACADEMIC SELF-CONCEPT

Academic Self Description Questionnaire I

Description

The Academic Self Description Questionnaire I (ASDQ–I; Marsh, 1990c) was designed to measure multiple subject-specific dimensions of academic self-concept, as well as a single dimension of general school self-concept. This scale represents an extension of the Self Description Questionnaire I (Marsh, 1992b),[1] a measure of multiple facets of self-concept to be described later in this chapter. Development of the ASDQ–I evolved from construct validity research related to the revised Shavelson et al. (1976) model, which was subsequently termed the *Marsh/Shavelson model.* To adequately test the validity of the revised model, an instrument was needed that was capable of measuring self-perceived competence regarding multiple aspects of academic performance; the ASDQ–I was designed to address this need. In consultation with school administrators, Marsh (1990c, 1993a) determined a set of school subjects taken by all students. A separate self-concept subscale was then constructed to match each content area: Spelling, Reading, Handwriting, Social Studies, Computer Studies, Science, Mathematics, Physical Education, Art, Music, Religion, and Health.

Target Population

The ASDQ–I is designed for use with children in Grades 4 through 6 (ages 8–12 years).

Scale Structure

The ASDQ–I is a 78-item self-report scale that comprises 12 subject matter subscales and one General-School subscale.[2] Items are structured on a 6-point Likert-type scale format, with 6 items constituting each subscale. The subject matter subscales measure self-perceived competence related to seven core subjects (Spelling, Reading, Handwriting, Social Studies, Computer Studies, Science, and Mathematics) and five noncore subjects (Physical Education, Art, Music, Religion, and

---

1. Although the reference is dated 1992 as a consequence of recent changes in its location of distribution, the instrument has been established since the early 1980s.
2. The instrument also includes eight items designed to measure a separate global self-concept, should the researcher wish to tap this higher order facet.

Health). The phrasing of item stems in each subscale is identical, with only the subject area being changed; for example, "Compared with others my age, I am good at [a specific school subject]" and "I get good marks in [a specific school subject] classes." For the General-School subscale, the term *most school subjects* replaces the specific academic area. One sample item from each of the Computer Studies and General-School subscales of the ASDQ–I, respectively, is presented in Exhibit 5.1.

Administration and Scoring

The ASDQ–I can be administered individually or in groups. Children are asked to respond to simple declarative statements by placing a check mark under one of the six alternatives that they believe best describes them (see Exhibit 5.1). Taking into account the additional time needed for reading the instructions, reviewing the response procedure based on an example item, and answering questions, completion of the ASDQ–I can take from 15 to 20 min, depending on the age range and number of children being tested.

Given a 6-point scale format, the score for each completed item will represent a value from 1 to 6. Subscale scores of the ASDQ–I are obtained through a simple summation of scores relative to all items constituting the scale in question.

Normative Data

Samples. Initial testing of the ASDQ–I was based on a sample of 234 boys in Grades 5 and 6, all of whom attended the same Catholic boys' school in Sydney, Australia.

Selection and Refinement of Items. I am unaware of any available information at this time regarding either the selection or refinement of the ASDQ–I items.

Psychometric Properties. Reliability. Marsh (1990c) reported internal consistency reliability coefficients ranging from .881 to .941 (median α = .909) for the 13 subscales of the ASDQ–I. No other reliability information is available at this time.

Validity. Both exploratory and confirmatory factor analyses of the ASDQ–I, based on item-pair responses, have yielded well-defined solutions related to each subject-specific, as well as the General-School, subscale (Marsh, 1990c). (The use of item pairs has been the pattern followed for all research conducted by Marsh and colleagues in testing for evidence of construct validity related to the set of SDQ instruments; the rationale and advantages of this approach are presented in Marsh,

Exhibit 5.1

Sample Items From the Academic Self Description Questionnaire I

	False	Mostly False	More False Than True	More True Than False	Mostly True	True
Work in Computer Studies classes is easy for me.	_____	_____	_____	_____	_____	_____
I have always done well in most school subjects.	_____	_____	_____	_____	_____	_____

1992b.) Results from the exploratory factor analysis clearly identified all 13 self-concept subscales constituting the ASDQ–I; these findings were strongly substantiated with the subsequent testing of several confirmatory factor analytic models.

Findings from Marsh's (1990c) research on the ASDQ–I reveal very clearly not only that academic self-concept is multidimensionally structured but also that its facets are easily discriminated by elementary school children. Thus, if researchers wish to measure children's perceptions of their competence in relation to different academic subjects, it is critically evident that an instrument specifically designed to measure these differential perceptions is necessary. At the present time, then, the ASDQ–I is unique in its ability to address this measurement focus.

Related Psychometric Research

By means of exploratory factor analytic procedures, Larocque (1996) examined the factorial validity of the ASDQ–I for 475 Canadian children in Grades 5 and 6 (236 boys and 239 girls; mean age = 10.8 years). Because the ASDQ–I can be adjusted to accommodate particular school curricula, Larocque tailored the instrument to measure self-concepts related to the 11 subject areas common across the three school districts from which the data were drawn; the General-School subscale was also included. The domain-specific self-concepts measured were reflective of the following subjects: listening in language arts, reading in language arts, speaking in language arts, writing in language arts, arithmetic; geometry, science, social studies, religion, physical education, and art.

Although results generally supported the multidimensional structure of the ASDQ–I, as tailored by Larocque (1996) to match appropriate and relevant subject areas, the differentiation was lower than expected, with the data being best described by a seven-factor model. Specifically, items tapping each of these four language arts subject areas loaded on one factor; additionally, items reflective of the social studies and science areas loaded on the same factor. It seems obvious, however, that these results derived from the children's perception of the four language arts subjects, not as separate entities, but rather as different components of one subject area. Similarly, Larocque reported that post-test information revealed also that children had been advised by their teachers that social studies and science represented the same subject area. Thus, although at first blush it may seem that Larocque's findings cast some doubt on the factorial validity of the ASDQ–I, I believe that such an interpretation would be very much in error; indeed, where clearly different subject areas were tapped, its factorial structure was found to be very sound. The problem would appear to lie not with the ASDQ–I per se, but rather with the subject areas a researcher tailors the instrument to measure.

Evaluation Summary

Although the ASDQ–I is a relatively new instrument, its design was patterned after the well-established SDQ–I (Marsh, 1992b). Given the abundance of sound psychometric data available on the latter, in addition to the other two SDQ scales, there is no question in my mind that the ASDQ–I will accrue the same high-quality and thorough psychometric investigative work as its parent instrument. The instrument is theoretically linked to the Marsh/Shavelson model of self-concept and fills an important void in the existing pool of measures designed to tap perceptions of academic competence by elementary school children. Indeed, it represents the first such instrument to measure multiple subject-area facets of academic self-concept. Thus, despite its relatively new measurement status, for each of these reasons, I consider it important to include the ASDQ–I in the present volume.

Although the item content of the ASDQ–I is rooted in the Australian educational system, it can easily be modified for use within other educational jurisdictions. In this regard, Marsh stated that researchers are free to alter the ASDQ–I item content to more appropriately match their own academic curriculum endeavors. However, he does request that findings from research that has used the ASDQ–I be forwarded to him as a courtesy only (H. W. Marsh, personal communication, February 13, 1995).

Source Information

Location: Herbert W. Marsh, School of Education and Language Studies, University of Western Sydney, P.O. Box 555, Campbelltown, New South Wales 2560, Australia

Cost: No manual is presently available. However, Dr. Marsh has recommended that interested users write to him for updated information.

Perception of Ability Scale for Students

Description

The Perception of Ability Scale for Students (PASS; Boersma & Chapman, 1992) is a self-report scale designed to measure children's self-perceptions of their academic abilities and school-related achievement. In particular, the instrument taps self-perceived competence in performing basic school-related tasks such as writing, spelling, and math, as well as perceptions and attitudes toward school in general. Its development is grounded in the theoretical work of Bloom (1976), who recognized the influence of school-related perceptions on children's motivation and perseverance in school tasks, and in the hierarchical model of self-concept proposed by Shavelson et al. (1976).

Although the PASS would appear to be a relatively new instrument, this is definitely not the case. It was originally developed in the late 1970s and was known, until only recently, as the Student's Perception of Ability Scale (Boersma & Chapman, 1979); since then, the instrument has undergone a continuous program of testing based on numerous independent samples across a variety of populations. As a result, the PASS is now a well-established measure of academic self-concept that is built on a solid foundation of psychometric research.

Boersma and Chapman (1992) emphasized that in developing the PASS, the intent was to design an instrument that could serve several purposes across a wide variety of settings. Accordingly, the authors identified several ways in which the PASS may be used. First, the PASS can serve effectively as a screening instrument to identify high-risk children or to monitor general program effects on school-related self-perceptions. Boersma and Chapman (1992) suggested that a typical setting might include regular and special education classrooms, counseling and psychological service facilities, residential treatment centers, and private office practices. Second, the PASS can be used to evaluate special or regular education programs in which specific efforts may have been implemented to improve either achievement or achievement-related activities; outcomes can be evaluated in terms of academic self-concept. Third, the PASS can be used effectively in combination with observational and other derived data for individual assessment in a variety of clinical and counseling settings. Finally, the PASS represents an important research instrument for providing multidimensional measurements of a student's academic self-concept; according to Boersma and Chapman, this remains its most important function. For example, the PASS has been used to evaluate academic self-concept characteristics relative both to gifted students and to students with learning disabilities and to determine the causal interplay between academic self-concept and academic achievement.

Target Population

The PASS was standardized for use with elementary school children in Grades 3 through 6 (ages 8–12 years). Although the instrument has been read aloud to children in Grade 2 and used successfully with children in grades ranging through to Grade 10, no systematic attempts have been made to standardize or validate it for these populations. The PASS is therefore most appropriately used with the population of children for which it was originally standardized.

Scale Structure

The PASS is a 70-item, dichotomously structured (yes/no) instrument that comprises six subscales: Perception of General Ability, Perception of Math Ability, Perception of Reading/Spelling Ability, Perception of Penmanship and Neatness Skills, School Satisfaction, and Confidence in Academic Ability. Items have been written at approximately the mid-second-grade level and represent statements describing feelings that students may have about themselves with respect to their schoolwork. Boersma and Chapman (1992) stated that to reduce the tendency toward acquiescence and negative response biases, positively and negatively worded items were balanced throughout the scale.

A sample item from the School Satisfaction subscale of the PASS is presented in Exhibit 5.2.

Administration and Scoring

The PASS can be administered individually or in groups. Children are asked to indicate whether each statement applies to them by marking either yes or no in the appropriate circle accompanying the item (see

---

Exhibit 5.2

Sample Item From the Perception of Ability Scale for Students

	YES	NO
I like going to school.	(Y)	(N)

Exhibit 5.2). As noted earlier, the PASS has been used with Grade 2 children and in grades higher than 6. Nonetheless, Boersma and Chapman (1992) urge caution in the interpretation of scores when the instrument is used with children outside the normative populations; the PASS should not be used with children younger than Grade 2 age. Completion of the PASS typically takes approximately 15 to 20 min when administered individually and approximately 20 to 25 min when administered to groups.

The PASS can be scored either by hand, by means of an autoscore answer form, or by means of a computer scan sheet (WPS Test Report), which is subsequently mailed to the publisher (Western Psychological Services [WPS]). In either case, responses are tallied to yield one general academic self-concept score based on a combined multifaceted perspective of school life and six separate and more specific academic self-concept scores. Three summary scores are made available: a total raw score, a percentile score, and a normalized T score.

A very nice additional feature of the PASS scoring procedure is the provision of three different validity checks of item responses with respect to the presence of response bias, inconsistent responding, and misrepresentation. The Response Bias Index assesses acquiescence and negative response bias based on a cutoff criterion of yes responses. The Inconsistency Index identifies random response patterns and is based on a set of paired items to which responses are logically inconsistent and occur infrequently. Finally, the Misrepresentation Index serves as an initial screen of inaccurate self-reporting.[3] Based on a total score of six items relating to perfection of work, this index flags students who show a tendency toward reporting unrealistic or inaccurate perceptions of their academic ability. One sample from this set of items is shown in Exhibit 5.3.

---

3. Boersma and Chapman (1992, p. 41) noted that this index is often termed a *Lie Scale*. However, they chose not to use the term *lie* because it connotes children's deliberate attempts to misrepresent their true feelings about school.

Exhibit 5.3

Sample Item Used in Calculating the Misrepresentation Index From the Perception of Ability Scale for Students

	YES	NO
I always understand everything I read.	Ⓨ	Ⓝ

Normative Data

Samples. Normative testing of the PASS was based on 831 children in Grades 3 through 6 attending one of nine schools sampled from Idaho, Oregon, and Washington; both urban and rural communities were represented. Although the majority of children were from middle-income families, the full range of socioeconomic backgrounds was represented in the normative sample. Boersma and Chapman (1992) presented a separate descriptive statistics summary (*M* and *SD*) for Grade 3 through Grade 6; percentiles, stanines, and T-score conversions are also provided. Both sets of information are furnished for boys and girls separately, as well as in combination.

Selection and Refinement of Items. From a pool of 200 items that tapped self-perceptions of general academic ability, subject-specific competence, and feelings, attitudes, and self-confidence about school in general, 143 were selected for the initial version of the PASS.[4] This scale was administered to 310 Grade 3 children attending five middle-income public elementary schools in Edmonton, Alberta, Canada (Boersma & Chapman, 1992). After both factor and item analyses of the data, the instrument was further reduced to its present 70-item form. The revised scale was then administered to 642 children in Grade 3 through Grade 6 attending two middle-income schools in Edmonton, Alberta; the sample comprised seven Grade 3, seven Grade 4, six Grade 5, and five Grade 6 classes. Satisfied with the adequacy of the factor structure based on this second development sample and with the full scale and subscale intercorrelations, the test authors retained the originally tested 70-item early version of the PASS.

Psychometric Properties. Reliability. Internal reliability estimates for the PASS full scale have been consistently high across the Canadian development samples ($N = 310$, $\alpha = .91$, Chapman, Boersma, & Maguire, 1977; $N = 642$, $\alpha = .92$, Boersma & Chapman, 1984) and the American normative samples ($N = 831$, $\alpha = .93$, Boersma & Chapman, 1992).

---

4. Known then as the Student's Perception of Ability Scale.

Cronbach alpha coefficients for the PASS subscales have also been consistent, with most values exceeding .80; estimates have ranged from .64 to .84 (mean α = .78) and from .69 to .86 (mean α = .78) for the first and second development sample, respectively, and from .69 to .85 (mean α = .79) for the normative sample. Whereas the Confidence in Academic Ability subscale has consistently yielded the lowest reliability estimate, the Reading/Spelling Ability subscale has consistently produced the highest estimate.

Test–retest reliability estimates have also been reported for the PASS. A full scale stability coefficient of .83 (for 4–6 weeks) was reported for the development sample of 603 children in Grade 3 through Grade 6 (Boersma & Chapman, 1984), and coefficients of .72 and .64 were reported for over 1 and 2 years, respectively, for 932 New Zealand children (Chapman, 1988b). Finally, data from both of these studies showed the Reading/Spelling Ability subscale to be the most stable PASS subscale and the School Satisfaction subscale to be the least stable.

Validity. In the light of the rigorous scrutiny and final selection of items from the original pool of 200, Boersma and Chapman (1992) contended that the content validity of the PASS was sound. They further noted that although the instrument does not balance the coverage of all subject areas evenly, it does tap a meaningful range of achievement and general school perceptions. It is in this sense that the test authors believe that the content of the PASS is valid for the assessment of academic self-concept in elementary school children.

Concurrent validity of the PASS has been tested through the examination of its relation with other measures of both academic and general self-concept. Validity with respect to academic self-concept has been tested with the Self-Concept of Ability Scale (Brookover, 1962) for Grade 10 LD and non-LD students (Chapman & Wilkinson, 1988) and with the Intellectual and School Status subscale of the Piers–Harris Children's Self-Concept Scale (PHCSCS; Piers, 1984) for children in Grade 3–Grade 6 (Boersma & Chapman, 1992; Chapman et al., 1977). These coefficients have ranged from .52 to .74 (mean r = .60). Validity coefficients bearing on general self-concept have derived from comparison with the PHCSCS for children in Grade 3 to Grade 6 (Boersma & Chapman, 1992; Chapman et al., 1977); with the Canadian Self-Esteem Inventory[5] for children in Grade 1 through Grade 7 (Battle, 1979); and

---

5. The name has since been changed to the Culture-Free Self-Esteem Inventory (Battle, 1981).

with the Tennessee Self-Concept Scale (Roid & Fitts, 1988/1994) for Grade 10 LD and non-LD children (Chapman, 1988b); these values have ranged from .25 to .70 (mean r = .53).

Evidence of construct validity related to the PASS has been substantiated on the basis of a principal-components analysis that yielded six well-defined subscales, as well as numerous studies of relations between both its full scale and separate subscale scores and various external criteria. These include affective and personality measures; intelligence measures; and academic achievement measures as indicated by report card grades, standardized test scores, teacher ratings, and parent perceptions. Because limitations of space preclude the full reporting of these values here, readers are referred to the comprehensive summaries presented in the manual (Boersma & Chapman, 1992).

Related Psychometric Research

Although numerous studies have tested for and found the validity of PASS scores to be adequate for various exceptional populations (for a review, see Chapman, 1989), most of this research has focused on the LD population (see Chapman, 1988a; Chapman & Boersma, 1991). As a consequence of findings that strongly support appropriate use of the PASS with LD children, a summary of this research is presented in chapter 8. In addition, the instrument has been used successfully to measure the academic self-concepts of other ethnic groups, such as New Zealand Maoris, Canadian Native Indians, and Spanish-speaking Mexican Americans (Arellano & Chapman, 1992).

Evaluation Summary

The PASS is a soundly constructed measure of academic self-concept that has undergone continuous testing of its psychometric properties for the past 18 years. The item content and instructions are easily understood by young children, and it is quickly and easily administered. An additionally unique and valuable feature of this instrument is valid and reliable use with academically handicapped children. One aspect of the psychometric research on the PASS that could be strengthened, however, is the provision of construct validity evidence. In particular, the instrument could benefit substantially from a rigorous testing of (a) its factorial structure, by means of confirmatory factor analytic procedures and (b) its convergent and discriminant validities, by means of the MTMM approach within the framework of covariance structure modeling. Overall, however, the PASS has been shown to be a psychometrically adequate measure of multidimensional academic self-concepts.

Source Information

Location: Western Psychological Services, 12031 Wilshire Boulevard, Los Angeles, California 90025-1251

Cost: Manual: $28.50

Kit: $70.00 (includes manual, 25 autoscore answer forms, and 2 prepaid WPS Test Report mail-in answer sheets for computer scoring and interpretation)

Measurement of Multiple Self-Concept Domains

Multidimensional Self Concept Scale

Description

The Multidimensional Self Concept Scale (MSCS; Bracken, 1992) is designed to measure multiple context-dependent dimensions of self-concept for preadolescent, as well as adolescent, children. On the basis of the perspective that self-concept is a behavioral construct rather than part of a larger cognitive self-system (see, e.g., Harter, 1983), Bracken (1992) argued for use of the unhyphenated term *self concept* in both the title and the theoretical rationale that underpins the instrument.[6] The MSCS can be used effectively in research endeavors that seek to examine relations between self-concept and other theoretical constructs. It can also be used in a wide variety of clinical settings that include "public and private schools, counseling centers, mental health centers, pediatric hospital settings, psychological and psychiatric centers for youth and adolescents, drug and alcohol units for youth, correction and social service agencies, and related clinical facilities" (Bracken, 1992, p. 11).

Development of the MSCS has been solidly grounded in the theoretical view that self-concept is multidimensionally and hierarchically structured. As such, it assumes that the multiple facets are moderately intercorrelated and subsumed by a general Self-Concept factor similar to Spearman's *g* (Bracken & Howell, 1991), a notion that parallels the underlying rationale of the Shavelson et al. (1976) model. The MSCS embraces three additional features that are, in part, in keeping with the Shavelson et al. model: (a) that self-concept develops in an organized

---

6. For consistency throughout this volume, however, use of the hyphenated form is maintained in reference to the construct in general.

manner, shaped by individuals' learned evaluations about themselves as derived from their successes and failures, reinforcement histories, and reactions from and interactions with others; (b) that, as with other learned behavioral response patterns, self-concept is a relatively stable construct; and (c) that self-concept is developmental in that, as with most acquired human characteristics, it becomes increasingly differentiated with age. Finally, the MSCS is based on a "perspective-by-standard" (Bracken & Howell, 1991, p. 323) self-concept acquisition model. This view holds that self-evaluation is based on information gleaned from two perspectives: that directly acquired through personal experience and that indirectly acquired through interaction with others. In addition, the evaluative process is based on four standards: absolute (success/failure), ipsative (performance of one activity in relation to one's general performance), comparative (performance in relation to that of others), and ideal (expected level of performance). (For a more intensive description of each of these features, see Bracken, 1992.)

Taken together, the theoretical underpinning of the MSCS reflects a taxonomic model of self-concept having three facets: context-specific domains, evaluative perspectives, and evaluative performance standards (Marsh & Hattie, 1996). In keeping with the taxonomic design, each of these facets, in turn, embraces multiple levels. Accordingly, the context-specific domains facet has six levels (social, competence, affect, academic, family, and physical); the evaluative perspectives facets has two levels (self [i.e., personal] and other); and the evaluative performance standards facet has four levels (absolute, ipsative, comparative, and ideal). (For an elaboration of these aspects of the MSCS within the framework of the taxonomic model, see chapter 1 of this volume.)

Target Population
The MSCS is designed for use with children in Grade 5 through Grade 12 (ages 9–19 years).

Scale Structure
The MSCS is a 150-item self-report scale that taps children's self-perceptions related to six contextual domains: social competence related to interactions with others (Social subscale); success/failure in attainment of goals (Competence subscale); recognition of affective behaviors (Affect subscale); academic achievement, as well as competence in other school-related activities (Academic subscale); competence related to in-

---

Exhibit 5.4

Sample Item From the Multidimensional Self Concept Scale

Strongly Agree (SA)	Agree (A)	Disagree (D)	Strongly Disagree (SD)	
				SCORE
My family makes me feel loved.		SA A D SD		

---

teractions with family members (Family subscale);[7] and physical attractiveness and prowess (Physical subscale). To offset response-set bias of a central tendency nature, items are structured on a 4-point Likert-type scale format with no neutral option; 25 items constitute each subscale.

Because of the wide age range for which the MSCS is designed, items have been carefully constructed to ensure that each is appropriate for use with younger children. For example, no item elicits a response that relates to dating. In addition, to protect against any possibility of bias due to ethnicity, gender, or geographical location (urban, rural, or suburban areas of the United States), items are intentionally worded as concisely, simply, and briefly as possible; no colloquialisms, slang, or other nonstandard words are used.

A sample item from the Family subscale of the MSCS is presented in Exhibit 5.4.

Administration and Scoring

The MSCS can be administered individually or in groups. Children are asked to respond to simple declarative statements by circling one of the four alternatives that they believe best describes them (see Exhibit 5.4). Items have been written at the third-grade reading level; thus, the MSCS is not recommended for use with children whose reading abilities are below this level. Although the full scale is typically completed in 20 to 30 min, Bracken (1992) noted that additional time may be necessary for young children who have poor reading abilities.

Scoring the MSCS is easily accomplished by merely adding the raw scores of each subscale. Of course, negative items must first be reversed before being added, to redistribute the weights in the positive direction. Bracken (1992) also provided a formula for computing prorated scores for incomplete questionnaires.

---

7. The term *family* is used in the generic sense to mean individuals upon whom the child is dependent for care, security, and nurturance (Bracken, 1992).

Normative Data

Samples. Normative testing of the MSCS was based on a total sample of 2,501 children in Grade 5 through Grade 12 inclusive (ages 9–19 years). The instrument was administered in 17 locations representing the South, West, North Central, and Northeast regions of the United States. Subsamples comprised children representative of both genders; all major ethnic heritages; urban, suburban, small town, and rural communities; and both regular and special education programs. Bracken (1992) noted that the MSCS standardization sample far exceeded those reported for other major self-concept measures designed for use with the same population (e.g., Piers–Harris Children's Self-Concept Scale [PHCSCS]; Piers, 1984). The following normative information is reported in the manual for each subscale: means and standard deviations by age, standard score equivalents by raw score, standard scores converted to T scores, and percentile ranks corresponding to standard scores.

Selection and Refinement of Items. Before pilot testing, a pool of initially developed items was subjected to two informal examinations and critiques by graduate psychology students, middle school teachers, and middle and high school students to identify those considered to be ambiguous, threatening, or otherwise problematic; dubious items were subsequently revised or discarded. After this initial screening, a 180-item field test version of the instrument was administered to a sample of 500 children in Grade 5 through Grade 8 from two separate school systems in Tennessee, and examiners were asked to report any problematic items. After an item analysis of the field test data, items exhibiting low reliabilities and those that were either strongly endorsed or denied by most students were either revamped or discarded. The entire refinement process subsequently yielded the present MSCS, comprising six subscales, each of which comprises 25 items.

Psychometric Properties. *Reliability.* Reported internal reliability estimates based on the field test sample for both the MSCS full and separate subscales (Bracken, 1992) are shown to be exceptionally high. For each grade sampled in the pilot testing, coefficient alpha reliabilities ranged from .97 to .99 (mean α = .98) for the full scale and from .85 to .97 for the subscales; mean subscale alpha values were .90, .87, .93, .90, .97, and .92 for the Social, Competence, Affect, Academic, Family, and Physical subscales, respectively.

Test–retest reliability estimates have also been reported for the MSCS. Based on a sample of 37 Grade 8 students, a test–retest reliability of .90 was reported for the full scale over a 4-week period (Bracken, 1992). Additionally, subtest test–retest coefficients for over the same interval ranged from .73 (Affect) to .81 (Academic and Physical), with a mean value of .78. In addition to the calculation of these stability coefficients, Bracken tested for significant differences across time; based on a Bonferroni correction of t test results, findings revealed no significant differences. On the basis of these findings, then, the MSCS appears to be both stable and resistant to chance-score fluctuations in the assessment of multiple dimensions of self-concept.

Validity. Given that the six domains measured by the MSCS represent a comprehensive decomposition of self-concept for preadolescent and adolescent children and are strongly linked to the theoretical literature, Bracken (1992) contended that the content validity of the MSCS is sound. Moreover, on the basis of a comparative review of 5 well-known self-concept measures and 70 personality measures designed for use with these populations, he reported that only the MSCS adequately tapped content representative of each of these domains.

Concurrent validity of the MSCS has been tested through the examination of both its full scale and separate subscale scores with other well-known self-concept measures. Results have shown full scale correlations between the MSCS and the Coopersmith Self-Esteem Inventory (CSEI; Coopersmith, 1967), the Piers–Harris Children's Self-Concept Scale (PHCSCS; Piers, 1984), the Self Description Questionnaire I (SDQ–I; Marsh, 1992b), and the SDQ–II (Marsh, 1992c) to be .73, .83, .69, and .80, respectively. Examination of theoretically similar subscale scores between the MSCS and these same instruments (except the CSEI) yielded values ranging from .66 (Social) to .75 (Academic) for the PHCSCS, from .47 (Academic) to .82 (Social) for the SDQ–I, and from .54 to .68 (Family) for the SDQ–II.[8]

Evidence of construct validity related to the MSCS has been investigated from three different perspectives. First, results from two studies found MSCS scores to accurately discriminate between normal elementary school children ($N = 39$; $N = 24$) and children previously identified as having low self-concepts ($N = 10$) and those in need of further psychological assessment ($N = 25$; Bardos, 1991). Second, based on the national standardization sample, Bracken and Kelley (in press) found the six facets of self-concept measured by the MSCS to be discriminable

---

8. Based on the mean correlation between the Social—Opposite Sex Relations and Social—Same Sex Relations subscale scores based on the SDQ–II.

from the respective constructs measured by the Assessment of Interpersonal Relations Scale. Finally, based on a multiple-instrument factor analysis (see Woodcock, 1990) that comprised the MSCS, PHCSCS, CSEI, Tennessee Self-Concept Scale, and Self-Esteem Index (Brown & Alexander, 1991), Bracken, Bunch, and Keith (1992) reported strong support for the six context-dependent factors measured by the MSCS.

Related Psychometric Research

Based on a study of students in Grades 5, 6, and 8, Delugach, Bracken, Bracken, and Schicke (1992) have reported further support for the multidimensional structure of self-concept and for the psychometric soundness of the MSCS. Full scale scores correlated significantly with those of the SDQ–I and SDQ–II, thereby underscoring the similarity of the instruments in assessing a global self-concept. Subscale correlations between and across instruments provided additional support for the multidimensionality of the construct.

Evaluation Summary

Although the MSCS is a relatively new self-concept measure, it comes equipped with solid psychometric credentials. In addition to a carefully constructed set of subscales that are solidly linked to a well-established theoretical framework, the instrument has been subjected to a rigorous and extensive testing program that provides important evidence of its psychometric properties. Findings stand in firm support of its use for both clinical and research applications. Nonetheless, additional construct validity research using the analysis of covariance structures would be beneficial in seeking further evidence of its factorial structure (confirmatory factor analyses) and convergent and discriminant validity (MTMM analyses). Overall, however, the MSCS represents an important new self-concept scale that is worthy of serious consideration when the measurement of preadolescent and adolescent self-concepts is of interest.

Source Information

Location: Pro-Ed Inc., 8700 Shoal Creek Boulevard, Austin, Texas 78758

Cost: Complete kit: $64.00 (includes manual and 50 record booklets)

Piers—Harris Children's Self-Concept Scale

Description

The Piers—Harris Children's Self-Concept Scale (PHCSCS; Piers, 1984), subtitled "The Way I Feel About Myself," is a self-report scale initially designed as a unidimensional measure of children's self-perceptions in relation to six areas of their daily functioning: behavior, intellectual and school status, physical appearance and attributes, anxiety, popularity, and happiness and satisfaction. Although the most recent test manual (Piers, 1984), as well as recent studies of the PHCSCS (e.g., Benson & Rentsch, 1988), emphasized its multidimensional structure, Marsh and Holmes (1990) remind us that the items of this instrument were never constructed a priori to measure these specific facets of self-concept; rather, the dimensions evolved from six a posteriori principal-component analyses, with items being retained only if they demonstrated a replicated loading pattern across studies (see also Cosden, 1984; Wylie, 1989). The PHCSCS is most clearly linked to the nomothetic model of self-concept described in chapter 1.

The PHCSCS was developed in the early 1960s to serve two purposes: (a) as a research instrument and (b) as an aid to clinical and educational evaluation in applied settings (Piers, 1984). Its construction is rooted in the theoretical rationale that the self-concept reflects a global perspective of self in relation to important aspects of one's life and that these perceptions are shaped by social interaction with others. This global perspective is based on several theoretical assumptions: (a) that self-concept has a phenomenological nature (see Wylie, 1974) and, as such, it must be inferred from an individual's behavior or from his or her self-report; (b) that self-concept has both global and specific components; (c) that self-concept is relatively stable; (d) that self-concept has both evaluative and descriptive components; (e) that self-concept is influenced by developmental factors; and (f) that self-concept is organized and plays a key role in motivation. (See Piers, 1984, for an elaborated discussion of these characteristics.) Overall, these theoretical notions are akin to those proposed by Shavelson et al. (1976).

The PHCSCS can be used effectively to measure children's self-concepts within three contexts. First, it can be used as a screening instrument in high-risk settings, with other methods of assessment. For example, Piers (1984) suggested that it could be used in special education and other classroom settings to screen for children who might benefit from further psychological evaluation. Second, the PHCSCS can be used in a variety of clinical and counseling settings in which it may be deemed important to integrate scores from this instrument with clinical observations and other test data to obtain an overall picture of a particular child. Finally, on the basis of reports that the PHCSCS is the most frequently cited test for preadolescents (see Marsh & Holmes, 1990), its use as a research instrument in providing quantitative self-reported scores of self-concept seems well established. Indeed, despite its popularity as an assessment measure in other settings, Piers (1984) maintained that the PHCSCS's function as a research instrument remains one of its primary purposes.

Target Population

The PHCSCS has been standardized for use with children in Grades 4 through 12 (ages 8–18 years). Although the instrument has been used experimentally with younger children (Kugle, Clements, & Powell, 1983), Piers (1984) stressed the lack of systematic validity research related to children younger than 8 years of age, thus the risk involved in making comparisons with the normative samples. Given the PHCSCS's self-report format, she also recommended that it not be used with children who either were emotionally disturbed or had low verbal ability, owing to "bilingual background, organic impairment, or moderate to severe mental retardation" (Piers, 1984, p. 3).

Scale Structure

The PHCSCS is an 80-item, dichotomously scaled (yes/no) self-report questionnaire that comprises six *cluster scales*: Behavior, Intellectual/School Status, Physical Appearance/Attributes, Anxiety, Popularity, and Happiness/Satisfaction.[9] Items have been written at the third-grade reading level and represent statements that describe how some people feel about themselves. For each statement, children are asked to indicate whether the situation described applies to them by circling either the yes or the no response alternative provided. To reduce the tendency toward acquiescence and negative response biases, positively and negatively worded items have been balanced throughout the scale.

A sample item from the Popularity cluster of the PHCSCS is presented in Exhibit 5.5.

---

9. Piers (1984) noted that, conceptually, cluster scores could be considered equivalent to multiple group factor scores (see Gorsuch, 1983).

Exhibit 5.5

Sample Item From the Piers–Harris Children's Self-Concept Scale

I am among the last to be chosen for games .... yes   no

---

Administration and Scoring

The PHCSCS can be administered either individually or with small groups of children. Because it is critically important that children fully understand both the item content and the response procedure, Piers (1984) suggested limiting the size of the group to no more than 10 when administering the instrument to children at the low end of the age scale. Completion of the PHCSCS typically takes approximately 15 to 20 min for most children.

The PHCSCS can be scored by hand using a scoring key or by computer using either a scan sheet (WPS Test Report) that is subsequently mailed to the publisher for scoring and interpretive information or the same program provided on a microcomputer disk. A total raw score is calculated by tallying the number of items marked in the positive direction (i.e., indicative of high self-concept). In addition, as an aid to detailed clinical interpretation, separate cluster scores can be obtained. Note, however, that the PHCSCS total score cannot be determined from a summation of the cluster scores. This is because, as noted earlier, these item clusters have not been derived a priori in a true factor analytic sense. As a consequence, many items are scored on more than one cluster scale, and some are completely deleted from the cluster scores; this is made easier by means of a scoring key. Both the total and cluster raw scores may be converted to percentiles, stanines, or T scores for interpretation purposes.

Finally, the computer-scoring procedure for the PHCSCS provides a Response Bias Index, reflective of the degree of yea-saying and nay-saying response bias, and an Inconsistency Index, indicative of the extent to which responses are consistent across items.[10]

Normative Data

Samples. The standardization sample for the total PHCSCS was based on 1,183 children in Grades 4 through 12 drawn from one school district in Pennsylvania; given findings of no consistent gender or grade

---

10. For a more detailed explanation of these indexes, see a description of the Perception of Ability Scale for Students (this chapter).

differences, the scores were pooled for normative purposes. Norms for the separate cluster scales, however, were based on a sample of 485 public school children (248 girls and 237 boys) drawn from 279 elementary, 55 junior high, and 151 senior high schools. The following normative information is reported in the manual: total score means and standard deviations for each of five grades (4, 6, 8, 10, and 12); cluster and total score means and standard deviations by sex and in combination; and percentile, stanine, and T-score conversions for both cluster and total score PHCSCS scores.

Selection and Refinement of Items. Construction of an original pool of 164 items was based on Jersild's (1952) research in which he asked children to describe in writing what they liked and disliked about themselves. Results were categorized as follows: physical characteristics and appearance; clothing and grooming; health and physical well-being; home and family; enjoyment of recreation; ability in sports and play; academic performance and attitudes toward school; intellectual abilities; special talents (i.e., music or art); "just me, myself"; and personality characteristics, inner resources, and emotional tendencies (Piers, 1984). These items were administered to a sample of 90 children enrolled in Grades 4, 5, and 6. Following the deletion of lie scale items, as well as determined problematic items, a subsequent pool of 140 items was tested on a sample of 127 Grade 6 students. From these data, the 30 highest and 30 lowest scores were identified, and then the retention of items was based on their power to discriminate significantly ($p < .05$) between these high and low groups; items that were not answered in the expected direction were also deleted. These screening procedures resulted in the present 80-item PHCSCS.

The initial intent in developing the PHCSCS was to have the instrument yield a total score that reflected a child's overall perspective of self. Piers (1984) was emphatic in her contention that this global score was still the most widely used and thoroughly researched score for the PHCSCS. Cluster scale scores were based on findings from principal-components analyses with varimax rotation, conducted on a series of six independent samples: Piers's (1963) Grade 6 sample ($N = 457$), Piers's (1973) follow-up Grade 6 ($N = 146$) and Grade 10 ($N = 151$) samples (see Piers, 1984), and three samples from a study by Michael, Smith, and Michael (1975); the latter samples represented 299 elementary, 302 junior high, and 300 senior high school students.[11] Only items

---

11. Piers (1984) referred to these analyses as *factor analyses*, which, technically speaking, is inaccurate.

that replicated across studies were retained (but see Marsh & Holmes, 1990, regarding this point).

Psychometric Properties. Reliability. Piers (1984) summarized internal consistency reliability coefficients for the PHCSCS total scale as derived from several studies. Accordingly, the following estimates have been reported: K–R 20 coefficients ranging from .88 to .90 (mean $r_{K-R\ 20}$ = .90; Grades 6 and 10), a Spearman–Brown coefficient of .91 (ages 7–12 years), and alpha coefficients ranging from .89 to .92 (mean α = .90; Grades 3–6, ages 6–12 years). Internal consistency estimates for the cluster scales have been shown to range from .73 (Happiness/Satisfaction) to .81 (Behavior, mean $r_{K-R\ 20}$) for 485 normal school children (no grade reported) and 97 children from three psychiatric and psychological outpatient clinics (Piers, 1984).

A substantial amount of test–retest reliability information based on time intervals ranging from 2 weeks to 1 year has also been reported for the PHCSCS; all relate to the total scale only. Given the number of studies reported in the manual and in the interest of space, findings specific to each are not reported here. As a general overview, however, note that the samples on which these stability coefficients were computed represented ages ranging from 7 to 20 years and represented children from both public and private schools; various ethnic groups; children with normal and abnormal speech patterns; and LD, mentally retarded, and emotionally disturbed children. In summary, reported test–retest results ranged from r = .42 (for mentally retarded or emotionally disturbed children; ages 11–16 years; N = 39; 8-month time interval) to r = .96 (for children with mild speech articulation disorders; Grades 3 and 4; N = 10; 3–4-week time interval), with a mean r of .73. No information is provided in the manual with respect to tests of stability related to the PHCSCS separate cluster scales.

Validity. Piers (1984) contended that in developing the initial set of 140 items, a conscious attempt was made to build content validity into the PHCSCS by defining the universe of items to be measured as the areas in which children reported various characteristics they either liked or disliked about themselves. However, as a consequence of the scale refinement process, the representation of certain areas may be less well covered. As a test of content validity, several studies have attempted to correlate PHCSCS total scale scores with various teacher- and peer-rating scores of self-concept. Although, typically, these correlations have been low and nonsignificant, a few significant correlations have been reported, the highest of which is .54 for teacher ratings of self-concept for children in Grades 3 and 4 (see Piers, 1984, for a full description of these studies). Given that self-concept scores derived from ratings by others are actually inferred, rather than actual perceptions of self, it is not surprising that these values are fairly low. Indeed, these findings support the argument that unless the rater knows the subject extremely well and completes the self-concept scale as if he or she were the subject, these values will tend to be low, because the self-concept is viewed from two different perspectives (see, e.g., Marsh & Byrne, 1993).

Concurrent validity of the PHCSCS has been tested through the examination of its relation with other unidimensional measures of self-concept. Seven such studies are reported in the manual and involve the following measures: Pictorial Self-Concept Scale (Bolea, Felker, & Barnes, 1971), Tennessee Self-Concept Scale (Fitts, 1965), Bills Index of Adjustment and Values (Bills, 1975), Coopersmith Self-Esteem Inventory (Coopersmith, 1967), Personal Attribute Inventory (Parish & Taylor, 1978), Nonsexist Personal Attribute Inventory (Parish & Rankin, 1982), and Lipsitt's (1958) Children's Self-Concept Scale.[12] Validity coefficients ranged from .32 (Personal Attribute Inventory; Grades 3–8; $N = 390$) to .85 (Coopersmith Self-Esteem Inventory; Grades 5–6; $N = 215$), mean $r = .54$. Of course, considering that the Coopersmith Self-Esteem Inventory is based on a rationale, questionnaire format, and target population similar to those of the PHCSCS, it is both reasonable and indeed expected that the correlation between the total scores of the two instruments should be fairly high.

Piers (1984) reported evidence of construct validity related to the PHCSCS on the basis of findings from several principal components analyses of its underlying structure, intercorrelations among cluster and total scale scores, five MTMM analyses of its convergent and discriminant validities, criterion between-groups analyses of its discriminability, and correlations with external criteria (i.e., between-network relations of its nomological network; see, e.g., Byrne, 1984; Cronbach & Meehl, 1955; Shavelson et al., 1976). Except for four studies, all other principal components analyses of the PHCSCS were described earlier; on the basis of what Piers considered to be strong dimensional structure similarities between her earlier findings (1963, 1973) and those from the Michael et al. (1975) study, she concluded reasonable evidence of construct validity. (Michael et al. [1975], however, reported consistency

---

12. Although two other measures are listed, they are not self-report measures of self-concept.

across their three samples relative to only three of the six intended PHCSCS dimensions.) The remaining studies (described in the manual) tested for the replication of structural findings for different racial and ethnic groups, as well as for a group of mentally retarded children. Based on findings from these studies that showed some dissimilarities as well as instability within the same (mixed-ethnic) group, Piers (1984) called for caution in the interpretation of the cluster scales. However, based on the clearly inadequate sample sizes used in each of these four studies, the results are not surprising and, in fact, cannot be meaningfully interpreted. Nonetheless, given the method by which the separate PHCSCS scales were constructed, thereby yielding a pattern of cross-loadings for several items, achievement of any simple principal components solution seems highly unlikely.

Intercorrelations among the cluster scales have been shown to range from .21 (for Behavior with Physical Appearance/Attributes) to .59 (for Physical Appearance/Attributes with Intellectual/School Status; mean $r = .42$). Logically, explanation of these moderate associations lies with the loading of several items on more than one component; Piers (1984), too, acknowledged this fact. The extent to which each of the cluster scales correlates with the total scale is reported to range from .67 (Behavior) to .78 (Intellectual/School Status; mean $r = .70$). Finally, Piers reported that most items exhibited higher correlations with the cluster scales to which they belonged than with the other nontarget scales, thereby arguing for further evidence of construct validity.

Findings from studies based on the traditional (Campbell & Fiske, 1959) approach to MTMM analyses (see, e.g., Byrne & Goffin, 1993) have generally been consistent in demonstrating strong evidence of convergent validity for general self-concept, as measured by the PHCSCS total scale, and lack of discriminant validity related to its separate cluster scales (see Piers, 1984). These findings argue strongly for use of the PHCSCS as a measure of general self-concept rather than as a measure of multidimensional self-concepts. In addition, Piers reported evidence of the PHCSCS total scale to discriminate between normal and mentally retarded adolescents and between preadolescent boys on the basis of having/not having a "chum" relationship. Discriminability of the instrument has also been shown for particular items relative to physically abused and nonabused preadolescents, as well as normal and clinical samples of elementary, junior high, and senior high school students. Finally, Piers reported evidence of construct validity based on significant correlations between the total scale and other behavioral and personality measures to which it is logically and theoretically linked.

Related Psychometric Research

Recent research has investigated various psychometric properties of the PHCSCS. First, based on a sample of 155 children (Grades 6–8; mean age 13.1 years), Cooley and Ayers (1988) reported internal consistency reliability to be adequate for both the total scale scores (α = .92) and cluster scale scores (mean α = .79), albeit inadequate evidence of discriminant validity based on the cluster scale correlations (mean r = .54).

Second, three studies have tested the a priori dimensional structure of the PHCSCS: (a) Based on exploratory factor analytic procedures that included both principal-components and iterative factor analyses, Collins, Kafer, and Shea (1985) found a comparatively clearer solution with the latter. They reported five factors (all but Happiness/Satisfaction) to be consistent across eight samples of 100 children ranging in age from 8 to 15 years; (b) Based on a sample of 290 Grade 5 children (mean age 10.5 years) for which an exploratory factor analytic approach with oblique rotation was used to take into account the noted correlations among the PHCSCS cluster scales, Marsh and Holmes (1990) reported weak support for a multifaceted scale that they argued "calls into question its continued use for inferring multiple dimensions of self-concept" (p. 113); (c) Benson and Rentsch (1988) used confirmatory factor analytic procedures to test both the dimensionality of the PHCSCS and the influence of item phrasing (positively or negatively worded items) on its dimensional structure. On the basis of responses from 885 Black, White, and Hispanic children in Grade 3 through Grade 6, these authors reported support for a three-factor model (one content factor and two phrasing factors), thereby suggesting that construct validity of the instrument is a function not only of content but also of manner of phrasing; the effect of negative response bias related to the PHCSCS has recently been supported (Marsh & Holmes, 1990). (Readers interested in detailed discussions of negative response bias are referred to Benson & Hocevar, 1985; Marsh, 1986c; Marsh & Holmes, 1990.) On the basis of their findings, Benson and Rentsch determined that the PHCSCS is unidimensional in terms of its content.

Finally, based on traditional MTMM analyses (Campbell & Fiske, 1959), Marsh and Holmes (1990) reported adequate convergent validity for the PHCSCS, albeit weak evidence of discriminant validity. They concluded that although the total score for this instrument may provide a reasonable measure of overall self-concept, the validity of its cluster scores is somewhat dubious. Indeed, these conclusions are in keeping with those expressed by many viewers (including Piers, 1984) that any interpretation of these separate scale scores should be made with caution.

Evaluation Summary

Historically, the PHCSCS has been the most widely used and highly recommended self-concept instrument for children (Hughes, 1984; Marsh & Holmes, 1990). However, with the recent development of measures that are more firmly grounded in theory than the PHCSCS and that have been more rigorously tested with respect to their psychometric properties, this tradition is gradually becoming eroded (see, for example, this chapter as well as chapter 6). In the light of (a) our current knowledge of both methodological approaches to, and substantive findings from, construct validity research related to self-concept and (b) the fact that the original 80-item PHCSCS has been neither renormed (J. H. Epstein, 1985) nor revamped (Cosden, 1984) since its original publication in the late 1960s, it seems clear that the instrument is due for both a reassessment and retesting of its current structure. Although the manual (in contrast to the earlier version [Marsh & Holmes, 1990]) emphasizes its multidimensional measurement capabilities, recent psychometric testing of the PHCSCS (as noted earlier) calls this claim into question.

On the basis of construct validity research, then, it appears that the PHCSCS is most appropriately used as a measure of general self-concept; at best, the cluster scale scores should be used only as a guide in identifying areas of particular concern for purposes of intervention program planning. Indeed, this conclusion would appear to support Piers's (1984) own perspective regarding effective use of the PHCSCS. I join other reviewers (Bentler, 1972a; J. H. Epstein, 1985) in commending the test author for her honest and candid recognition of the scale's limitations and for her caveat to exercise caution in the interpretation of its scores.

Source Information

Location: Western Psychological Services, 12031 Wilshire Boulevard, Los Angeles, California 90025-1251

Cost: Manual: $45.00

Kit: $115.00 (includes 25 test booklets, 1 scoring key, 1 manual, 2 prepaid WPS Test Report answer sheets for computer scoring and interpretation, and 25 profile forms)

Self Description Questionnaire I

Description

The Self Description Questionnaire I (SDQ–I; Marsh, 1992b) is designed to measure multiple dimensions of self-concept for preadolescents. In particular, the scale taps self-perceptions relative to four nonacademic areas (Physical Ability, Physical Appearance, Peer Relations, and Parent Relations) and three academic areas (Reading, Mathematics, and school in general), as well as a global perception of self. The instrument is solidly grounded in the multidimensional/hierarchical self-concept model originally proposed by Shavelson et al. (1976), but subsequently revised and retitled by Marsh (Marsh et al., 1988; Marsh & Shavelson, 1985). Indeed, it was the SDQ–I that was used in testing several specific hypotheses bearing on the Shavelson et al. (1976) model and that eventually led to its reformulation as the Marsh/Shavelson model of self-concept.

The SDQ–I has served as a prototype from which all subsequent SDQ instruments (SDQ–II, SDQ–III, Academic Self Description Questionnaire I [ASDQ–I], ASDQ–II, and Physical Self-Description Questionnaire [PSDQ]) have been developed. It is the product of an exceptionally rigorous construct validity research portfolio that over this past decade, has continuously focused on the interplay between theory and empirical research.

Target Population

Although the SDQ–I was originally designed for use with children in Grades 4 through 6 (ages 8–12 years), results from several studies have shown its additional suitability for use with Grade 2 children.

Scale Structure

The SDQ–I is a 76-item self-report scale that comprises eight subscales: (a) four nonacademic (Physical Ability, Physical Appearance, Peer Relations, and Parent Relations); (b) three academic, two of which are subject-matter specific (Reading and Mathematics) and one that relates to school in general (General—School); and (c) one that measures overall global self-concept (General—Self). The items are structured on a 5-point Likert-type scale format, with each subscale comprising eight positively worded items. In addition, Marsh (1992b) reported that there are 12 negatively worded items that are included solely for the purpose of disrupting any tendency toward positive response bias. However, based on research that has shown the validity of responses to negatively worded items to be problematic for young children and pread-olescents (Benson & Hocevar, 1985; Benson & Rentsch, 1988; Marsh, 1986c; Marsh & Holmes, 1990), these items are not included in the computation of self-concept scores. One sample item from each of the Physical Appearance and General—Self subscales of the SDQ–I, respectively, is presented in Exhibit 5.6.

Administration and Scoring

The SDQ–I can be administered individually or in groups. For each statement provided in the questionnaire, children are asked to identify which one of the five alternative responses listed at the top of each page best describes them by placing a check mark in the appropriate box accompanying each item (see Exhibit 5.6). Marsh (1992b, 1992c) recommended that each SDQ–I item be read aloud, with children concomitantly reading the same item quietly to themselves. Taking into account the additional time needed for reading the instructions, reviewing the response procedure based on a sample item, and answering questions, completion of the SDQ–I can take from 15 to 20 min, depending on the age range and number of children being tested.

Responses to the SDQ–I can be scored either manually, by means of the Scoring and Profile Booklet provided, or by computer, by means of the scoring program disk provided. The booklet provides for the calculation of subscale raw scores, total scale raw scores (nonacademic, academic, and total self), and optional control scores (i.e., checks for various types of response bias). Raw scores related to each subscale, as well as the total raw score, may be converted to midinterval percentile ranks and nonnormalized T scores. The norms tables in the manual

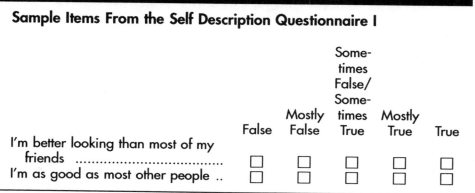

Exhibit 5.6

Sample Items From the Self Description Questionnaire I

	False	Mostly False	Some-times False/ Some-times True	Mostly True	True
I'm better looking than most of my friends	☐	☐	☐	☐	☐
I'm as good as most other people ..	☐	☐	☐	☐	☐

provide information for both boys and girls, separately and in combination.

Finally, the manual provides directions related to the calculation of six different control scores bearing on the following information: (a) inconsistency on correlated-item pairs, (b) consistency on uncorrelated-item pairs, (c) noncontingent summary (the difference between [a] and [b]), (d) negativity bias, (e) positivity bias, and (f) individual profile variation (i.e., the standard deviation of a child's individual raw scale scores, not including the General—Self subscale). Each control score is accompanied by a comprehensive explanation, along with the related rationale. Norms for the control scores are presented as midinterval percentiles and normalized T scores.[13]

Normative Data

Samples. Norms development and standardization of the SDQ–I were based on a series of research studies involving a total sample of 3,562 elementary school children (Grades 2–6) in New South Wales, Australia. Drawn from geographically diverse regions of Sydney, Australia, the samples represented schools in working-class, middle-class, and upper-class areas; single-sex and coeducational schools; and both public and Catholic schools. Marsh (1992b) noted that because the General—Self subscale is a relatively recent addition to the SDQ–I, normative data related only to the remaining seven scales are presented for the total sample (*N* = 3,562); norms relative to the General—Self scale are based on a sample of 1,118. Information provided in the norms tables is exceedingly comprehensive. For each subscale, total scale (nonacademic and academic), Total Self (nonacademic and academic), as well as the General—Self scale, Marsh provides the following information: midinterval percentile, nonnormalized T score, mean, median, standard deviation, skewness coefficient, internal consistency reliability coefficient, correlation with grade level, and correlation with gender.

Selection and Refinement of Items. Although not explicitly stated in the manual, the present set of SDQ–I items evolved from two preliminary versions of the instrument. Items were generated to match the Shavelson et al. (1976) model of self-concept and then later selected and refined on the basis of findings from exploratory and confirmatory factor and item analyses (H. W. Marsh, personal communication, February 13, 1995). In particular, substantial research was conducted to

---

13. The basic rationale and underlying assumptions related to the use of normalized and nonnormalized T scores are fully explained in the manual.

determine the appropriateness of using negatively worded items with young children (for an extensive discussion of this topic, see Marsh, 1986a, 1992b).

Psychometric Properties. Reliability. Based on the full normative sample, Marsh (1992b) reported internal consistency reliability coefficients ranging from .81 to .94 (mean α = .86) for the seven nonacademic and academic subscales of the SDQ–I, and .91, .92, and .94 for the Total Nonacademic, Total Academic, and Total Self scales, respectively; based on a sample of 739, Marsh (1992b) also reported an alpha coefficient of .81 for the General—Self scale.

Test–retest reliability is reported for the SDQ–I based on samples of 528 Grades 5 and 6, and 143 Grade 4 children over a period of 6 months. Coefficients ranged from .54 (General—School) to .74 (Physical Ability, mean r = .62) for the fifth and sixth graders and from .27 (Parent Relations) to .71 (General—School, mean r = .58) for the fourth graders. Marsh (1992b) noted the lack of any reasonable explanation for the unusually low stability estimate for the Parent Relations scale relative to Grade 4 children; indeed, deletion of this aberrant value yields a mean stability coefficient of .62.

Validity. Prerequisite to presenting findings regarding the concurrent validity of the SDQ–I, it is critically important to first note that most, if not all, findings reporting the extent to which scores on one instrument converge with those on another are based on total scale scores; the explanation given for this phenomenon seems to lie with the traditionally poor factor structure associated with most self-concept scales (Marsh, 1992b; Wylie, 1974). A more rigorous test of such validity can be attained, however, when the subscales of both instruments are structured to measure the same constructs.

Based on this more reasonable approach and designed within the framework of MTMM analyses, concurrent validity of the SDQ–I has been tested for agreement between matching scales of the Coopersmith Self-Esteem Inventory (CSEI; Coopersmith, 1967; Marsh & Richards, 1988a); the Perceived Competence Scale for Children (PCSC; Harter, 1982;[14] Marsh & Gouvernet, 1989; Marsh & Holmes, 1990); and the Piers–Harris Children's Self-Concept Scale (PHCSCS; Marsh & Holmes, 1990; Piers, 1984). Although Marsh (1992b) reported adequate support for the Parent Relations and Peer Relations subscales with the CSEI

---

14. This version of the instrument preceded the current version, which is known as the Self-Perception Profile for Children (Harter, 1985b).

Home (median $r = .53$) and CSEI Social (median $r = .50$) subscales, respectively, he found little to no convergence between the CSEI Academic and the three SDQ–I academic subscales (Reading, Mathematics, General—School). However, given the reported instability of the CSEI (median $r = .39$), as well as its low correlations with academic achievement measures (median $r = .15$), this is not surprising. In contrast to these results, convergence between the SDQ–I and matching PCSC subscales (Physical, Social, General, and Cognitive) has been strong. Marsh and Gouvernet (1989) reported validity coefficients of .67, .74, .57, and .60, respectively, whereas Marsh and Holmes (1990) reported values of .69, .68, .56, and .60, respectively. Finally, tests of convergence between subscales of the SDQ–I and matching scales of the PHCSCS (those dealing with physical appearance, popularity, and intellectual ability) revealed validity coefficients of .68, .59, and .60, respectively. Taken together, these findings make it clear that when subscales of the SDQ–I are tested for convergence with appropriately matched subscales from other instruments, evidence of concurrent validity is extremely good.

Most validity research bearing on the SDQ–I has focused on tests of its construct validity. Indeed, the scope and comprehensiveness of this research are clearly overwhelming! In the light of the magnitude of this literature, it is not possible to present any reasonable review of this research here; readers are referred, instead, both to the manual (Marsh, 1992b) and to an important review of this literature (Marsh, 1990b). I can, however, paint a relatively broad scape of the type of research that Marsh and his colleagues conducted in their endeavors to establish the construct validity of the SDQ–I. This research addressed both the within- and between-network aspects of construct validity. As noted elsewhere, within-network studies focus on the dimensionality of self-concept, whereas between-network studies attempt to demonstrate evidence of a theoretically consistent, or at least logical, pattern of relations between measures of self-concept and other constructs.

Within-network research related to the SDQ–I has used exploratory and confirmatory factor analyses, as well as MTMM analyses, a few of which have been conducted within the confirmatory factor analysis framework.[15] Findings from these studies have determined the soundness of the SDQ–I's factorial structure for all populations for which it is intended to be used. By means of rigorous confirmatory factor anal-

---

15. All factor analyses of the SDQ–I conducted by Marsh and colleagues have been based on item pairs rather than single items. For the rationale underlying this approach, see Marsh (1992c).

ysis testing strategies, the instrument has further been found to be invariant across gender, age, and culture. Between-network research related to the SDQ–I has examined relations between particular subscales of the instrument and a wide array of other constructs, such as gender, age, academic performance, inferred self-concepts (by significant others such as teachers, parents, and peers), family background characteristics, self-attribution, and experimental conditions associated with intervention programs designed to enhance self-concept. In the process of testing these relations, Marsh and colleagues addressed important theoretical issues in self-concept research, such as frame-of-reference effects, causal predominance between academic self-concept and academic achievement, self-attributions for academic success and failure, self–other agreement, and intervention effects. Findings from the research just discussed provide exceptionally strong support for the construct validity of the SDQ–I.

Related Psychometric Research

Marsh, Craven, and Debus (1991) recently adapted the SDQ–I to an individual-interview format for use with children younger than 8 years of age. On the basis of a sample of children in kindergarten ($n = 163$; mean age = 5 years), Grade 1 ($n = 169$; mean age = 6 years), and Grade 2 ($n = 169$; mean age = 7 years), Marsh, Craven, and Debus found this approach to be very effective in assessing multidimensional self-concepts for these young children. Despite concern that the children might experience fatigue or boredom toward the end of the testing period, these researchers found this not to be the case. Indeed, results yielded psychometric properties for this SDQ–I adaptation that were stronger than those reported for the Pictorial Scale of Perceived Competence and Social Acceptance for Young Children (Harter & Pike, 1984; see chapter 4, this volume), an instrument specifically designed for use with children of this age group (Marsh, Craven, & Debus, 1991). In light of these findings, the SDQ–I interview technique is currently being tested with the Head Start program (H. W. Marsh, personal communication, February 13, 1995).

In addition to Marsh and associates, others have investigated various aspects of the psychometric soundness of the SDQ–I. For example, the factorial structure of the SDQ–I has been examined by means of an exploratory factor analytic approach with samples of Nepalese ($N = 404$; Watkins, Lam, & Regmi, 1991), Nigerian ($N = 462$; Watkins & Akande, 1992), and Zimbabwean ($N = 270$; Watkins & Mpofu,

1994) children; a translated version has also been tested with a sample of 231 Chinese children (Watkins & Dong, 1994). Results from these studies have generally supported the validity of interpretations based on each of the SDQ–I subscales. Watkins and colleagues have also reported strong support for the internal consistency reliability of these components. Finally, as part of a larger study, Byrne and Schneider (1988) examined the extent to which the SDQ–I and Perceived Competence Scale for Children (Harter, 1982), an earlier version of the Self-Perception Profile for Children (Harter, 1985b), converged in their measurement of general, academic, social, and physical self-concepts for gifted Canadian Grade 5 ($n = 44$) and Grade 8 ($n = 46$) children. Strong evidence of concurrent validity was reported for each of the four subscales; validity coefficients ranged from .54 to .86 (mean $r = .73$) for Grade 5 and from .66 to .88 (mean $r = .80$) for Grade 8.

Evaluation Summary

There is absolutely no doubt that the SDQ–I is clearly the most validated self-concept measure available for use with preadolescent children. For more than a decade, it has been the target of a well-planned research strategy to firmly establish its construct validity, as well as its other psychometric properties. In using the SDQ–I, researchers, clinicians, counselors, and others interested in the welfare of preadolescent children can feel confident in the validity of interpretations based on responses to its multidimensionally sensitive items. Information that would be helpful to users of the SDQ–I, however, and that is currently not available in the manual relates to (a) the reading level of the items and (b) the process used in determining the universe of items from which the current set of SDQ–I items was drawn.

Source Information

Location: Publication Office, School of Education and Language Studies, University of Western Sydney, P.O. Box 555, Campbelltown, New South Wales 2560, Australia

Cost: Kit: $50.00 (includes SDQ–I, manual, and scoring key)

Self-Perception Profile for Children

Description

The Self-Perception Profile for Children (SPPC; Harter, 1985b) is designed to measure multiple dimensions of self-concept for preadolescents.[16] The scale was specifically constructed to reflect Harter's contention that self-concept is a multidimensional construct that reflects both domain-specific evaluations and overall judgments of self-worth (Harter, 1990b). In particular, construction of the SPPC embraced the notion that global self-worth must be tapped directly, as well as independently of self-perceptions related to specific domains. As such, the SPPC is designed to measure five specific domains (Scholastic Competence, Athletic Competence, Social Acceptance, Physical Appearance, and Behavioral Conduct) and a separate facet of Global Self-Worth.[17] Indeed, as emphasized by Harter (1985b), this approach to measuring global self-concept differs substantially from that determined through the summation of, or averaging across, items that tap specific self-concepts (e.g., Coopersmith Self-Esteem Inventory; Coopersmith, 1967). Whereas the latter method presumes that global self-worth is merely a composite of self-perceptions related to specific domains in one's life, the SPPC argues that its existence is separate and apart from these specific dimensions. The SPPC is theoretically linked to the correlated-factor model of self-concept described in chapter 1.

The SPPC, like the Self Description Questionnaire I, is currently one of the most widely used instruments for the measurement of preadolescent self-concept. The question format originally developed for the SPPC has been used as the model for all subsequently constructed instruments by Harter and her colleagues.

Target Population

The SPPC was originally designed for use with children in Grades 3 through 6 (ages 8–12 years). Although Harter (1985b) noted that the instrument could be used with adolescents, she cautioned that it did not provide a sufficiently rich and differentiated picture of self-concept with this age group. Thus, a more appropriate measure of self-concept for adolescents would be the Self-Perception Profile for Adolescents (Harter, 1988c), which is reviewed in the next chapter.

Harter (1985b) also advised that the SPPC not be used with children below the third grade (less than 8 years of age) for several reasons. First, the question format is not easily understood by children of this

---

16. The present scale represents a version of the original one, entitled the Perceived Competence Scale for Children (Harter, 1982).

17. I have recently been advised that the name of the Self Acceptance subscale will be changed to Peer Likeability in an upcoming revision of the SPPC to better reflect the fact that items constituting this subscale tap characteristics of self rather than the behavior (e.g., acceptance) of peers (S. Harter, personal communication, October 27, 1994).

age. Second, the reading skills of these younger children are not sufficiently developed for them to fully understand the item content. Third, because generalized descriptors such as trait labels (e.g., *popular, smart,* and *good-looking*) do not emerge until middle childhood, these specific labels can be misinterpreted by young children. Finally, because a concept of overall global self-worth as a person is not fully developed in children of this age, they are unable to comprehend the questions being asked in this subscale. As a consequence, the reliability of the scale becomes very distorted.

Scale Structure

The SPPC is a 36-item self-report scale that comprises six subscales. Five scales are designed to measure self-perceptions in relation to specific domains of one's life (Scholastic Competence, Athletic Competence, Social Acceptance, Physical Appearance, and Behavioral Conduct), and one is designed to measure perception of self in general (Global Self-Worth). Each subscale is composed of six items, with three being worded in the positive direction and three in the negative direction. The items are structured in a 4-point structured-alternative format, with the intent to offset the tendency for children to respond in a socially desirable manner. One sample item from each of the Scholastic Competence and Global Self-Worth subscales of the SPPC is presented in Exhibit 5.7.

In addition to the descriptive information provided by the SPPC, the manual includes the similarly structured Importance Rating Scale that also taps perceptions of importance in relation to each domain. On the 4-point format, children are asked to rate how important each dimension is in determining how they feel about themselves; there are 10 rating items, with 2 items for each specific self-concept domain.

Administration and Scoring

The SPPC can be administered either individually or in groups. As can be seen from the items displayed in Exhibit 5.7, children respond to each item by deciding first which of the two statements best describes them and then, relative to that statement, whether it is really true for them or just sort of true for them. Once they have decided which of the four alternatives is most appropriate for them, they indicate their choice by placing a check mark in the appropriate box accompanying the item. Before having children complete the questionnaire, it is highly recommended that the administrator guide them through a few sample

Exhibit 5.7

Sample Items From the Self-Perception Profile for Children

Really True for Me	Sort of True for Me				Sort of True for Me	Really True for Me
☐	☐	Some kids do very well at their classwork	BUT	Other kids don't do very well at their classwork.	☐	☐
☐	☐	Some kids are happy with themselves as a person	BUT	Other kids are often not happy with themselves.	☐	☐

items so that they are clearly informed regarding the response procedure. Harter (1985b) further suggested that although she recommended that the items be read aloud for third and fourth graders, children in the higher grades could respond to the items without this assistance. Although there is no indication of the amount of time required for completion of the SPPC reported in the manual, Marsh and Gouvernet (1989) found it to be approximately the same as for the Self Description Questionnaire I (15–20 min).

Item responses to the SPPC are scored as either 1, 2, 3, or 4, with 4 being indicative of high self-concept; negative items require reversal before the computation of subscale scores. In scoring the SPPC, item scores are averaged within each subscale, thereby providing a total profile of six scores, each of which represents a mean ranging from 1 to 4. For ease of calculation, a scoring key is included in the manual.

In addition to providing a self-perception profile, Harter (1985b) provided the means for calculating a discrepancy score, which is based on the mean discrepancy between the level of perceived competence and the importance attached to each dimension. She noted that this discrepancy score would be typically negative, because the importance ratings tend to be higher than the perceived-competence scores. Overall, the larger the total discrepancy score (with a negative sign), the more the child's importance ratings exceed his or her competence and, ultimately, the lower will be the level of self-concept. (For a more extensive discussion of importance and discrepancy scores, see chapter 1 of this volume; see also Bogan, 1988; Cronbach & Furby, 1970; Hattie, 1992; Marsh, 1986b, 1993e; Wells & Marwell, 1976; Wylie, 1989.)

Normative Data

Samples. Norms development for the SPPC was based on four independent samples of Colorado elementary school children ranging from Grade 3 through Grade 8; approximately 90% of the children were White and were from families representative of the lower-middle through upper-middle socioeconomic strata (Harter, 1985b). Specifically, the samples can be described as follows: Sample A (Grade 6, n = 432; Grade 7, n = 316); Sample B (Grade 6, n = 126; Grade 7, n = 122; Grade 8, n = 142); Sample C (Grade 3, n = 60; Grade 4, n = 57; Grade 5, n = 54); Sample D (Grade 3, n = 73; Grade 4, n = 60; Grade 5, n = 45). Subscale means and standard deviations relative to each sample, by grade and gender, are reported in the manual.

Selection and Refinement of Items. As footnoted earlier, the SPPC represents a revised version of the original scale, the Perceived Competence

Scale for Children (Harter, 1982). The original version was designed to measure children's self-perceptions related to three specific domains (Cognitive Competence, Social Acceptance, and Athletic Competence) as well as global self-worth. Items for the original scale were developed from information gathered during interviews with children. A pilot 40-item version of this scale was administered to a sample of children registered in Grades 3 through 6 (*N* = 215). Exploratory factor analytic results revealed the response data to be adequately described by a four-factor solution. On the basis of stringent inclusion criteria (i.e., high loading on target factors[18] and minimal loadings on nontarget factors, mean value near the midpoint, acceptable variability, and high contribution to internal consistency of the subscale), three or four items were subsequently replaced with new ones. Analysis of data derived from the administration of this revised scale to 133 children was considered to be satisfactory, with all items meeting the inclusion-criteria standards (Harter, 1982).

Numerous analyses of the Perceived Competence Scale for Children response data derived from a total of 2,271 elementary school children representing four discrepant geographical locations in the United States revealed strong psychometric properties related to this revised scale (Harter, 1982). However, in the process of further instrument refinement, Harter determined that two additional subscales were needed to measure self-perceptions of physical appearance and behavioral conduct. Addressing these concerns, Harter subsequently constructed the present SPPC scale, which includes six rather than four subscales. She noted that the name of the instrument was changed to better reflect its focus on self-adequacy as well as self-competence (i.e., the PCSC focused solely on competence). Moreover, the new title conveyed the notion that children's perceptions of themselves were being measured and that a child's profile of scores across various domains in his or her life "provides the richest and most accurate picture of one's self-concept" (Harter, 1985b, p. 5). Other modifications to the SPPC included a renaming of the original four subscales to more accurately reflect the domain being measured and the revision of several items related to the original four scales. A subsequent revision to the SPPC is noted below.

Psychometric Properties. *Reliability.* Across Samples A through D, noted earlier, Harter (1985b) reported internal consistency reliability

---

18. Loading of the item on the factor it was designed to measure.

coefficients for each of the six subscales; these ranged from .80 to .85 (mean α = .82) for Scholastic Competence, from .75 to .80 (mean α = .78) for Social Acceptance, from .80 to .86 (mean α = .83) for Athletic Competence, from .76 to .82 (mean α = .80) for Physical Appearance, from .71 to .77 (mean α = .74) for Behavioral Conduct, and from .78 to .84 (mean α = .80) for Global Self-Worth. Following an item analysis, Harter (1985b) reported that one item in the Behavioral Conduct scale (Item 35) was replaced and that two additional items underwent a revision of content (Social Acceptance [Item 14] and Global Self-Worth [Item 6]). No test–retest reliability estimates are reported in the manual.

Validity. The only validity research reported in the SPPC manual relates to exploratory factor analytic findings for each of Samples A, B, and C. Results demonstrated a very clear six-factor structure, with all loadings, except one, exceeding .30, and most (72/108) exceeding .50; no cross-loadings exceeded .18. On the basis of both the strength of the factor loadings and the replicability of their loading pattern across the three samples, then, these findings provide strong support for the factorial validity of the SPPC. Of the six subscales, Behavioral Conduct appeared to be the weakest, with factor loadings ranging from .33 to .82 (M = .57).

Harter (1985b) also reported factor correlations across the three samples and noted several interesting patterns. First, these interfactor relations were found to be higher for the younger children (Grades 3 and 4). Second, among the specific domains, Scholastic Competence correlated highest with Behavioral Conduct, thereby suggesting that children who perceive themselves as doing well in school also perceive themselves as being well-behaved. Third, Athletic Competence, Physical Appearance, and Social Acceptance tended to cluster together; these findings would suggest that greater acceptance by peers is linked to both a child's athletic prowess and his or her physical attractiveness. Finally, across all samples, Physical Appearance correlated the highest with the Global Self-Worth, with values ranging from .62 to .73 (mean r = .67).

Related Psychometric Research

Although I am aware of no additionally reported psychometric research conducted by Harter and colleagues on the SPPC, the instrument has been tested in relation to the Self Description Questionnaire I (Marsh, 1992b). As noted earlier, Marsh and colleagues (Marsh & Gouvernet, 1989; Marsh & Holmes, 1990), as well as Byrne and Schneider (1988), found evidence of strong concurrent validity between the SPPC and the Self Description Questionnaire I.[19] Additionally, based on factor and MTMM analyses, and correlations with other criterion measures, Marsh and Gouvernet concluded that there is strong evidence of convergent and discriminant validity for responses to both instruments. Finally, based on a gradual building of norms related to the Perceived Competence Scale for Children for emotionally disturbed preadolescent boys, there is some evidence that the SPPC may be used satisfactorily with this population (see H. E. Kaplan & Moon, 1987). To the best of my knowledge, psychometric properties related to the Importance Rating Scale have not been reported.

Evaluation Summary

Taking into account the careful and systematic development of its parent instrument, the Perceived Competence Scale for Children, the SPPC can now be regarded as a well-established and psychometrically sound instrument that is proving to be a very popular measure of self-concept for preadolescent children. Built on a strong theoretical foundation that reflected the author's theoretical view of self-concept, the SPPC was developed to facilitate research bearing on the impact of domain-specific judgment on global self-worth in children. It has since been used to generate considerable information related to the determinants of global self-worth in children (Friedman, 1992). However, given that most psychometric research has been conducted on its parent instrument, the SPPC could benefit substantially from rigorous construct validity work based on the analysis of covariance structures. In particular, it would be of interest to test for the validity and invariance of its factorial structure using a confirmatory factor analytic model and, also, to test for evidence of convergent, criterion-related, and discriminant validity based on an MTMM model. Although Marsh and colleagues have partially tested for the construct validity of the SPPC, their work was based on the earlier version of the instrument. Indeed, in the light of Harter's (1985b, p. 7) gracious generosity in granting permission to copy the instrument, researchers are encouraged to validate the factorial structure of SPPC responses with data representative of various child populations.

Source Information

Location: Susan Harter, University of Denver, Department of Psychology, 2155 South Race Street, Denver, Colorado 80208-0204

Cost: Manual: $18.00

---

19. Each of these analyses, however, was based on the Perceived Competence Scale for Children (Harter, 1982).

6

Measures of Self-Concept for Adolescents (Grades 9–12; Ages 13–19 Years)

By adolescence, children are substantially more sophisticated in their ability to describe themselves. Two major features characterize these self-descriptions. First, adolescents are capable of using abstract concepts (or traits) such as *tolerant, moody, affectionate,* and the like, in reference to self (Harter, 1988b). Second, adolescents have the capability of forming self-perceptions in relation to particular contexts or situations (e.g., at school, at home, or at hockey practice) and roles (e.g., as student, as granddaughter, or as lead in the school play). In keeping with these developmental advances, the domain-specific facets of self-concept are more clearly delineated for adolescents than they are for preadolescents.

Of the 30 adolescent self-concept measures reviewed, 7 are included here. One instrument (the Rosenberg Self-Esteem Scale) is a unidimensional measure of general (i.e., global) self-concept. All other measures represent multidimensional scales; 2 tap multiple facets of academic self-concept (Academic Self Description Questionnaire II and Dimensions of Self-Concept [Form S]), 1 taps multiple facets of physical self-concept (Physical Self-Description Questionnaire), 2 tap multiple domain-specific facets of self-concept as well as a separate facet of general (i.e., global) self-concept (Self Description Questionnaire II and Self-Perception Profile for Adolescents), and the remaining 1 taps multiple domain-specific facets of self-concepts, albeit from both an internal and external perspective (Tennessee Self-Concept Scale). To the best of my knowledge, there is no available instrument designed to measure multiple facets of social self-concept for adolescents. We turn first to the two instruments designed to measure academic self-concept.

Measurement of Single Self-Concept Domains

ACADEMIC SELF-CONCEPT

Academic Self Description Questionnaire II

Description

The Academic Self Description Questionnaire II (ASDQ–II; Marsh, 1990c), as was the case for the ASDQ–I, measures multiple subject-matter dimensions of academic self-concept, as well as a single dimension of general school self-concept. In contrast to the ASDQ–I, however, this scale is designed for use with early adolescents and therefore represents an extension of the Self Description Questionnaire II (SDQ–II; Marsh, 1992c), a measure of multiple facets of self-concept to be described later in this chapter.[1] As was the case for the ASDQ–I, development of the ASDQ–II evolved from construct validity research related to the Marsh/Shavelson model (Marsh & Shavelson, 1985). Similarly, school administrators were consulted to identify the set of school subjects taken by all students, and a separate self-concept subscale was then constructed to match each content area. The subject areas tapped by the ASDQ–II are English language, English literature, foreign languages, history, geography, commerce, computer studies, science, mathematics, physical education, health, music, art, industrial art, and religion (Marsh, 1990c, 1992a).

Target Population

The ASDQ–II is designed for use with junior high and high school students (Grades 7–12; ages 12–19 years).

Scale Structure

The ASDQ–II (Marsh, 1990c) is a 96-item self-report scale that comprises 15 subject-matter subscales and one General School subscale.[2]

---

1. In keeping with Footnote 1 in chapter 5 regarding the SDQ–I, the reference here is also dated as 1992 due to recent changes in its location of distribution. The instrument, however, has been established since the early 1980s.

2. As with the ASDQ–I, the instrument also includes eight items designed to measure a separate global self-concept, should the researcher wish to tap this higher order facet.

Items on the ASDQ–II parallel those of its parent instrument, the SDQ–II; as such, items are structured on a 6-point Likert-type scale format, with 6 items constituting each subscale. The subject-matter subscales measure self-perceived competence related to nine core subjects (English language, English literature, foreign languages, history, geography, commerce, computer studies, science, and mathematics) and six noncore subjects (physical education, health, music, art, industrial art, and religion). As with the ASDQ–I, the phrasing of item stems in each subscale is identical, with only the name of the subject area being altered; for example, "Compared with others my age, I am good at [a specific school subject]" and "I get good marks in [a specific school subject] classes." For the General School subscale, the term *most school subjects* replaces the specific academic area. One sample item from the Foreign Languages subscale of the ASDQ–II is presented in Exhibit 6.1.

Administration and Scoring

The ASDQ–II can be administered individually or in groups. Students are asked to respond to simple declarative statements by placing a check mark under one of the six alternatives that they believe best describes them (see Exhibit 6.1). Although the instructions are self-explanatory and easily understood by adolescents, the administrator is advised to orally review them before having the students complete the form. Typically, most adolescents respond to all items in less than 20 min.

Given a 6-point scale format, the score for each completed item will represent a value from 1 to 6. Subscale scores of the ASDQ–II are obtained through a simple summation of scores relative to all items constituting the scale in question; negative items, of course, will require reversal before summation.

Exhibit 6.1

Sample Item From the Academic Self Description Questionnaire II

	False	Mostly False	More False Than True	More True Than False	Mostly True	True
I'm hopeless when it comes to foreign language classes.	___	___	___	___	___	___

Normative Data

Samples. Initial testing of the ASDQ–II was based on a sample of 524 boys in Grades 7 through 10, all of whom attended the same Catholic boys' school in Sydney, Australia.

Selection and Refinement of Items. Marsh (1990c) has not yet provided information related to either the initial pool of items from which the present set was chosen or the process used in retaining particular items.

Psychometric Properties. *Reliability.* Marsh (1990c) reported internal consistency reliability coefficients ranging from .885 to .949 (median $\alpha = .921$) for the 16 subscales of the ASDQ–II. No other reliability information is available at this time.

Validity. Although results from exploratory and confirmatory factor analyses of the ASDQ–II, based on item-pair responses,[3] revealed reasonably well defined 16-factor solutions, Marsh (1990c) reported some ambiguity of structure across the English Language and English Literature factors; all remaining factors, however, were sharply delineated and clearly represented the relevant academic and General School subscales. Thus, although the ASDQ–II can satisfactorily tap multiple facets of adolescent academic self-concept, its measurement of separate English subject areas is more difficult to achieve. However, given the often vague distinction between these two academic subjects and the fact that the content and focus of each will vary both between and within countries, cities, and even schools within the same educational jurisdictions, these findings are not unexpected.

Based on path analyses, as well as MTMM analyses within a confirmatory factor analytic framework, Marsh (1992a) further tested for the construct validity of the ASDQ–II by investigating the strength of relations between the eight core subject-matter self-concept facets and their matching academic achievement scores and for evidence of their convergent and discriminant validities.[4] On the basis of these analyses, Marsh (1992a) determined (a) support for the convergent validity of the academic self-concept ratings and their matching achievement scores (mean $r = .572$), (b) support for the discriminant validity of academic self-concept ratings and the content specificity of relations be-

---

3. As noted in chapter 5 regarding the ASDQ–I, this pattern has been used in all testing of the SDQ instruments by Marsh and colleagues. For an elaboration of the rationale, see Marsh (1992c).

4. Based on findings from the initial factor analytic work reported earlier (Marsh, 1990c), items from both the English Language and English Literature subscales were postulated to load on a single English factor.

tween academic self-concept and achievement (mean $r = .332$), and (c) support for the hypothesis that different areas of self-concept are more distinct (mean $r = .343$) than are the corresponding areas of achievement (mean $r = .581$).

In keeping with his research on the ASDQ–I (Marsh, 1990c), Marsh's study of the ASDQ–II reveals not only that adolescent academic self-concept is multidimensionally structured but also that its facets are clearly discriminable. Thus, for research bearing on adolescents' perceptions of their academic competence to be meaningful, it is clearly evident that one must measure self-concept relative to each academic subject area. The ASDQ–II is therefore unique in its capability to measure self-perceptions of academic performance related to several subject-matter contents for the targeted age group.

Related Psychometric Research

In a recent investigation of weighted models and issues raised by Marsh (1986b) and Pelham and Swann (1989), Marsh (1993e) examined relations among the 15 ASDQ–II subject-matter subscales, importance ratings associated with each of these core/noncore academic areas, the single global academic subscale, and the single, eight-item global self-esteem subscale (see Footnote 2). He found little support for the use of individually weighted averaging in computing self-concept scores; rather, results strongly supported constant differentially weighted models in which the same weight for each content domain is assigned to all subjects. Accordingly, these results imply that the influence of any particular subject-matter self-concept on global academic self-concept and the higher order global self-esteem varies minimally for individuals who rate this dimension as more or less important; similarly, these specific facets vary little for individuals who are more or less certain about their overall self-views.

On the basis of these rigorously derived findings, Marsh (1993e) concluded that "no matter how global self-concept is defined, it cannot adequately represent the diversity of content-specific domains of self" (p. 990). As further clarification of this statement, Marsh (1993e) explained that he is not arguing against the use of general esteem scales per se, but, rather, is merely suggesting that self-concept researchers should also consider multiple dimensions of the construct that, at the very least, include those facets most pertinent to the aims of their research.

Evaluation Summary

As with the ASDQ–I, the ASDQ–II is a relatively new instrument, with its basic structure being patterned after the well-established SDQ–II (Marsh, 1992c). Given the abundance of sound psychometric data available on all three SDQ instruments, as noted in chapter 5, I am clearly confident that the ASDQ–II will accrue the same high quality and thorough psychometric investigative work as the other Marsh instruments. Thus, despite its relatively new measurement status, the ASDQ–II is included here because it provides for a critically important means for testing for multidimensional academic self-concepts for adolescents. As noted in chapter 5, although the item content is rooted in the Australian educational system, it can be easily modified for use within other educational jurisdictions. In this regard, Marsh stated that researchers are free to alter the ASDQ–II item content to more appropriately match their own academic curriculum endeavors. However, he does request that findings from research that has used the ASDQ–II be forwarded to him, as a courtesy only (H. W. Marsh, personal communication, February 13, 1995).

Source Information

Location: Herbert W. Marsh, School of Education and Language Studies, University of Western Sydney, P.O. Box 555, Campbelltown, New South Wales 2560, Australia

Cost: No manual presently available. However, Dr. Marsh has recommended that interested users write to him for updated information.

Dimensions of Self-Concept (Form S)

Description

The Dimensions of Self-Concept scale (Form S; DOSC/S; Michael & Smith, 1976) is a self-report scale designed to measure multiple non-cognitive factors associated with adolescent self-concepts bearing on the junior high and secondary school settings. As such, each item represents either an activity or attitude related to various school learning situations or environments. The revised manual (Michael, Smith, & Michael, 1989, p. 1) considers the purposes of the DOSC/S to be twofold: (a) to identify children who exhibit low levels of self-esteem in relation to the school environment and who may ultimately experience difficulty in their schoolwork and (b) to diagnose, for purposes of counseling or guidance by teachers, professional counselors, or administrators, the areas and related activities believed to be contributing to low self-esteem scores (i.e., scores falling below average—possibly in the bottom third of the score distribution [Michael et al., 1989]).

The original development of the DOSC/S was undertaken as a means for measuring the self-concepts of gifted students in an enrichment program of a large metropolitan school district in California, which teachers and other professionals perceived as being perplexingly low. In structuring the dimensionality of the DOSC instruments in general,[5] Michael and Smith (1976) focused on aspects of the school environment considered most likely to impact on the self-concepts of both gifted and nongifted students, with respect to which self-concept intervention programs were feasible. Based on their own rationale of affectivity related to school learning, the test authors determined that academic self-concept was most adequately defined by five major dimensions, which are described below.

Although the authors of the DOSC do not explicitly link the instrument to a specific theoretical model, I consider it to be most appropriately affiliated with the nomothetic model of self-concept, described in chapter 1.

Target Population
The DOSC/S is appropriate for use with junior high and secondary school children in Grades 7 through 12 (ages 13–19 years).

Scale Structure
The DOSC/S (Michael & Smith, 1976) is a five-dimensional, 70-item instrument based on a 5-point Likert-type scale format; each subscale is composed of 14 items. The five dimensions of noncognitive academic self-concept measured are as follows:

1. Level of Aspiration, a reflection of behavior patterns indicative of the extent to which academic performance and activities are consistent with children's perceptions of their scholastic potentialities
2. Anxiety, a reflection of behavior patterns and perceptions as-

---

5. There is also a Form E for use with elementary school children (Grades 4–6) and a Form H for use with college students (see chapter 7). Because of limited and relatively weak psychometric findings reported for the DOSC/E, this version of the instrument is not included in the present volume.

sociated with emotional instability, lack of objectivity, and ex-aggerated concern with respect to tests and self-esteem preservation in relation to academic performance

3. Academic Interest and Satisfaction, reflective of the degree of intrinsic motivation and love of learning for its own sake that students derive from their academic work

4. Leadership and Initiative, reflective of behavior patterns and perceptions associated with mastery of knowledge and skills in a particular area, with the ability and willingness to guide others in attaining the same level of mastery

5. Identification Versus Alienation, reflective of the extent to which a student feels accepted and respected, as opposed to isolated and rejected, by his or her teachers and peers

A sample item from the Anxiety subscale of the DOSC/S is presented in Exhibit 6.2.

Administration and Scoring

The DOSC/S can be administered individually or in groups. Children are asked to respond to simple declarative statements by filling in the circle representing the one alternative of five that they believe best describes them (see Exhibit 6.2). Although the instructions are self-explanatory, examiners are advised to demonstrate the respondence procedure based on an illustration other than the ones contained in the questionnaire. Children at this level typically require 15 to 35 min to complete the answer sheet.

Scoring of the DOSC/S can be performed either manually or by returning completed forms to the publisher for machine scoring. As noted earlier in the description of the scale format, five different weights are assigned to the response alternatives for each item. As such, the manual scoring of subscale scores is easily accomplished by adding

Exhibit 6.2

Sample Item From the Dimensions of Self-Concept (Form S)

	Never	Seldom	About Half the Time	Very Often	Always
Some of my classes are so interesting that I do much more work than is required	○	○	○	○	○

the selected response weights associated with all items constituting a particular subscale. Negative items, of course, must be reversed in order that high scores represent high levels of academic self-concept.

Normative Data

Samples. Initial testing of the DOSC/S was based on separate samples of approximately 200 children in each of Grades 7, 8, and 9 and 275 children in each of Grades 10, 11, and 12, all drawn from a large metropolitan school district in Los Angeles, California.

Selection and Refinement of Items. The DOSC/S was initially structured as two separate tests: one for junior high school (Grades 7–9) and the second for secondary school (Grades 10–12) students. Each form comprised 150 items—30 for each of the five subscales. Before pilot testing the instrument, the content validity of all items was scrutinized by 25 professional members of the Los Angeles Unified School District. Inappropriate items were subsequently deleted or revised, and the instrument was tested in a pilot administration; a second revision and pilot testing led to further revisions of the items and an amalgamation of the junior high and secondary versions, thereby leading to the present 70-item version of the DOSC/S.

Psychometric Properties. Reliability. Michael and Smith (1976) reported internal reliability coefficients of the DOSC/S to range from .84 to .90 ($M = .86$) for children in Grades 7 through 9 and from .79 to .89 ($M = .85$) for children in Grades 10 through 12 across the six samples; results from a later study of Grade 8 students ($N = 234$) ranged from .75 to .86 ($M = .82$; Michael et al., 1989).

Validity. To validate relations between the noncognitive academic self-concept factors comprising the DOSC/S and academic performance, Michael, Smith, and Michael (1978) examined correlations between the DOSC/S subscales and measures of reading comprehension and critical thinking skills. Although somewhat atypical (see, e.g., Heilbrun, 1985), these values were interpreted as concurrent validity coefficients. Based on the original version of the DOSC/S, Michael et al. (1978) found the Leadership and Initiative subscale to demonstrate the highest validity (mean $r = .42$) for junior high school students and the Anxiety subscale to demonstrate the highest validity (mean $r = -.40$) for secondary school students. More recent validity research has been based on the Revised Form S of the instrument. In a study of Mexican American Grade 7 children ($N = 234$), Michael et al. (1989) determined scores from the Level of Aspiration and Anxiety subscales to demonstrate the highest correlations with a standardized achievement measure ($r = .62$ and $r = -.47$, respectively). In a second study, Michael et al. (1989) correlated DOSC/S scores with overall grade point average and with grades in mathematics and English for a sample of 179 American Grade 7 children. They found the Level of Aspiration, Leadership and Initiative, and Identification Versus Alienation subscales to correlate the highest with overall grade point average ($r = .53$, .42, and .40, respectively) and grades in mathematics and English (mean $r = .44$, .35, and .35, respectively; Michael et al., 1989).

Extrapolating from several studies, Michael et al. (1989) summarized long-term predictive validities related to the DOSC/S subscales for four separate samples of students as follows: Grade 7 (over three semesters, $n = 179$), Grade 9 (over four semesters, $n = 147$), Grade 11 (over two semesters, $n = 141$), and Grade 12 (over two semesters, $n = 161$). Based on correlations with total grade point average and grades in mathematics and English courses, the Level of Aspiration subscale (mean $r = .45$ and .39, respectively) was found to exhibit the highest degree of predictive validity; the Anxiety subscale failed to demonstrate statistically significant evidence of predictive validity. Short-term predictive validity (7-week period) for an ethnically diverse sample of Grade 11 students once again revealed the Level of Aspiration subscale to demonstrate the highest validity with respect to grades in three academic courses (mean $r = .34$) and overall grade point average ($r = .36$); the Anxiety subscale again demonstrated the weakest level of predictive validity.

Reported evidence of construct validity for the DOSC/S has been based solely on exploratory factor analyses. Although results based on item-level data led to a second-order structure of dubious interpretability, those based on sets of items were shown to yield a reasonably adequate five-factor structure that supported the theoretical framework underlying instrument development.

Evaluation Summary

In contrast to the ASDQ–II, the DOSC/S provides for the measurement of noncognitive adolescent academic self-concepts. Although its related psychometric research suffers from some limitations, the test authors are to be commended for their steadfast and continuous efforts in testing for the validity of its test scores. Indeed, most of this work has focused on validating the link between the DOSC/S subscales and various aspects of academic performance. However, evidence of test–retest reliability should be reported; given the number of longitudinal studies conducted on the instrument (see Michael et al., 1989), this issue would appear to be easily addressed. Perhaps a more critical limitation of the DOSC/S lies with the relative lack of strong construct validity investigations of its factor structure; analyses of covariance structures within the frameworks of confirmatory factor and MTMM analyses are highly recommended. Finally, virtually all psychometric investigations of the DOSC/S have been conducted by Michael and his colleagues. Thus, although the DOSC/S has been the subject of a number of psychometric studies, its credibility as a measuring instrument could benefit substantially from rigorous testing by researchers other than those directly associated with the test authors.

Source Information
Location: Edits, P.O. Box 7234, San Diego, California 92167

Cost:　　Manual: $3.25
　　　　　Test forms: $8.75/pkg 25; $31.25/pkg 100; $117.00/pkg 500
　　　　　Specimen set: $6.25

PHYSICAL SELF-CONCEPT

Physical Self-Description Questionnaire

Description
The Physical Self-Description Questionnaire (PSDQ; Marsh et al., 1994) is a 70-item scale designed to measure 10 facets of physical self-concept, along with general self-esteem. More specifically, the instrument is composed of 11 subscales, 9 of which are designed to tap perceptions of self related to specific areas of physical fitness and competence, 1 that measures self-perceptions of global physical competence, and 1 that measures global self-esteem. In keeping with the ASDQ–II, development of the PSDQ evolved from construct validity research related to both the Shavelson et al. (1976) hierarchical model of self-concept and the Self Description Questionnaire II (SDQ–II; see section on SDQ–II later in this chapter). In particular, the PSDQ reflects three subscales from the SDQ–II (Physical Ability, Physical Appearance, and General Self); subscales constituting an earlier version of the instrument, as presented by Marsh and Redmayne (1994); and components of physical

fitness as delineated by Marsh (1993b) in a confirmatory factor analysis of data from the Australian Health and Fitness Survey (Marsh et al., 1994).

Target Population

The PSDQ is designed for use with adolescents. Although Marsh (in press-a; Marsh et al., 1994) postulated that the instrument also should be appropriate for use with adults, there is as yet no construct validity research to substantiate this claim.

Scale Structure

The PSDQ (Marsh et al., 1994) is a 70-item self-report scale that taps nine specific components of physical self-concept (strength, body fat, activity, endurance/fitness, sports competence, coordination, health, appearance, and flexibility), a single global physical self-concept, and overall general self-esteem. Paralleling the SDQ–II, items constituting the PSDQ are structured in a 6-point Likert-type scale format; two subscales comprise 8 items (Health and Global Self-Esteem), whereas the remainder comprise 6 items each. One sample item from the Endurance/ Fitness subscale of the PSDQ is presented in Exhibit 6.3.

Administration and Scoring

The PSDQ can be administered individually or in groups. Students are asked to respond to simple declarative statements by circling one of the six alternatives that they believe best describes them (see Exhibit 6.3). Although the instructions are self-explanatory and easily understood by adolescents, the administrator is advised to orally review them, along with one sample item (not related to the PSDQ), before having the

Exhibit 6.3

Sample Item From the Physical Self-Description Questionnaire

	False	Mostly False	More False Than True	More True Than False	Mostly True	True
I am good at endurance activities like distance running, aerobics, bicycling, swimming, or cross-country skiing.	1	2	3	4	5	6

students complete the form. Typically, most adolescents respond to all items in less than 20 min.

Normative Data

Samples. Initial testing of the present 70-item PSDQ was based on a sample of 395 adolescents (n = 217 boys, n = 178 girls; mean age = 15 years, approximately) who attended a private comprehensive high school in metropolitan Sydney.[6]

Selection and Refinement of Items. Selected items for the PSDQ have been drawn from a number of studies involving both the SDQ–II and at least two preliminary versions of the instrument. Marsh's rationale in constructing a separate SDQ instrument designed to measure multiple physical self-concepts derived from studies of the SDQ–II that demonstrated substantial correlation between Physical Ability subscale scores and (a) athletic participation by high school adolescents and young adult women (Jackson & Marsh, 1986) and (b) physical fitness indicators for high school girls (Marsh & Peart, 1988). In addition, findings from a study of the Australian Health and Fitness Survey showed physical fitness self-concept to be strongly related to a variety of fitness indicators for boys and girls 9 to 15 years of age (Marsh, 1993e). The initial version of the PSDQ comprised only six subscales: Physical Ability and Physical Appearance (from the SDQ–II), and Strength, Balance, Flexibility, and Endurance. The construct validity and psychometric adequacy of this instrument were tested on a sample of 105 Grade 8 girls (mean age = 14 years) attending one of two private schools in Sydney, Australia (Marsh & Redmayne, 1994). Provided with strong support for a hierarchical structure of physical self-concept based on these six subscales, Marsh et al. (1994) went on to construct the present version of the scale. As a preliminary step to investigations of a final version of the PSDQ, Marsh et al. (1994) first tested a longer version of the instrument for a sample of 315 high school adolescents (n = 208 boys, n = 107 girls; mean age = 14.8 years) who were participants in the Australian Outward Bound school program. On the basis of findings from item, reliability, and factor analyses, weak items were identified and subsequently deleted, resulting in the present 70-item version.

Psychometric Properties. Reliability. For each of two samples of adolescents (Sample 1, n = 315; Sample 2, n = 385), Marsh et al. (1994)

---

6. These adolescents served as the validation sample in a cross-validation study of the PSDQ in which a longer version of the instrument was first tested with the calibration sample described later (see Marsh et al., 1994).

reported internal consistency reliability coefficients for boys and girls separately, as well as in combination for each group. Alpha coefficient estimates were reported as ranging from .86 (Flexibility and General Self-Esteem) to .96 (Body Fat; mean α = .91) across the two samples. Taking gender into account, these estimates ranged from .79 (Health) to .96 (Body Fat) for boys (mean α = .88) and from .87 (Health) to .96 (Global Physical; mean α = .92) for girls across the two samples. The authors noted that no other reliability information was available.

Validity. Based on an MTMM analysis within the framework of a confirmatory factor analytic model, Marsh et al. (1994) investigated evidence of concurrent validity between related scales of the PSDQ and those constituting two other physical self-concept measures; these were the Physical Self-Perception Profile (PSPP; Fox & Corbin, 1989) and the Physical Self-Concept Scale (PSCS; Richards, 1988). Results demonstrated good evidence of concurrent validity between the PSDQ and the other two instruments. Estimates ranged from .61 to .86 (mean r = .76) for relations with the PSPP and from .66 to .90 (mean r = .80) for relations with the PSCS. As determined from these analyses also, Marsh et al. (1994) reported evidence of convergent and discriminant validity related to the PSDQ, as well as to the other two instruments.

Results from confirmatory factor analyses of the PSDQ not only have provided exceptional support for the clarity and strength of its 11 subscales but also have shown the factorial structure of the instrument to be invariant across gender. More specifically, when factor loadings and factor correlations were constrained to be equal across boys and girls, and then the model was estimated simultaneously for both groups, Marsh et al. (1994) determined no significant difference from a model in which the estimates were freely estimated for each group separately. These results imply not only that the PSDQ items are being interpreted in exactly the same way by boys and girls, but also that the underlying theoretical structure of physical self-concept is equivalent.

Based on a subsample of 258 students from Sample 2 of the Marsh et al. (1994) study (i.e., the validation sample described under Normative Data, earlier), the construct validity of the PSDQ was further tested through examination of its subscale relations with external criteria to which they should be logically linked (see Marsh, in press-a). These criteria included both self-report and behavioral observation measures such as a silhouette-matching task, an objective test of body fat, participation in adherence and exercise programs, and so on (see Marsh, in press-a, for the extended list and explanation of these criteria). Findings from this investigation revealed that except for the Flexibility subscale, all external physical criteria were more closely related to the specific PSDQ scales with which they should be logically linked than they were to the other PSDQ scales, and to global physical self-concept and general self-esteem. The nonsignificant relation between the Flexibility subscale and a sit-and-reach test of flexibility is curious and requires more intensive scrutiny; the problem lies either with inferences based on the PSDQ, or with the sit-and-reach test, or with both instruments. On the basis of results from this study, Marsh (in press-a) concluded that there was good support for the construct validity of the PSDQ responses with respect to a wide variety of external criteria.

Related Psychometric Research

The PSDQ, although a product of its parent instrument, the SDQ–II, is a relatively new presence on the scene of physical fitness and sport. In keeping with his now widely known theoretically and psychometrically sound approach to instrument development, Marsh has embarked on a carefully orchestrated and logical program of construct validity research that tests both the multidimensional and hierarchical structure of physical self-concept and the factorial validity of the PSDQ, which is tied to this theoretical premise. Although a few of these studies were briefly described earlier, it is worthwhile to note at least two others that focus on important aspects of measuring physical self-concept, in general, and measuring it with the PSDQ, in particular.

The first of these addresses the issue of the hierarchical structure of physical self-concept and evaluates relations between its specific dimensions and the higher order constructs of global physical self-concept and general self-esteem (Marsh, 1994a). As with his earlier work in this area (Marsh, 1986b, 1993e), Marsh compared a series of theoretical models that incorporated a variety of perspectives related to the notion of importance ratings. The second study (Marsh, in press-b) tackled the problem of establishing the link between a measuring instrument and logically related external criteria as an important link in the construct validity process. In particular, Marsh (in press-b) assessed the similarity of external criteria as measured by two instruments: the Perceptions of Success Questionnaire (Roberts, 1993), designed to measure mastery and competitiveness orientations, and the Sports Orientation Questionnaire (Gill, 1993), designed to measure competitiveness, win, and goal orientation. Findings from this research pointed to the need for sports psychologists to pursue more rigorous construct validity research endeavors and to be cognizant of the *jingle* (i.e., scales with the same label that reflect the same construct) and *jangle* (scales with different labels that reflect different constructs) fallacies.

Evaluation Summary

As with the Academic Self Description Questionnaire instruments, the PSDQ is a relatively new instrument. Its basic structure was patterned after the well-established SDQ–II (Marsh, 1992c). Nonetheless, Marsh has already begun a series of rigorous studies to establish the instrument's construct validity and overall psychometric reputation. Although the within-network structure of the PSDQ has been shown to be relatively sound, Marsh et al. (1994) noted the need for construct validity research that focused on between-network relations with appropriate external criteria. As noted earlier, progress in this direction has already been initiated (Marsh, in press-b). The instrument could also benefit from research that addresses the generalizability of PSDQ interpretations across cultures and research that investigates the extent to which it can discriminate between known criterion groups; the latter bears importantly on intervention work designed to enhance particular aspects of physical self-concept. Indeed, Marsh (in press-b; Marsh et al., 1994) has already noted these present limitations. In light of the psychometric history of the three SDQ instruments, I have no doubt that the PSDQ will rapidly accrue the same exceptionally strong psychometric properties. Indeed, researchers are encouraged to conduct construct validity work, as well as other psychometric work, which will contribute to our knowledge of physical self-concept, in general, and of the PSDQ, in particular. Toward this end, Marsh has permitted interested researchers to copy the scale items free of charge (see Marsh et al., 1994). As a courtesy only, however, he would appreciate receiving information related to any research in which the PSDQ has been used.

Source Information

Location: Herbert W. Marsh, School of Education and Language Studies, University of Western Sydney, P.O. Box 555, Campbelltown, New South Wales 2560, Australia

Cost: No manual is presently available. However, Dr. Marsh has recommended that interested users write to him for updated information.

GENERAL SELF-CONCEPT

Rosenberg Self-Esteem Scale

Description

The Rosenberg Self-Esteem Scale (SES; Rosenberg, 1965, 1989) was designed to measure global self-esteem in the sense intended by Rosenberg (1965, 1979, 1989), as opposed to other philosophical perspectives on the topic. That is to say, "the self-concept is not a *collection* but an organization of parts, pieces, and components, and . . . these are hierarchically organized and interrelated in complex ways (Rosenberg, 1979, p. 73). In developing the SES, Rosenberg (1965, 1989) worked from the premise that individuals acknowledge the phenomenological experience of general self-worth over and above the evaluations of the more discrete characteristics of the self (Harter, 1985a). As such, Rosenberg (1979) argued that whereas both aspects of the self exist as separate and distinguishable entities within a person's phenomenological field, each can and should be studied in its own right.

The SES, then, is a unidimensional scale designed to measure only perceptions of global self-esteem. In other words, it taps the extent to which a person is generally satisfied with his or her life, considers him- or herself worthy, holds a positive attitude toward him- or herself, or, alternatively, feels useless, desires more respect, and so on. Thus, it is important to distinguish Rosenberg's perspective from that of others who consider general self-esteem to represent a sum of self-judgments relative to specific aspects of one's daily functioning; that is to say, a summation of subscale scores from a single instrument designed to measure multidimensional self-concepts.

Rosenberg's theoretical perspective regarding global self-esteem, along with the item content of his SES, provided the template from which the global self-esteem subscales of the Harter (1985b, 1988c; Messer & Harter, 1986; Neemann & Harter, 1986; Renick & Harter, 1988) and Marsh (1992a, 1992b, 1992c, 1993d) series of instruments were developed. In each case, global self-esteem is measured as a separate and distinct entity by items constituting a single subscale; it is not measured through the summation of multidimensional subscale scores. The SES is theoretically linked to the true unidimensional model of self-concept described in chapter 1.

Exhibit 6.4

Sample Item From the Rosenberg Self-Esteem Scale

I am able to do things as well as most other people.

Target Population

The SES was originally designed for use with junior and senior high school adolescents. Presumably, it is intended for use with children in Grades 7 to 12 (ages 12–19 years), although this population is not specifically identified (see also Bracken & Mills, 1994). Over the intervening years, however, the instrument has also become a popular measure of self-esteem for adults. Nonetheless, I am not aware of any studies that have tested the validity of its use with this population.

Scale Structure

Rosenberg (1965, 1989) noted that in constructing the SES, he was guided by the important practical constraints of ease of administration, economy of time, the ability to rank individuals along a single continuum of global self-esteem, and face validity. The resulting instrument is a 10-item self-report scale designed to measure a unidimensional factor of global self-esteem. To accomplish the goal of unidimensionality, items constituting the SES were originally structured as a Guttman-type scale,[7] with possible responses ranging from *strongly disagree* to *strongly agree*. However, reviewers (Blascovich & Tomaka, 1991; Wylie, 1989) noted that most researchers preferred scoring the instrument as a 4-point Likert scale. In fact, Blascovich and Tomaka further noted that some authors have preferred to expand this Likert-type format into 5- or 7-point scales, thereby resulting in a broader range of self-esteem scores. Rosenberg (1965) reported that to control for response bias (i.e., acquiescence), positively and negatively worded items were alternated. A sample item from the SES is presented in Exhibit 6.4.[8]

Administration and Scoring

The SES can be administered either individually or in groups, although these conditions are not specifically mentioned in Rosenberg's (1965, 1989) discussion of the instrument. Given that it has become customary

---

7. As such, item content moves sequentially from weaker to stronger expressions of self-perception so that agreement with the stronger statements implies agreement with those that are milder (Cohen et al., 1988).

8. Because the number of scale points can vary across researchers, only the item itself is included here.

to score the SES as a Likert-type scale (see above), the total score is derived from a simple summation across the 10-item response values (after reflection of negative items); a score of 40 (based on a 4-point scale) thereby would represent high self-esteem. Because no actual manual exists for the SES, and Rosenberg neither elaborated on nor demonstrated the scale-point format used in his original study, researchers have devised their own set of instructions for responding to the SES items. Typically, however, this has meant preceding the list of items with a presentation of possible responses and then asking the respondents to either tick or circle one of the four (or more) response alternatives for each of the 10 declarative statements. Although, again, Rosenberg provided no guidelines regarding the expected length of time required to complete the SES, my own experience has shown 5 min to be ample.

Normative Data

Samples. Initial testing of the SES was based on Rosenberg's (1965) study of 5,024 adolescents drawn from 10 high schools that, in turn, were chosen randomly from all high schools in the state of New York; schools were stratified by size of community.

Selection and Refinement of Items. Rosenberg provided no information related to either the initial pool of items from which the present set was chosen or the process used in retaining particular items (see also Wylie, 1989).

Psychometric Properties. *Reliability.* Several indicators of internal consistency reliability have been reported for the SES. For example, based on personal communication with Rosenberg, Wylie (1989) reported an alpha coefficient of .77 for the standardization sample. In addition, she reported coefficients of reproducibility for Guttman-scale scores of .92 and "slightly higher" (p. 26) for this sample and a sample of 560 British adolescents, respectively. Other reported alpha coefficients for the SES included in both the Wylie (1989) and Blascovich and Tomaka (1991) reviews have been based on samples of noninstitutionalized persons 60 years or older ($N = 323$, $\alpha = .74$; Ward, 1977); men 60 years or older ($N = 1,332$, $\alpha = .72$; Dobson, Goudy, Keoth, & Powers, 1979); civil servants ($N = 873$, $\alpha = .83$; Schmitt & Bedeian, 1982); first-year university students ($N = 259$, $\alpha = .88$; Fleming & Courtney, 1984); Grades 11 and 12 Canadian high school students ($N = 832$, $\alpha = .87$; Byrne & Shavelson, 1986); and parents ($N = 116$, $\alpha = .80$; Orme, Reis, & Herz, 1986).

In their reviews, Wylie (1989) and Blascovich and Tomaka (1991) have reported evidence of only four test–retest reliability coefficients related to the SES. From a methodological perspective, however, only two are worth reporting here. One study was based on a sample of 990 suburban Canadian high school students over a 7-month interval ($r = .63$; Byrne, 1983); the other was based on a sample of 259 first-year university students over a 1-week interval ($r = .82$; Silber & Tippett, 1965).

Validity. Although reported correlations have been cited as evidence of convergent validity between the SES and other self-concept measures (Blascovich & Tomaka, 1991; Wylie, 1989), most of these make little sense in the light of the distinction already noted with respect to Rosenberg's versus others' conceptualizations of global self-esteem. For example, both reviewers cited a validity coefficient of .55 between the SES and the Coopersmith (1967) Self-Esteem Inventory, as reported by Demo (1985). Yet, as noted earlier, Harter (1985a) emphasized the vivid distinction between these two instruments in their measurement of global self-esteem. Whereas the SES measures self-esteem directly, the Coopersmith instrument measures it by summing together subscale scores representative of more specific self-concepts; this latter approach is clearly counter to Rosenberg's intended conceptualization of the construct.

Indeed, of the studies cited by Blascovich and Tomaka and by Wylie as providing evidence of convergent validity, I consider only two to represent evidence of concurrent validity. In the one study (Byrne & Shavelson, 1986 [cited in Wylie, 1989]), an MTMM analysis was used to investigate evidence of convergent and discriminant validity related to a postulated multidimensional self-concept as represented by four self-concept facets (general, academic, English, and mathematics) and measured by three divergent methods (Guttman, Likert, and semantic differential); elements of this matrix relevant to the SES revealed its convergent validity with the General—Self subscale of the SDQ–III (Marsh, 1992d) to be .79 and its convergent validity with the Self Concept subscale of the Affective Perception Inventory (A. T. Soares & Soares, 1979) to be .64. In the second study (Savin-Williams & Jaquish, 1981 [cited in Blascovich & Tomaka, 1991]), the SES was shown to correlate .72 with the Lerner Self-Esteem Scale, .24 with "beeper" self-reports of self-esteem, and .27 with peer ratings for an adolescent sample.

In their reviews, Blascovich and Tomaka (1991) and Wylie (1989) also cited correlations between SES scores and a variety of other constructs as providing evidence of convergent validity. Here again, I fail to find the meaningfulness of many of these reported correlations. For example, citing from the Fleming and Courtney (1984) study, both reviewers reported a validity coefficient of .42 with physical appearance, as measured by a subscale of the revised Janis–Field Scale. However, some cited correlations can be meaningfully interpreted as the extent to which self-esteem, as measured by the SES, is related to other constructs in its nomological network (between-network relations). In this sense, then, the validity coefficients reflect the link between self-esteem and other external variables with which it should be logically and theoretically related. Accordingly, Fleming and Courtney found the SES to correlate negatively with anxiety ($r = -.64$), depression ($r = -.59$), and anomie ($r = -.43$) and to correlate positively with general self-regard ($r = .78$) and social confidence ($r = .51$) for college students ($n = 246$).

As further evidence of construct validity, Wylie (1989) summarized findings from seven factor analytic studies of the SES; all were conducted using an exploratory, as opposed to a confirmatory, approach to the data analyses. Two of the seven studies reported strong support for a unidimensional structure based on samples of female undergraduate students ($N = 206$; O'Brien, 1985) and college students ($N = 1,194$; Hensley, 1977). Findings from the other five studies argued for a two-factor structure based on samples of boys 16 years and older ($N = 3,000$; Kohn, 1969); adults of all ages ($N = 500$; H. B. Kaplan & Pokorny, 1969); university students ($N = 479$; Hensley & Roberts, 1976); men 60 years or older ($N = 1,322$; Dobson et al. 1979); and high school students ($N = 340$; Carmines & Zeller, 1979). Despite considerable agreement among these five studies concerning which items define each factor, there is some inconsistency regarding interpretation of the two factors. Whereas H. B. Kaplan and Pokorny concluded the first factor to represent general self-esteem and the other, a related but independent construct, which they termed Self-Derogation, others (Carmines & Zeller, 1979; Hensley & Roberts, 1976) concluded that the second factor represented a combination of the same first factor (i.e., Self-Esteem) plus a response set or method factor reflective of a response pattern that was implemented irrespective of item content. Taken together, then, although factor analytic findings have been somewhat discrepant in terms of the underlying structure of the SES, it would appear that the instrument is basically unidimensional.

Related Psychometric Research

Using a confirmatory factor analytic approach, two recent studies have sought to replicate findings from two of the exploratory factor analytic studies noted earlier. Based on the Carmines and Zeller (1979) correlation matrix, the first study (Goldsmith, 1986) tested for the validity of their reported two-factor solution, as well as the one reported by H. B. Kaplan and Pokorny (1969); Goldsmith also tested for the replicability of the factor solutions with two additional samples of college students ($N = 97$) and other adults ($N = 87$), using Heise and Bohrnstedt's (1970) formulas for validity, invalidity, and reliability. Goldsmith's findings concurred with those from past research that the SES is best described by a two-factor structure. However, he further determined that this factorial structure appears to vary across populations, thereby providing support for both the Carmines and Zeller and the H. B. Kaplan and Pokorny findings. Whereas the SES was basically unidimensional (with the second factor representing systematic error) with the adult sample, it was multidimensional (with the second factor representing a negative attitude toward self, or self-derogation) with the college sample.

The second study (Shahani, Dipboye, & Phillips, 1990) tested for the factorial validity of the SES with a sample of government employees in the American Southwest ($N = 1,726$). These researchers tested three hypotheses: (a) that the SES is unidimensional, as postulated by Rosenberg (1965, 1979), (b) that the SES has a two-factor structure with a pattern of loadings consistent with those described by H. B. Kaplan and Pokorny (1969), and (c) given findings of a two-factor SES structure, that the factors would be correlated. Although Shahani et al. generally found support for the superiority of H. B. Kaplan and Pokorny's two-factor structure, they determined model fit to the data to be somewhat inadequate. Based on findings from a post hoc exploratory analysis that investigated the possibility that careless responding led to the negative factor (see, e.g., Schmitt & Stults, 1985), they concluded that the two factors represent psychologically meaningful dimensions of self-esteem. Nonetheless, Shahani et al. noted that their findings do not necessarily rule out a methodological interpretation. Clearly, more research is needed to further clarify the underlying structure of the SES.

Evaluation Summary

As evidenced from a review of the substantive literature in which self-esteem is a variable under study, it is clear that the SES is the most popular instrument used for its measurement. The theoretical underpinning of the SES is consistent with Rosenberg's (1965, 1979, 1989) conceptualization of a hierarchically ordered, albeit separate, self-esteem construct.

Although the instrument has savored a generally positive reputation over the years, I believe that rigorous testing of its psychometric properties based on updated methodological procedures and large samples is long overdue. In particular, the SES could benefit from a stringent testing of both the validity and invariance of its factorial structure across diverse adolescent and adult populations using confirmatory factor analytic procedures. Indeed, findings from past factor analytic research have opened the door to numerous questions bearing on its postulated unidimensionality that are in need of answers. In the light of our current knowledge of the multidimensionality of self-concept, and the widely known research of Harter (e.g., 1985a) and Marsh (e.g., 1986b) regarding the structure of global self-esteem, the question of whether this construct is itself multidimensionally structured is intuitively intriguing and cries out for investigation. Although the construct validity of a measuring instrument and its underlying theory cannot be tested simultaneously (because the testing of one presumes the validity of the other), researchers are urged to tackle this issue with respect to either the SES or the structure of global self-esteem. Over time, findings from both research pursuits should provide a wealth of information that may help clarify this important construct validity contention.

Source Information

Location: Rosenberg, M. (1989). *Society and the adolescent self-image* (Rev. ed.). Middletown, CT: Wesleyan University Press.
Permission for use can be obtained from copyright holder:
University Press of New England
23 South Main Street
Hanover, New Hampshire 03755

Measurement of Multiple Self-Concept Domains

Multidimensional Self Concept Scale

The Multidimensional Self Concept Scale (MSCS; Bracken, 1992) is designed to measure multiple context-dependent dimensions of self-concept for adolescents, as well as for preadolescent children. For details on this instrument, see chapter 5.

Piers—Harris Children's Self-Concept Scale

The Piers—Harris Children's Self-Concept Scale (PHCSCS; Piers, 1984), designed for use with adolescents as well as preadolescents (ages 8–18 years), is a self-report unidimensional measure of self-concepts in relation to six areas of daily functioning: behavior, intellectual and school status, physical appearance and attributes, anxiety, popularity, and happiness and satisfaction. For details on this instrument, see chapter 5.

Self Description Questionnaire II

Description

The Self Description Questionnaire II (SDQ–II; Marsh, 1992c) is designed to measure multiple dimensions of self-concept for adolescents. This instrument was built from its companion instrument, the SDQ–I; thus, the multidimensional structure of the two instruments is very similar. In particular, the SDQ–II is designed to measure the same four nonacademic areas (physical ability, physical appearance, peer relations, and parent relations), three academic areas (reading, mathematics, and school in general), and a global perception of self as the SDQ–I. One important difference between the two instruments, however, relates to the Peer Relations subscale. Consonant with developmental theory, this subscale in the SDQ–II is made more specific by tapping perceived social relations with same-sex peers and opposite-sex peers (i.e., two subscales in lieu of one). Beyond this change, the SDQ–II includes two additional subscales: Emotional Stability and Honesty/Trustworthiness. As was true for the SDQ–I, the SDQ–II is solidly grounded in the Shavelson et al. (1976) multidimensional/hierarchical self-concept model.

Target Population

Although the SDQ–II was originally designed for use with younger adolescents attending junior high and high schools (Grades 7–10), extensive research has now firmly established its appropriateness for students in Grades 7 through 12. Although its later companion instrument, the SDQ–III (see chapter 7) can and has been used with late adolescents in high school (Grades 11–12; Byrne, 1988a, 1988b; Marsh & O'Neill, 1984), Marsh (1992c) noted that this instrument was designed primarily for use with college students and other adults.

Scale Structure

The SDQ–II is a 102-item self-report scale that comprises 11 subscales: (a) seven nonacademic (Physical Ability, Physical Appearance, Peer

Relations—Same Sex, Peer Relations—Opposite Sex, Parent Relations, Emotional Stability, and Honesty/Trustworthiness); (b) three academic, two of which are subject-matter specific (Reading and Mathematics) and one of which relates to school in general (General—School); and (c) one that measures overall global self-concept (General—Self). In contrast to the SDQ–I, the items are structured on a 6-point Likert scale format; some subscales are composed of 8 items, and other subscales are composed of 10 items. To disrupt acquiescence response biases, half of the items in each subscale are worded negatively. One sample item from the Peer Relations—Same Sex subscale of the SDQ–II is presented in Exhibit 6.5.

Administration and Scoring

As with the SDQ–I, the SDQ–II can be administered either individually or in groups. For each statement provided in the questionnaire, adolescents are asked to identify which one of the six alternative responses listed at the top of each page best describes them by placing a check mark in the appropriate box accompanying each item (see Exhibit 6.5). Although Marsh (1992c) recommends that for group administration, the examiner verbally review instructions for completing the SDQ–II, the procedure described on the initial page of the instrument is self-explanatory. He reported that most adolescents complete the questionnaire in approximately 20 min.

Responses to the SDQ–II can be scored either manually, by means of the Scoring and Profile Booklet provided, or by computer, by means of the scoring program disk provided. The booklet provides for the calculation of subscale raw scores and total scale raw scores (Nonacademic, Academic, and Total Self). Raw scores related to each subscale, as well as the total raw score, may be converted to midinterval percentile ranks

---

Exhibit 6.5

Sample Item From the Self Description Questionnaire II

	False	Mostly False	More False Than True	More True Than False	Mostly True	True
It is difficult to make friends with members of my own sex	☐	☐	☐	☐	☐	☐

and nonnormalized T scores. The norms tables in the manual provide information for both boys and girls separately and in combination.

Normative Data

Samples. Norms development and standardization of the SDQ–II were based on a series of research studies involving a total sample of 5,494 students (2,658 boys and 2,836 girls) from junior high and high schools (Grades 7–12) in metropolitan Sydney, Australia. Drawn from geographically diverse regions of Sydney, Australia, the samples represented schools in working-class, middle-class, and upper-class areas; single-sex and coeducational schools; and both public and Catholic schools. For each subscale, total scale (Nonacademic and Academic), Total Self scale (Nonacademic and Academic), and General—Self scale, Marsh (1992c) provided the following information in the norms tables: midinterval percentile, nonnormalized T score, mean, median, standard deviation, and coefficients of skewness and kurtosis.

Selection and Refinement of Items. After several early revisions of the instrument, an initial pool of 153 items was constructed to tap the 11 self-concept dimensions measured by the SDQ–II. Based on the first large-scale study of the SDQ–II (N = 901; Marsh, Parker, & Barnes, 1985), this item pool was subsequently reduced to 122 for purposes of analyses. Reduction of items was based on item-analysis statistics, as well as the decision to retain 10 items per subscale, with an approximate balance between positively and negatively worded statements. Using the same criteria, the final (i.e., present) 102-item version of the SDQ–II was based on the entire normative sample (N = 5,494). Marsh (1992c) reported that reduction of total instrument length and maintenance of appropriate levels of subscale reliabilities were the primary determinants underlying the final selection of SDQ–II items.

Psychometric Properties. *Reliability.* Based on the full normative sample (N = 5,494), Marsh (1992c) reported internal consistency reliability coefficients ranging from .83 (for Emotional Stability) to .91 (for Physical Appearance), with a mean alpha over the 11 subscales of .87. As additional indicators of internal consistency, he also reported corrected item–scale correlations (i.e., correlation between an item and the summed responses from other items in the same scale) for each item. These coefficients ranged from .35 (Item 98, measuring Emotional Stability) to .80 (Item 35, measuring Physical Appearance), with an overall mean correlation coefficient of .60.

Test–retest reliability related to the SDQ–II is reported in the manual, based on a study by Marsh and Peart (1988) in which they examined responses by 137 high school girls before and after an intervention program designed to enhance their physical fitness. Over a period of 7 weeks, stability coefficients in relation to the SDQ–II were found to range from .73 (Honesty/Trustworthiness) to .88 (Mathematics), with an overall mean correlation coefficient of .80. Although admittedly based on a single, relatively small, and gender-specific sample, these indicators of measurement stability are nonetheless substantial and reflect strong evidence of test–retest reliability in relation to the SDQ–II.

Validity. In keeping with the SDQ–I, most validity research bearing on the SDQ–II has focused on tests of its construct validity. Once again, in the light of the volume of research conducted in this regard, I refer readers both to the manual (Marsh, 1992c) and to the two review articles previously noted (Marsh, 1990b; Marsh & Hattie, 1996) for a more in-depth treatment of the various aspects of construct validity tested. Included here is a brief summary of both within- and between-construct validity research.

Within-network research related to the SDQ–II has used both exploratory and confirmatory factor analyses. In keeping with Marsh's testing for the validity of all SDQ instruments, these analyses were based on paired rather than single items; for the rationale underlying this approach, readers are referred to Marsh (1992c). The initial test of factorial validity was based on 901 students (Grades 7–12) from one large high school in metropolitan Sydney, Australia (Marsh et al., 1985). Results revealed a very strong factor structure, with each of the 11 subscales of the SDQ–II being clearly identified. Furthermore, in keeping with the underlying theory, factors were intercorrelated, albeit these relations were small (median $r = .14$). More specifically, Marsh et al. (1985) reported the highest correlations to occur between the General—Self and all other subscales (median $r = .20$), between the General—School and the two subject-matter subscales ($r = .33$ and .30), and between the Physical Appearance and Peer Relations—Opposite Sex subscales ($r = .33$).

To provide a definitive study of the SDQ–II factor structure, a single factor analysis was conducted on the 5,494 sets of responses from the normative sample. As expected, findings revealed an exceptionally clear 11-factor structure; specifically, (a) target loadings (item loadings on the factor they were hypothesized to measure) were substantial, with values ranging from .48 to .80 (median = .68), (b) nontarget loadings were substantially smaller and ranged from −.12 to .27 (median = .03), and (c) correlations among the factors were modest, ranging from −.03 to .39 (median = .15). In a follow-up test of these data, factor analytic results showed this factor structure to replicate across separate samples of boys and girls at the junior high level (Grades 7–8) as well as boys and girls at the senior high level (Grades 9–11). Overall, factor analytic findings relative to the SDQ–II stand in strong support of its clear 11-factor structure, the similarity of this structure across both sex and age, and the validity of its hypothesized structure within the framework of the Shavelson et al. (1976) theoretical model on which it is based.

Between-network research related to the SDQ–II has examined relations between particular subscales of the instrument and a wide array of other constructs such as gender; age; academic performance; inferred self-concepts (by significant others such as teachers, parents, and peers); family background characteristics; self-attribution; experimental conditions associated with intervention programs designed to enhance self-concept; and masculinity, femininity, and androgyny. In the process of testing these relations, Marsh and colleagues have addressed important theoretical issues in self-concept research, such as frame-of-reference effects, causal predominance between academic self-concept and academic achievement, self-attributions for academic success and failure, self–other agreement, and intervention effects. Findings from the research just described provide exceptionally strong support for the construct validity of the SDQ–II.

Related Psychometric Research

In a cross-cultural study that included Australian (n = 1,147) and American (n = 17,544)[9] Grade 10 students, Marsh (1994b) used responses from five SDQ–II subscales (Mathematics, Reading, Parent Relations, Peer Relations—Same Sex, and Peer Relations—Opposite Sex) to compare the validity of several theoretical models in general, and the validity of SDQ–II scores in particular, across the two groups of adolescents. Of specific relevance here are findings bearing on the score reliabilities and factorial structure of the SDQ–II. Except for one subscale (Peer Relations—Opposite Sex), coefficient alpha estimates of internal consistency reliability were basically equivalent across the two cultural groups and ranged from .74 to .88 (mean α = .83); estimates related to the Peer Relations—Opposite Sex subscale were .83 for Australian ad-

---

9. This was a nationally representative sample.

olescents and .73 for American adolescents. Findings provided good support for the hypothesized factor structure of the SDQ–II for both groups of adolescents and for the invariance of this structure across Australian and American cultures; moreover, the factorial structure of the SDQ–II was found to be equivalent across gender within both countries.

A second study recently investigated the reliability of SDQ–II scores and relations among its subscale scores for a sample of middle school and junior high school students ($N = 763$) in the Midwestern United States (Vispoel, Forte, & Bleiler, 1995). Findings yielded internal consistency reliability estimates ranging from .85 (Honesty/Trustworthiness) to .93 (Mathematics) with a mean coefficient alpha value of .88. In contrast to the findings of Marsh et al. (1985) that demonstrated minimal correlations among self-concept factors (median $r = .14$), Vispoel et al. determined the median correlation to be .36.

Evaluation Summary

In keeping with my evaluation of the SDQ–I, I consider the SDQ–II to be the most validated self-concept measure available for use with adolescent children. Following a similarly planned program of research as that of its predecessor over the past 10 years or so, the SDQ–II has undergone extensive testing to establish its psychometric soundness as a measure of self-concept. Once again, researchers, clinicians, counselors, and others interested in the welfare of adolescent children can feel confident in the validity of interpretations based on responses to its multidimensionally sensitive items. I do suggest, however, that information related to the reading level of SDQ–II items be included in the next version of the manual; such information may be helpful to researchers wishing to test for the validity of SDQ–II responses based on samples representative of various exceptional or cultural populations.

Source Information

Location: Publication Office, School of Education and Language Studies, University of Western Sydney, P.O. Box 555, Campbelltown, New South Wales 2560, Australia

Cost: Kit: $50.00 (includes SDQ–II, manual, and scoring key)

Self-Perception Profile for Adolescents

Description

The Self-Perception Profile for Adolescents (SPPA; Harter, 1988c) represents an upward extension of Harter's (1985b) Self-Perception Profile for Children (SPPC; see chapter 5). As such, it builds on the same theoretical assumption that perceptions of self reflect multidimensional, specific domains of one's life, as well as a separate domain of global self-worth. In keeping with developmental theory related to self-concept (e.g., Harter, 1988b; Shavelson et al., 1976), the SPPA is designed to measure self-perceptions related to more specific domains than was the case for the SPPC. That is, in addition to global self-worth and the five specific self-concept dimensions measured by the SPPC, the SPPA also taps perceptions of job competence, close friendship, and romantic appeal. Thus, the SPPA is theoretically linked to the correlated-factor model of self-concept described in chapter 1.

In providing her rationale for the inclusion of the three additional subscales, Harter (1988c) explained that Job Competence, for example, was added because most teenagers begin to work at part-time jobs. Thus, their perception of competence on the job represents a new and relevant domain of self-evaluation. The inclusion of the Close Friendship domain is in keeping with developmental theory that has shown that the ability to make and maintain close friendship ties takes on more salience in the early adolescent years. Moreover, Harter (1988d) contended that this ability differed to some extent from the notion of peer acceptance or popularity among classmates. Finally, it is evident that during adolescence, teenagers become romantically interested in others and in Western societies, at least, the process of dating is initiated. For this logical reason, then, perceptions of self with respect to the domain of romantic appeal seemed relevant for this age group.

Harter (1988c) noted that for the most part, the content of the original six scales of the SPPC have been kept parallel across the child and adolescent versions of the instrument. Whereas the wording of many items is identical, that of several others has been changed to make the SPPA more appropriate for the adolescent age group. Harter (1988c) noted that one major advantage of such content overlap across the SPPC and SPPA is that it allows researchers interested in developmental issues to comfortably switch from one instrument to the other at the appropriate age level and yet still be able to compare subscale scores across the two versions.

Target Population

According to Harter (1988c), the SPPA is appropriate to use with adolescents for whom, in the researcher's judgment, the three additional scales (Job Competence, Romantic Appeal, and Close Friendship) are salient. As a result, no specific age has been proscribed. For example, in the case where young adolescents (ages 13–15 years) are not yet involved with jobs or dating, the SPPC may be used effectively; indeed, norms related to children in Grades 7 and 8 are included in the SPPC manual. However, Harter (1988c) recommended that for adolescents in Grades 9 through 12, the SPPA should be the instrument of choice. She further cautioned that in its present form, the SPPA may not be appropriate for use with special populations such as adolescents with learning disabilities or mental impairments.

Scale Structure

The SPPA is a 45-item self-report scale that comprises nine subscales. Eight scales are designed to measure self-perceptions in relation to specific domains of one's life (Scholastic Competence, Athletic Competence, Social Acceptance, Physical Appearance, Job Competence, Close Friendship, Romantic Appeal, and Behavioral Conduct), and one is designed to measure perception of self in general (Global Self-Worth). (Harter [1988c]) emphasized that the Global Self-Worth subscale was not intended as a measure of general competence.) Each subscale is composed of five items, with all but two having three items worded in the positive direction and two in the negative direction; the Physical Appearance and Close Friendship subscales have three negative and two positive items. As with the SPPC, items are structured in a 4-point structured-alternative format to offset socially desirable responding.

The question format of the SPPA parallels that of the SPPC. As such, adolescents are first presented with a description of two types of teenagers and then asked to identify which one of the two most resembles them. Harter (1988c) stated that the effectiveness of this question format lies in the implication that half of the adolescents in the world view themselves one way, whereas the other half hold opposing views. In this way, either choice is legitimized. Once the respondents have chosen between these two groups, they then determine whether the behavior described is really true, or just sort of true for them. Harter (1988c) noted that on the basis of verbal elaborations by adolescents when asked to rationalize their choices, she feels confident that their SPPA responses represented accurate self-perceptions rather than ones that were socially desirable. One sample item from the Close Friendship subscale of the SPPA is presented in Exhibit 6.6.

As was true for the SPPC, the manual for the SPPA includes a separate scale that enables researchers to also tap perceptions of im-

Exhibit 6.6

Sample Item From the Self-Perception Profile for Adolescents

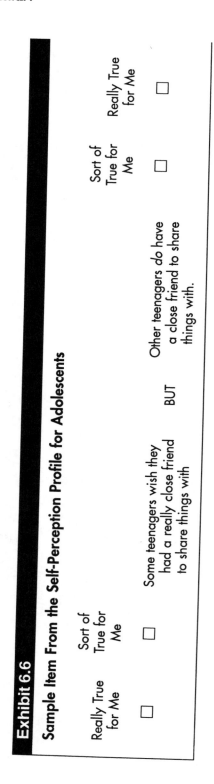

Really True for Me	Sort of True for Me			Sort of True for Me	Really True for Me
☐	☐	Some teenagers wish they had a really close friend to share things with	BUT	Other teenagers *do* have a close friend to share things with.	☐ ☐

portance in relation to each domain. Based on the same scale format as the SPPA, the Importance Rating scale, for adolescents, comprises 16 items, with 2 items for each domain-specific self-concept.

Administration and Scoring

In keeping with the administration and scoring of the SPPC described in chapter 5, the SPPA can be administered either individually or in groups, and the mode of responding and scoring is identical. Harter (1988c) pointed out that in explaining the question format, it is essential that the researcher clarify that for any given item, respondents must check only one box on either side of the item statement; they do not check both sides. A scoring key and instructions for the computation of discrepancy scores are provided in the manual. (For a more extensive discussion of importance and discrepancy scores, see chapter 1 of this volume; see also Bogan, 1988; Cronbach & Furby, 1970; Hattie, 1992; Marsh, 1986b, 1993e; Wells & Marwell, 1976; Wylie, 1989.)

Normative Data

Samples. Norms development for the SPPA was based on four independent samples of adolescents drawn from schools in Colorado (Grades 8–11). In keeping with sampling for the SPPC, approximately 90% of the children were White and represented the lower-middle through upper-middle socioeconomic strata (Harter, 1988c). These samples can be described as follows: Sample A (Grade 8, $n = 56$; Grade 9, $n = 38$; Grade 10, $n = 48$; and Grade 11, $n = 35$); Sample B (Grade 8, $n = 109$); Sample C (Grade 10, $n = 62$; Grade 11, $n = 180$); and Sample D (Grade 9, $n = 123$).

Selection and Refinement of Items. In the light of the fact that the SPPA is a relatively new instrument, decisions regarding the modification of items were based on findings related to data yielded by Samples A, B, and C. As a consequence of less than adequate internal consistency reliabilities for the Job Competence and Behavioral Conduct subscales, aberrant items contributing to this attenuation were subsequently revised before administration of the scale to Sample D. Harter (1988c) reported that data are currently being collected from 2,000 additional students in Grades 9 through 11 ($n = 500$ per grade) to whom the revised scale is being administered.

Psychometric Properties. Reliability. Based on each of the above four samples, Harter (1988c) reported internal consistency reliability coefficients for each of the nine subscales; as noted in the previous paragraph, however, the scale administered to Sample D represented a version in which items constituting the Job Competence and Behavioral Conduct scales were revised. For Samples A, B, and C, then, Harter reported internal consistency reliabilities ranging from .77 to .91 (mean α = .83) for Scholastic Competence, from .77 to .90 (mean α = .83) for Social Acceptance, from .86 to .90 (mean α = .88) for Athletic Competence, from .84 to .89 (mean α = .86) for Physical Appearance, from .58 to .60 (mean α = .59) for Behavioral Conduct,[10] from .79 to .85 (mean α = .81) for Close Friendship, from .75 to .85 (mean α = 81) for Romantic Appeal, from .55 to .93 (mean α = .71) for Job Competence, and from .80 to .89 (mean α = .85) for Global Self-Worth. Sample D coefficient alpha estimates were .81, .78, .92, .86, .78, .83, .80, .74, and .88, respectively. To date, no test–retest reliability estimates have been reported.

Validity. The only validity research reported in the SPPA manual relates to exploratory factor analytic findings for each of the four normative samples; only responses related to the eight specific domains were analyzed. Findings from these analyses yielded a relatively clear eight-factor structure that was replicable across the four groups of students. Except for four subscales (Social Acceptance, Close Friendship, Job Competence, and Behavioral Conduct), all factor loadings exceeded .30, and most (76/80) exceeded .50. Findings revealed the Job Competence (7 loadings <.30; 6 loadings between .30 and .50) and Social Acceptance (3 loadings <.30; 10 loadings between .30 and .50) factors to be the weakest, followed by the Behavioral Conduct (4 loadings <.30; 5 loadings between .30 and .50)[11] and Close Friendship (3 loadings <.30; 4 loadings between .30 and .50) factors. In the table reporting these results, Harter (1988c) noted that one item belonging to the Close Friendship subscale and two belonging to the Behavioral Conduct subscale were subsequently revised.

Reporting factor intercorrelations across the four samples, Harter (1988c) drew attention to several interesting patterns that are very similar to those reported for the SPPC. First, Scholastic Competence was found to be moderately related to Behavioral Conduct (mean r = .43), thereby suggesting that adolescents who perceive themselves as doing well in school also consider themselves to be well-behaved. Second, the three specific domains, Social Acceptance, Romantic Appeal, and Phys-

---

10. This subscale was not administered to Sample A.
11. Results are not reported for Sample D.

ical Appearance tended to cluster as moderately related constructs (mean $r = .47$). These findings suggest that physical attractiveness may lead to greater acceptance or popularity among one's peers and, ultimately, to greater perceived romantic appeal; they are also consistent with the inability of self-concept hierarchies to distinguish second-order social and physical factors (see Marsh, 1987b; Vispoel, 1995c). Third, Harter (1988c) noted that whereas Scholastic Competence was found to be fairly highly correlated (mean $r = .54$) with Social Acceptance for younger children (Grades 3 and 4), the relation was much weaker for adolescents (mean $r = .29$). Finally, across all samples, and in keeping with findings for preadolescents, Physical Appearance was found to be the specific domain that correlated the highest with Global Self-Worth (mean $r = .69$).

Related Psychometric Research

I am aware of no additionally reported psychometric research related either to the SPPA or to its Importance Rating scale.

Evaluation Summary

The SPPA is a relatively new instrument; thus, more time is needed to collect data and test for its psychometric soundness as a measure of multidimensional self-concepts for adolescents. Nonetheless, the instrument is grounded in the same solid theoretical base as its companion scale, the SPPC. Therefore, although information related to the validity of SPPA responses is sparse at this time, I have full confidence that the scale will quickly prove to be an important and well-established self-concept measure for this population. For this reason then, despite its short life span, the SPPA is included in this volume because of its strong theoretical foundation and because of the established construct validity of its companion instrument, from which six of its nine subscales were derived. In the work of establishing the psychometric soundness of the SPPA, however, I encourage the author, and others, to use various confirmatory factor analytic strategies in testing for both the validity and invariance of its factorial structure and for evidence of convergent, criterion-related, and discriminant validity. Indeed, this call is facilitated by Harter's (1988c, p. 5) gracious generosity to interested researchers in granting permission to copy the instrument for their own purposes.

Source Information

Location: Susan Harter, University of Denver, Department of Psychology, 2155 South Race Street, Denver, Colorado 80208-0204

Cost: Manual $15.00

Tennessee Self-Concept Scale

Description

The Tennessee Self-Concept Scale (TSCS; Roid & Fitts, 1988/1994), despite the complexity of its structure and history of controversial reviews over the years, continues to be one of the most popularly used personality instruments and is, by far, the most widely used self-concept measure (Marsh & Richards, 1988b). In developing the original version of the TSCS, Fitts (1965) wanted the instrument to be (a) easily completed by the respondent, (b) appropriate for use with a wide range of age groups and across a variety of settings, and (c) multidimensional in its description of self-concept (Roid & Fitts, 1988/1994). With respect to this last criterion, and in contrast to other instruments of its vintage, the TSCS was certainly ahead of its time in its postulated multifaceted structure of self-concept. Overall, the intent was to develop a self-concept scale that could serve as a common thread for tying together findings derived from research as well as from applied clinical settings.

As noted in chapter 1, the structure of the TSCS exemplifies the taxonomic model. As such, the instrument was originally designed as a 5 (external frame of reference) $\times$ 3 (internal frame of reference) $\times$ 2 (positively versus negatively worded items) facet design (Marsh & Richards, 1988b). The five external scales represent physical, moral–ethical, personal, family, and social self-concepts; they are akin to similar constructs measured by other multidimensional self-concept scales. The internal scales represent identity (the private internal self), behavior (a manifestation of the self that is observable to others), and satisfaction (a reflection of actual–ideal discrepancy; Marsh & Richards, 1988b). The third facet (positive/negative items), applicable only with use of the Clinical and Research Form, was intended as a check for various response biases, albeit Fitts (1965) suggested that any discrepancy in this regard may represent psychological conflict. Two forms of the TSCS are available: (a) a Counseling Form and (b) a Clinical and Research Form. The Counseling Form provides scores for the five external and three internal dimensions, a self-criticism score, four variability scores, and a time score (13 scores in total, not counting the Self-Criticism subscale). The information provided for the Clinical and Research Form is the same as for the Counseling Form, but in addition, it provides more detailed variability scores, additional lie and faking scores, and a number of empirically derived scores found to separate various comparative clinical and nonclinical groups (29 scores in total).

The 1988/1994 revision of the TSCS and its related materials differ from the original in several ways. First, the instrument now includes five supplementary scales; these include a new validity scale, three indexes of personality integration and self-actualization, and measures of psychological harmony. However, Roid and Fitts (1988/1994) noted that these scales are more appropriate for use with individuals 19 years of age or older. Second, the publisher provides improved hand-scoring answer sheets and a new computerized scoring and interpretation service. Third, the revised manual (Roid & Fitts, 1988/1994) now includes normative data for adolescents. Finally, the revised manual, in addressing previous negative reviews, includes substantially more information related to the reliability and validity of the scale (Archambault, 1992; Dowd, 1992).

Target Population

Roid and Fitts (1988/1994) advised that the TSCS is appropriate for use with individuals who are 13 years of age or older and who are capable of reading at approximately a Grade 4 level or higher. The instrument is applicable to the full range of psychological adjustment, from healthy, well-adjusted individuals to those identified as psychotic.

Scale Structure

The TSCS is composed of 100 self-descriptive statements, 10 of which are used to measure Self-Criticism, a factor that serves the purpose of a lie scale. The remaining 90 items tap perceptions of the self from two vantage points—an internal frame of reference and an external frame of reference; each represents the juncture of one dimension of the external facet and one of the internal facet. In other words, each item taps one aspect of the external perspective, as manifested in one aspect of the internal perspective. Items are structured on a 5-point Likert-type scale format ranging from 1 (*completely false*) to 5 (*completely true*), with half of the items in each subscale being worded in the negative direction.

Items constituting the TSCS internal-frame-of-reference component are designed to tap three aspects of an individual's personal perception of self: identity, self-satisfaction, and behavior. The Identity facet represents the private, internal self-concept that essentially taps the "what I am" aspect of the self. The Self-Satisfaction facet is derived from items that tap the extent to which the individual feels satisfied with his or her self-image, or the "how acceptable I am" aspect; as such, scores on this dimension reflect an actual–ideal discrepancy (Marsh & Richards, 1988b). Finally, the Behavior facet taps into the "what I do" and "how I act" aspect of the self-concept, thereby representing the manifestation of self that is observable to others (Marsh & Richards, 1988b).

The TSCS external-frame-of-reference facet reflects how an individual uses outside sources in forming his or her perceptions of self. As such, Marsh and Richards (1988b) suggested that the five dimensions constituting this module are similar to the constructs posited on other multidimensional measures of self-concept. The five dimensions are (a) Physical Self—perception of one's physical appearance, body build, state of health, skills, and sexuality; (b) Moral–Ethical Self—perceptions of one's moral worth, relationship to God, self as a "good" or "bad" person, and satisfaction with one's religion or lack of it; (c) Personal Self—perception of one's personal worth, sense of adequacy as a person, and personality, separate and apart from the body or relationships with others; (d) Family Self—perception of one's sense of adequacy, worth, and value as a family member; and (e) Social Self—perception of one's sense of adequacy and worth with respect to his or her social interaction with others.

Finally, items on the Self-Criticism scale represent mildly derogatory statements, or "common frailties," as Roid and Fitts (1994, p. 3) refer to them, that most people would freely disclose when responding candidly. Whereas high scores on this subscale are indicative of a healthy openness and capacity for criticism, low scores suggest that other TSCS scores may be spuriously high as a consequence of a defensiveness on the part of the respondent to present himself or herself in a positive light. On the other hand, Roid and Fitts noted that an extremely high Self-Criticism score (i.e., above the 99th percentile) indicates that the respondent may be totally lacking in defenses and, in fact, may be pathologically undefended.

To illustrate how TSCS items represent the juncture of both the external and internal frames of reference, three sample items representing the external facet are presented in Exhibit 6.7. The first item taps perception of one's social self with respect to the Identity dimension of the internal facet; the second, with respect to the Self-Satisfaction dimension; and the third, with respect to the Behavior dimension.

As noted earlier, the 1994 version of the TSCS also includes five supplementary scales available only for the Clinical and Research Form. These are as follows: (a) The Stanwyck–Garrison Faking Good Scale (Stanwyck & Garrison, 1982), a 9-item validity scale for normal, highly

Exhibit 6.7

Sample Items From the Tennessee Self-Concept Scale

Completely False	Mostly False	Partly False and Partly True	Mostly True	Completely True
1	2	3	4	5

I am a friendly person ....   _____

I am as sociable as I want to be ....   _____

I get along well with other people ....   _____

verbal respondents; high scores indicate a possibly invalid protocol. (b) The Seeman Personality Integration Index (Seeman, 1966), which when applied to particular scores on the TSCS, yields a measure of adaptive functioning; this index has been shown empirically to discriminate between individuals identified as clinically well-adjusted and those identified as falling in the range from normal to pathological. High scores indicate a well-adjusted, highly functioning person. (c) The Number of Integrative Signs (Fitts, 1972 [cited in Roid & Fitts, 1994]), used to identify highly functioning individuals; this index is determined in conjunction with particular TSCS scores and measures the number of positive assets. (d) The Self-Actualization Index (Fitts, 1972 [cited in Roid & Fitts, 1994]), used in identifying self-actualized individuals. As with Fitts's previous measure, this index is based on particular TSCS scores. (e) The Physical Harmony Index (no author was referenced in Roid & Fitts, 1994); this index, also calculated from specific TSCS scores, measures the presence of consistency versus dissonance or discomfort within the respondent's perception of self. High scores are indicative of a positive self-concept with absence of conflict or variability. For further details regarding these five scales, see the most recent edition of the manual (Roid & Fitts, 1994).

Administration and Scoring

The TSCS can be administered either individually or in groups. Roid and Fitts (1994) contended that because little explanation is needed beyond that which is provided in the test instructions, the instrument is essentially self-administered. Typically, completion of the TSCS requires 10 to 20 min, with the average time approximating 13 min.

Although two versions of the TSCS are available—one that is hand scorable and one that is computer scorable—both versions use exactly the same items (albeit in a different order). One difference between the two versions is that the one that is hand scorable can be profiled in two ways: (a) using the Counseling Form and (b) using the Clinical and Research Form.

As noted in the Description section, the Counseling Form provides scores for 13 basic scales (excluding the Self-Criticism subscale). Because the Counseling Form involves fewer scales, it can be scored in approximately 6 to 7 min. Furthermore, Roid and Fitts (1994) suggested that examiners do not need an extensive background in psychometric or psychopathology to interpret the Counseling Form results; these results can also be discussed with the respondents. The Clinical and Research Form yields the same 14 scores as the Counseling Form, with an additional 15 scores that can be used in research and clinical settings. In contrast to the Counseling Form, however, this version is much more complex in terms of scoring, analysis, and interpretation. The Clinical and Research Form requires approximately 30 min to score and is inappropriate for use as direct feedback to the respondent. Finally, the computer-scored version provides the same 29 scores yielded by the hand-scored Clinical and Research Form; in addition, however, it furnishes a few supplementary scores, an array of profiles, a full-color plotted graph, interpretive information, and a separate report, written in simplified language, that can be given directly to the respondent.

Normative Data

Samples. The original normative sample comprised 626 respondents representing various geographical areas of the United States. Ages ranged from 12 to 68 years and comprised an approximate balance of males and females, Blacks and Whites, socioeconomic classes, ability levels, and educational levels from the sixth grade through to the doctoral level (Roid & Fitts, 1994). Norms related to this original sample were subsequently tested against a number of other adolescent and adult samples; the latter included college students, working adults, and elderly adults in nursing homes and self-sufficient community residences. Details related to both the original norms and these validation samples are outlined in the TSCS manual.

Of particular import in this chapter are norms related to the adolescent population. In this regard, updated norms relevant to a more contemporary sample were sought for comparison with the previous composite of scores for adolescents, representing a broad spectrum that crossed grade (9 to 12), location (urban and rural), and school type (private and public). Accordingly, Sherman (1983, [cited in Roid & Fitts, 1994]) reported means related to a sample of Los Angeles high school students (N = 495). Findings revealed minimal differences (within 2/10 of a standard deviation) in TSCS scores between the composite of scores based on geographically and demographically diverse samples and the new normative group (Roid & Fitts, 1994).

Selection and Refinement of Items. Development of the TSCS began in 1955, with the original pool of items being derived from several self-concept measures available at that time, as well as from written self-descriptions from both clinical and nonclinical individuals. The development of a phenomenological system for purposes of item classification followed next. This system evolved into the current 3 (internal) $\times$ 5 (external) pattern of scoring. Finally, items were edited and subsequently presented to seven clinical psychologists whose task was to classify all items in keeping with the 3 $\times$ 5 systematic scheme developed by Fitts (1965); each item was also judged as being positive or negative. The 90 items that now constitute the TSCS are those for which the seven judges demonstrated perfect agreement.

Psychometric Properties. Reported psychometric properties for the TSCS, as presented in the revised manual (Roid & Fitts, 1994), are both extensive and very complete. As a consequence, limitations of space preclude their summary here. Because these statistics relate to a variety of populations that involve clinical as well as nonclinical samples, readers are directed to the manual for a more complete review. Of important note, however, is that the authors of the revised manual have taken great pains to address limitations noted by reviewers of the early version of the TSCS. In particular, psychometric properties of the instrument that were either missing or identified as being weak with respect to the previous editions have now been addressed. Thus, most of my discussion here relates to this updated information.

Reliability. Although the manual reports several internal consistency results, two recent studies are of interest here; they essentially reflect findings that are similar to those of the earlier studies. Based on one clinical sample (first offenders in a pretrial diversion program; N = 132) and two college samples (n = 132; n = 138), Tzeng, Maxey, Fortier, and

Landis (1985) reported internal consistency reliability coefficients for 90-, 30-, and 18-item subsets of the TSCS. For each sample, alpha coefficients based on pooled subsets of items exceeded .80; positively and negatively keyed items yielded coefficients ranging from .89 to .94.

More recently, Roid and Fitts (1994) reported internal consistency reliability findings based on a sample of 453 individuals who were subsequently partitioned into an adolescent sample (n = 122) and an adult sample (n = 331). Most coefficient alpha values range from .70 to .87; not surprisingly, estimates were highest for the total score across adolescent (α = .91), adult (α = .94), and total sample (α = .94).

Roid and Fitts (1994) reported test–retest reliability information based on three groups of adolescents (N = 81), one group of college students (N = 38), and three groups of adults (N = 44) over a period of from 2 hr to 10 weeks (Md = 6 weeks); scores for all 29 scales from the Clinical and Research Form of the TSCS were calculated at pretest and posttest. They reported that the average absolute difference (ignoring sign) was .146, or approximately 1/7 of a standard deviation, which Roid and Fitts considered to be minimal.

Validity. Roid and Fitts (1994) reported extremely extensive information bearing on the validity of the TSCS; this includes linkage of the instrument to empirically validated theoretical models of self-concept; confirmatory factor analyses, as well as reviewers' comments regarding exploratory factor analyses; MTMM analyses; and correlations with numerous personality scales. As such, they have addressed previous criticisms related to a lack of theoretical underpinning (Wylie, 1979) and information bearing on the internal structure of the scale (e.g., Bentler, 1972b).

As Roid and Fitts (1994) aptly noted, previous exploratory analyses did much to undermine the validity of the TSCS. Indeed, given the taxonomic structure of the instrument, not only is this mode of factor analysis inappropriate, but most studies have not even taken into account correlations among the factors by using oblique rotation (an unfortunately too common event in the application of factor analysis to psychological assessment scales). The more appropriate approach to validating the TSCS factor structure is the use of confirmatory factor analyses that can allow for the testing of a priori factor structures.

Findings from two early confirmatory factor analytic studies are reported in the manual, both based on the multiple-group-factoring approach. Based on samples of university students (N = 678) and male juvenile offenders (N = 341), B. McGuire and Tinsley (1981) reported sound evidence of three internal and five external factors, albeit no support for the External × Internal cross-classification; no support for the scale was found for the juvenile offenders. In a similar approach, based on a sample of 404 incarcerated men (mean age = 29 years), Walsh, Wilson, and McLellarn (1989) reported substantial support for only one of the internal facets (Identity) and three of the five external facets (Physical Self, Moral-Ethical Self, and Family Self). These results provided stronger support for the TSCS than was evident from the McGuire and Tinsley study.

Related Psychometric Research

Marsh and Richards (1988b) recently conducted a confirmatory factor analysis of the TSCS based on covariance structure modeling. As such, their study was able to test, more rigorously, the factorial structure of the instrument than other previously reported confirmatory factor analytic studies. Overall, the Marsh and Richards (1988b) investigation of the TSCS involved a two-stage strategy. First, exploratory and confirmatory analyses, as well as an ANOVA approach, were used to examine the internal structure of TSCS responses. Second, MTMM analyses were used to examine the convergent and discriminant validity of these responses in relation to those derived from another self-concept measure (the Self Description Questionnaire III; see chapter 7), as well as those from inferred self-concept ratings by external observers. Based on a sample of 343 participants in one of nine Outward Bound courses in Australia, Marsh and Richards reported consistent support for the TSCS external Family, Physical, and Social Self scales but little support for the remaining scales.

Evaluation Summary

The TSCS is a well-established self-concept measure that has been available for at least three decades; one particular strength of the instrument lies in its applicability to clinical samples. Although it has received many critical and negative reviews over the years, the current authors are to be commended for taking positive action to address many of the cited limitations. As noted earlier, many of the comments directed toward the absence of specific psychometric information have been addressed. Furthermore, the publisher is actively seeking additional samples representative of different adolescent and adult groups on which to further test for the validity of TSCS structure. In particular, I am aware of research currently being conducted on samples of individuals aged 65 years and older; unfortunately, I have no information to report at this time. Given the positive approach being taken by both the authors and the publisher toward improving the amount of information available on the TSCS, I feel confident that this instrument can serve the needs of researchers and clinicians well in the measurement of self-concept for diverse clinical and nonclinical populations from adolescence through late adulthood.

Source Information

Location: Western Psychological Services, 12031 Wilshire Boulevard, Los Angeles, California 90025-1251

Cost: Kit: $125.00 (includes 1 manual, 5 reusable test booklets, 10 hand-scored answer-profile sheets, 1 set of hand-scoring keys, and 2 prepaid Test-Report Mail-In Answer Sheets)

Measures of Self-Concept for Adults

7

One anomaly associated with self-concept measures designed for use with adults (20 to 64 years) is that most have been normed on college students. Indeed, of the instruments included in this chapter, all except one (the Adult Self-Perception Profile) were normed on college students; however, Self Description Questionnaire III scores based on noncollege samples have since been tested and found to be valid. In general, instruments designed for use with college students include self-concept facets (e.g., academic self-concept) that may not be relevant to the noncollege adult; by the same token, they often exclude critically relevant facets that relate to one's work environment, family responsibilities, and the like. Thus, there appears to be a genuine need for the development of measuring instruments designed specifically for use with adults who are not affiliated with a university or college on a full-time basis.

With one exception (Eden, 1981), to the best of my knowledge, there are no self-concept self-report measures designed specifically for use with adults 65 years of age and older. It appears that the most common approach to the tapping of self-concepts for the elderly has been the use of interview techniques. However, these measures for the most part are poorly described and provide little to no evidence of construct validity research; where such findings have been reported, they are the product of extremely weak and poorly conducted analytic work. As a consequence of this state of affairs, and because I sincerely wanted to be able to provide readers with at least one self-concept measure appropriate for use with the senior population, I have made an exception and included an interview-type instrument (the Self-Perception Genesis Method).

Of the 23 adult self-concept self-report measures reviewed, 6 are described in this chapter; all represent multidimensional scales. One instrument measures academic self-concept (Dimensions of Self-Concept [Form H]), two measure physical self-concept (Body Esteem Scale and Physical Self-Perception Profile), and the remaining three measure multiple domain-specific self-concepts, in addition to a separate facet of general (i.e., global) self-concept. We turn first to the measure of academic self-concept for college students.

EARLY TO LATE ADULTHOOD (20–64 YEARS)

Measurement of Single Self-Concept Domains

ACADEMIC SELF-CONCEPT

Dimensions of Self-Concept (Form H)

Description
The Dimensions of Self-Concept scale (Form H, DOSC/H, Michael et al., 1984) is a self-report scale designed to measure multiple noncognitive factors associated with academic self-concept related to college and university settings. As with the DOSC/S, each item of the DOSC/H taps either an activity or an attitude related to various school-learning situations or environments, and the purposes are twofold: (a) to identify students with low levels of self-esteem, in relation to the educative environment, who may ultimately experience difficulty in their schoolwork and (b) to diagnose, for purposes of counseling, the areas and related activities believed to be contributing to the low self-esteem scores (i.e., scores falling below average—possibly in the bottom third of the score distribution [Michael et al., 1989]).

Although the DOSC manual does not explicitly link the instrument to a particular theoretical model of self-concept, I consider it to be most closely affiliated with the nomothetic model of self-concept described in chapter 1.

Target Population

The DOSC/H is appropriate for use with college and university students.

Scale Structure

The DOSC/H (Michael et al., 1984) is a five-dimensional, 80-item instrument based on a 5-point Likert-type scale format; each subscale is composed of 16 items. The five measured dimensions of noncognitive academic self-concept are the same as those described in chapter 6 for the DOSC/S; they are as follows:

1. Level of Aspiration, a reflection of behavior patterns indicative of the extent to which academic performance and activities are in keeping with a person's perceptions of their scholastic potentialities
2. Anxiety, a reflection of behavior patterns and perceptions associated with emotional instability, lack of objectivity, and exaggerated concern with respect to tests and self-esteem preservation in relation to academic performance
3. Academic Interest and Satisfaction, reflective of the degree of intrinsic motivation and love of learning for its own sake that students derive from their academic work
4. Leadership and Initiative, reflective of behavior patterns and perceptions associated with mastery of knowledge and skills in a particular area, with the ability and willingness to guide others in attaining the same level of mastery
5. Identification Versus Alienation, reflective of the extent to which a student feels accepted and respected, as opposed to isolated and rejected, by his or her teachers and peers

A sample item from the Leadership and Initiative subscale of the DOSC/H is presented in Exhibit 7.1.

Administration and Scoring

The DOSC/H can be administered individually or in groups. Subjects are asked to respond to simple declarative statements by filling in the circle representing the one alternative of five that they believe best describes them (see Exhibit 7.1). Although the instructions are self-explanatory, examiners are advised to demonstrate the respondence procedure based on an illustrative statement other than the ones contained in the questionnaire. The authors suggest that typically 15 to 35 min are required for completion of the answer sheet.

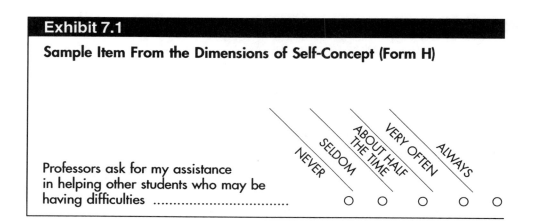

Exhibit 7.1

Sample Item From the Dimensions of Self-Concept (Form H)

Professors ask for my assistance
in helping other students who may be
having difficulties ....   NEVER SELDOM ABOUT HALF THE TIME VERY OFTEN ALWAYS
                                                       ○   ○   ○   ○   ○

Scoring of the DOSC/H can be performed either manually or by returning completed forms to the publisher for machine scoring. As noted earlier in the description of the scale structure, five different weights are assigned to the response alternatives for each item. As such, the manual scoring of subscale scores is easily accomplished by adding the selected response weights associated with all items constituting a particular subscale. Negative items, of course, must be reversed in order that high scores represent high levels of academic self-concept.

Normative Data

Samples. Initial testing of the DOSC/H was based on two independent samples (N_1 = 189, N_2 = 208) of daytime community college students from Los Angeles suburban campuses (Michael et al., 1984).

Selection and Refinement of Items. The DOSC/H was initially structured with 25 items in each of the five subscales and used with Sample 1 noted earlier; after a review of reliability coefficients related to this form, 5 items from each subscale were deleted, and the resulting five 20-item subscales were administered to Sample 2. Subsequent to findings related to the Sample 2 study, the instrument was eventually trimmed to the 16-item subscales consistent with its present form.

Psychometric Properties. Reliability. Michael et al. (1984) reported internal reliability coefficients of the DOSC/H to range from .85 to .90 (M = .88) for Sample 1 of the normative group of community college students and from .83 to .91 (M = .86) for Sample 2. Although no additional reliability data were reported for the normative sample, subsequent studies have yielded information that is reported below.

Validity. In keeping with earlier research bearing on the DOSC/S, Halote and Michael (1984) sought evidence of concurrent validity by correlating the noncognitive academic self-concept subscales of the DOSC/H and academic performance—as represented by (a) average or typical high school grade (i.e., mark), (b) academic rank in high school, (c) estimated college grade point average (GPA) to date, and (d) estimated future grade in tested class—for a sample of 202 community college students. Reported findings revealed little to no relation between the DOSC/H and indicators of academic performance in high school; only relations with estimated college academic performance were significant. Of these, scores from the Level of Aspiration subscale exhibited the highest level of convergent validity ($r = .40$, $r = .38$), followed by the Leadership and Initiative ($r = .34$, $r = .24$) subscale. In a similar study based on 239 undergraduate students, Caracosta and Michael (1986) examined correlations between the DOSC/H subscales and three measures: anticipated overall GPA to be earned, grade earned in class in which DOSC/H was administered, and high school GPA as recalled. Again, correlations with the high school indicator were negligible, and the Level of Aspiration and Leadership and Initiative subscales demonstrated the highest validity coefficients ($r = .32$, $r = .32$; $r = .27$, $r = .27$, respectively).

On the basis of these convergent validity findings, Halote and Michael (1984) argued for the potential promise of the Level of Aspiration subscale as an important predictor of college achievement. To date, however, no evidence in support of this postulation appears to have been reported in the literature.

As was the case for the DOSC/S, reported evidence of construct validity for the DOSC/H has been grounded in findings derived solely from exploratory factor analyses. Based on at least three such studies (Caracosta & Michael, 1986; Halote & Michael, 1984; Michael, Denny, Ireland-Galman, & Michael, 1986–1987), results support a relatively clean and adequately strong five-factor structure. Curiously, however, in each case, the authors used varimax rotation procedures. Nonetheless, given the strength of factor correlations reported in each of the mentioned studies (range = $-.26$ to $.63$, median $r = .30$; range = $-.13$ to $.63$, median $r = .41$; range = $-.26$ to $.62$, median $r = .34$, respectively), it would be more appropriate to base the final solution on oblique rotational procedures. Indeed, this approach would quite likely improve both the size and clarity of the factor loadings.

Related Psychometric Research

As a follow-up to previous testing of the DOSC/H, two subsequent studies have reported on the internal reliability of the instrument. One of these studies examined data from 239 undergraduate students at a private university (Caracosta & Michael, 1986) and reported internal reliability values ranging from .86 to .88 (M = .86); the other examined data from 181 community college students (Michael et al., 1986–1987) and reported values ranging from .85 to .90 (M = .88).

Evaluation Summary

The DOSC/H is unique in its measurement of multidimensional non-cognitive academic self-concepts for college students. Although the authors have reported important construct validity information related to the instrument, it is hoped that they will continue to seek further evidence in this regard. In particular, the instrument could benefit from a more rigorous testing of its factorial structure, based on the analysis of covariance structures within the frameworks of both confirmatory factor analytic and MTMM models. As such, a more powerful test of both its hypothesized factor structure and convergent and discriminant validities could be ascertained. Additionally, the authors need to provide evidence in support of the test–retest reliability of the DOSC/H, as well as substantially stronger evidence in support of its criterion validity. Finally, to the best of my knowledge and as noted with the secondary school version of the instrument (DOSC/S), virtually all psychometric investigations of the DOSC/H have been conducted by Michael and his colleagues. Researchers, other than those directly associated with the test authors, are encouraged to test for and report findings from construct validity research related to the DOSC/H. Indeed, such information would be extremely valuable in further establishing the soundness of the instrument for use in college settings.

Source Information

Location: Edits, P.O. Box 7234, San Diego, California 92167

Cost: Manual: $3.25
          Test forms: $8.75/pkg 25; $31.25/pkg 100; $117.00/pkg 500
          Specimen set: $6.25

PHYSICAL SELF-CONCEPT

Body Esteem Scale

Description

The Body Esteem Scale (BES; Franzoi & Shields, 1984) is designed to measure multidimensions of body esteem separately for men and women. Essentially, the general framework and rationale underlying the BES flows from its predecessor, the Body-Cathexis Scale (Secord & Jourard, 1953), an instrument that has been widely used in studies of body attributes for clinical as well as nonclinical samples (C. D. Thomas & Freeman, 1990). *Body-cathexis*, the extent to which individuals feel satisfied or dissatisfied with various parts or processes of their body (Secord & Jourard, 1953), was measured as a unidimensional construct in the initial scale; respondents rated 40 body parts and functions on a 5-point Likert-type scale, with higher scores representing higher satisfaction with one's body.

Based on findings that identified three gender-specific factors, derived from factor analyses of the Body-Cathexis Scale conducted separately for male ($n = 257$) and female ($n = 366$) college students, Franzoi and Shields (1984) determined that body esteem is more appropriately measured as a multidimensional construct that takes gender specificity into account. To address this concern, Franzoi and Shields (1984) subsequently developed the BES.

Although the authors do not explicitly link the BES to a particular model of self-concept, I consider it to be most closely affiliated with the correlated-factor model described in chapter 1.

Target Population

On the basis of research findings related to the BES to date, the instrument appears to be most aptly used with young adult populations. Although Franzoi and Shields (1984) noted that their original normative sample included a few older adults, they pointed to the need for specific norms in relation to a range of adult age groups.

Scale Structure

The BES (Franzoi & Shields, 1984) is a gender-specific three-dimensional, 35-item instrument that is structured on a 5-point Likert-scale format, with scores of 1 and 5 representing strong negative and strong positive feelings, respectively. On the basis of their early factor analytic work with the Body-Cathexis Scale, Franzoi and Shields determined that whereas body esteem represented attitudes toward physical attractiveness, upper body strength, and physical condition for men, it represented attitudes toward sexual attractiveness, weight concern, and physical condition for women.

In structuring the BES, Franzoi and Shields (1984) took these gender differences into account; thus, interpretation and scoring of the scale must be consistent with the gender of the respondent. For men, the Physical Attractiveness subscale taps attitudes bearing on their facial features, as well as aspects of their physique that in some way act as determinants of the extent to which they are judged as handsome or good-looking. The Upper-Body Strength subscale measures attitudes toward men's upper body, an aspect of their body that can be improved through specific kinds of anaerobic exercise (e.g., weight lifting) and that culturally has been equated with manly vigor and power. Finally, the Physical Condition subscale assesses perceptions of stamina, agility, and general strength.

For women, the Sexual Attractiveness subscale taps attitudes toward body parts and functions linked to facial attractiveness and sexuality. Although the Weight Concern subscale also elicits responses reflective of physical appearance, it focuses more on the measurement of attitudes toward body parts that can be physically altered by controlling food intake and toward body functions associated with food intake. Finally, the Physical Condition subscale taps attitudes toward stamina, strength, and agility.

Presented with a list of body parts and functions, respondents are asked to indicate how they feel about each, with respect to their own body, by rating each according to a 5-point scale. A sample block of eight items is shown in Exhibit 7.2.

Administration and Scoring

The BES can be administered either individually or in a group. Scoring of the scale is very easy and simply requires the addition of all items

---

Exhibit 7.2

Sample Items From the Body Esteem Scale

1 = Have strong negative feelings
2 = Have moderate negative feelings
3 = Have no feeling one way or the other
4 = Have moderate positive feelings
5 = Have strong positive feelings

_____ 1. body scent
_____ 2. appetite
_____ 3. nose
_____ 4. physical stamina

_____ 19. arms
_____ 20. chest or breasts
_____ 21. appearance of eyes
_____ 22. cheeks/cheekbones

deemed to represent each subscale, specific to men or women. For example, in tabulating a Physical Condition subscale score for women, the following items would be added: physical stamina, reflexes, muscular strength, energy level, biceps, physical coordination, agility, health, and physical condition. Tabulation of this subscale score for men would include a summation of appetite, physical stamina, reflexes, waist, energy level, thighs, physical coordination, agility, figure or physique, appearance of stomach, health, physical condition, and weight.

Normative Data

Samples. Initial testing of the BES was based on a sample of undergraduate male ($n = 331$) and female ($n = 633$) university students at the University of California at Davis (Franzoi & Shields, 1984).

Selection and Refinement of Items. As noted earlier, construction of the BES began with a factor analytic study of its predecessor, the Body-Cathexis Scale (Secord & Jourard, 1953), using data from 623 undergraduate university students. On the basis of the results of this study, Franzoi and Shields (1984) subsequently deleted all items that yielded low factor loadings (<.35) and added new items whose content they deemed to be relevant to the three extracted factors for men and women. The resulting BES was composed of 23 items from the Body-Cathexis Scale and 16 new items. This new 39-item scale was then administered to a second independent sample of male ($n = 182$) and female ($n = 301$) undergraduate students. Presented with findings of low factor loadings for 4 items, the authors subsequently deleted these items, which thus resulted in the present 35-item BES.

Psychometric Properties. Reliability. Franzoi and Shields (1984) reported internal reliability coefficients of the BES for each of the three subscales across gender. For men, coefficient alphas ranged from .81 (Physical Attractiveness) to .86 (Physical Condition; mean $\alpha = .84$); for women, they ranged from .78 (Sexual Attractiveness) to .87 (Weight Concern; mean $\alpha = .82$). Although not reported for the normative sample, Franzoi (1994) recently reported test–retest reliability results for a sample of undergraduate college students. This information is reported below.

Validity. To provide an estimate of convergent validity, Franzoi and Shields (1984) correlated scores from the BES with the Rosenberg (1965) Self-Esteem Scale for 44 male and 78 female undergraduate students. They reported correlations of .50, .45, and .51 for men, with respect to the Physical Attractiveness, Upper-Body Strength, and Physical Condition subscales, respectively; for women, the correlations were .32, .19, and .35 for the Sexual Attractiveness, Weight Concern, and Physical Condition subscales, respectively.

On the basis of findings from a discriminant function analysis that showed only the Weight Concern subscale of the BES to discriminate significantly between women diagnosed as either anorexic or nonanorexic and the Upper-Body Strength subscale to discriminate significantly between male weight lifters and non–weight lifters, Franzoi and Shields (1984) argued for some evidence of discriminant validity.

Evidence of construct validity for the BES is basically limited to the original factor analytic study of the instrument. On the basis of a principal components analysis with oblique rotation, Franzoi and Shields (1984) argued for three relatively distinct factors for both men and women, albeit the items loaded differently for each sex; only two items for men loaded on multiple factors. All items for both men and women loaded greater than .35 on their target factors (i.e., the factor they were designed to measure).

Related Psychometric Research

Findings from three additional studies have provided further support for the psychometric adequacy of the BES as a measure of attitudes toward different dimensions of male and female body esteem. First, on the basis of a sample of 150 male and 193 female undergraduate students, Franzoi and Herzog (1986) determined further evidence of its convergent and discriminant validity. They again found significant positive relations between the Rosenberg (1965) Self-Esteem Scale and each of the BES subscales; values ranged from .26 (Physical Attractiveness) to .40 (Physical Condition; mean r = .30) for men and from .21 (Sexual Attractiveness) to .39 (Physical Condition; mean r = .32) for women. Additionally, for both men and women, Franzoi and Herzog reported expected correlations between particular BES subscales and those of the Consciousness Questionnaire (Miller, Murphy, & Buss, 1981), as well as several questions pertaining to exercise, food intake, and attractiveness. Finally, on the basis of a second study of 63 male and 92 female undergraduate students, Franzoi and Herzog tested relations between the male Physical Attractiveness and female Sexual Attractiveness subscales of the BES and subjects' evaluations of their overall attractiveness. Surprisingly, no substantial correlation was found for men. On the basis of findings from this study, Franzoi and Herzog concluded that except for the Physical Attractiveness subscale for men, the remaining five dimensions of the BES demonstrated relatively good evidence of convergent and discriminant validity.

In a more recent study of the convergent and discriminant validity of the BES subscales for females, C. D. Thomas and Freeman (1990) tested relations between body dimensions measured by these scales and by the Eating Disorder Inventory (Garner, Olmstead, & Polivy, 1983), the Self-Consciousness Scale (Fenigstein, Scheier, & Buss, 1975), the Tennessee Self-Concept Scale (Fitts, 1965), a figure-rating task (Stunkard, Sorenson, & Schulsinger, 1983), a phototechnical body-size estimation procedure (Freeman, Thomas, Solyom, & Hunter, 1984), and items tapping weight satisfaction and attractiveness in a sample of female student volunteers from one Canadian university ($N = 200$; mean age = 27.6 years). They determined that whereas the BES Weight Concern subscale was most highly related to weight variables and other body-image measures, the Sexual Attractiveness and Physical Condition subscales were more strongly correlated with less specific self-perceptions and attitudes. On the basis of their findings, Thomas and Freeman concluded that the construct validity of the BES female subscales had been supported.

Finally, addressing concerns expressed by both Blascovich and Tomaka (1991) and Wylie (1989) concerning the lack of information related to both the stability and social desirability of the BES, Franzoi (1994) recently investigated both of these issues with 73 male and 145 female undergraduate students. On the basis of a time span of 3 months, he reported high test–retest reliability for each of the male and female scales. Estimates ranged from .58 (Physical Attractiveness) to .83 (Physical Condition; $r = .72$) for men and from .75 (Physical Condition) to .87 (Weight Concern; mean $r = .81$) for women. Tests of socially desirable responding, based on scores from the Self-Presentation Scale (Roth, Snyder, & Pace, 1986), revealed the BES not to be susceptible to denial of negative self-attitudes responding (as measured by the Denial subscale) and only slightly susceptible to positive self-attitudes responding (as measured by the Attribution subscale). Franzoi argued for continued support of the BES as a reliable and valid measure of body esteem.

Evaluation Summary

Given both the incidence and heightened awareness of eating and other body-image disorders, the BES would appear to be a potentially important instrument for use by both practitioners and researchers whose

concerns focus on populations at risk for these psychological disturbances. Although the instrument is slowly gathering support for the
construct validity of both its male and female scales, substantially more
evidence of construct validity is needed before it can be firmly established as a psychometrically sound scale. In particular, the BES could
benefit from rigorous construct validity research designed within the
framework of confirmatory factor analytic models; these can include
tests of both the validity and invariance of its dimensional structure
across various age populations, as well as tests of the convergent and
discriminant validity of its subscales through MTMM analyses. Additionally, evidence of the convergent validity of the BES can (and should)
be made stronger by testing relations between its scales and those of
other instruments designed to measure physical rather than general
self-concept (see, e.g., the Physical Self-Perception Profile, this chapter);
indeed, given our present knowledge of the hierarchical structure of
self-concept, it is evident that examining relations between the BES
subscales and measures of general self-concept, as has been done in the
past, provides a relatively weak test of convergent validity (see also Wylie,
1989). Overall, however, although the BES is still in need of strong
construct validation research, it nonetheless represents a potentially valuable measure of body esteem. My suggestions here, then, are given
with a view to making a very worthwhile and potentially sound instrument even better.

Source Information

Location: Stephen L. Franzoi, Department of Psychology, Marquette
University, Milwaukee, Wisconsin 53233

Cost: No manual presently available. However, Dr. Franzoi has recommended that interested users write to him for updated
information.

Physical Self-Perception Profile

Description

The Physical Self-Perception Profile (PSPP; Fox & Corbin, 1989) is designed to measure self-perceptions related to four specific subdomains
and one global domain of physical competence. In contrast to the Body
Esteem Scale, the PSPP focuses on perceived competence, rather than
self-acceptance, as it relates to physical self-esteem (Sonstroem, Speli-

otis, & Fava, 1992).[1] The instrument is strongly linked to both the Shav-elson et al. (1976) hierarchical model of self-concept and the Harter (1985b) methodology of scale construction. As a consequence, the PSPP is a theoretically and psychometrically well-developed assessment mea-sure that allows for testing of both the multidimensionality and hier-archical structure of physical self-concept.

In developing the PSPP, Fox and Corbin (1989) were guided by the desire to produce a theoretically grounded instrument that could measure, simultaneously, multiple facets of the physical self. They con-tended that such a measure would then facilitate much needed insight into the mechanisms of self-esteem change through exercise, as well as a more comprehensive appraisal of postulated models that include self-perception as a factor in exercise choice and persistence. Furthermore, Fox and Corbin believed that given the availability of a theoretically and psychometrically sound measuring instrument, researchers could then test for potentially important antecedent variables in the development of physical self-concept.

In keeping with the Self-Perception Profiles developed by Harter and colleagues, the PSPP is accompanied by an importance-rating scale, which Fox (1990) labeled the Perceived Importance Profile (PIP). This scale was developed concurrently with the PSPP and comprises four 2-item subscales, with each pair tapping perception of importance in re-lation to one of the four domain-specific subscales. The scale formats of the PSPP and the PIP are identical; four of the eight items are worded in the negative direction.

Target Population

Although the PSPP was originally normed on university students, the instrument has also demonstrated strong evidence of reliability and va-lidity with adults in the middle and later years (see, e.g., Sonstroem, Harlow, & Josephs, 1994; Sonstroem et al., 1992).

Scale Structure

The PSPP is a 30-item self-report instrument comprising four domain-specific subscales that measure perceived sport competence, body at-tractiveness, physical strength, and physical condition and one subscale that taps a global perception of overall physical competence (Physical Self-Worth). To offset socially desirable responding, the item-response

---

1. As noted by Sonstroem et al. (1992), some theorists (e.g., S. Epstein, 1973; Harter, 1983) consider self-esteem to consist of at least two dimensions: competence and self-acceptance.

format is patterned after that used in the Harter scales and, thus, each is written as a 4-point structured alternative; 6 items constitute each subscale. One sample item from each of the Physical Strength and Physical Self-Worth subscales, respectively, is presented in Exhibit 7.3.

Administration and Scoring

Development of the PSPP has been geared to administration with large groups. In reacting to each item statement, respondents are asked to first decide whether they are like the person described on the left side of the page or like the person described on the right side of the page. Having made this decision, they then decide whether the statement is really true for them or just sort of true for them; they indicate their preference by checking the appropriate box accompanying each item. Several pilot tests of the PSPP led to its present set of instructions. Although he designed the PSPP as a self-explanatory instrument, Fox (1990) advised that instructions for the instrument's completion be read aloud to the group as a whole, with elaboration as required, to clarify any confusion regarding this process. Indeed, Fox noted that even with college students, he found a 2%–4% error rate in their marking of the box most appropriate for their determined response.

Scoring the PSPP is simply a matter of adding the scores of all items that constitute each subscale; negative items, of course, require reversal so that high scores reflect high self-concept. A manual scoring sheet and an SPSS–X (SPSS, 1988) input file for computerized scoring is provided in the manual (Fox, 1990) for both the PSPP and the PIP. In addition, instructions for the computation of discrepancy scores are provided.

Normative Data

Samples. Initial testing of the PSPP was based on four independent samples of undergraduate students that yielded a total of 1,191 subjects. Three samples represented students at a university in northern Illinois ($n = 234$, $n = 355$, and $n = 377$); the other one represented students at a college in Missouri ($n = 225$). Fox (1990) reported mean ages of 19.7 and 23.2 years for the Illinois and Missouri participants, respectively. For purposes of comparison, Fox also reported on tests of the PSPP with a sample of obese adults ($n = 558$; mean age = 41.7 years) who were in the process of enrolling for treatment for their medical condition.

Selection and Refinement of Items. Selection of PSPP subscale domains, and their related items, was determined through a three-stage

Exhibit 7.3

Sample Items From the Physical Self-Perception Profile

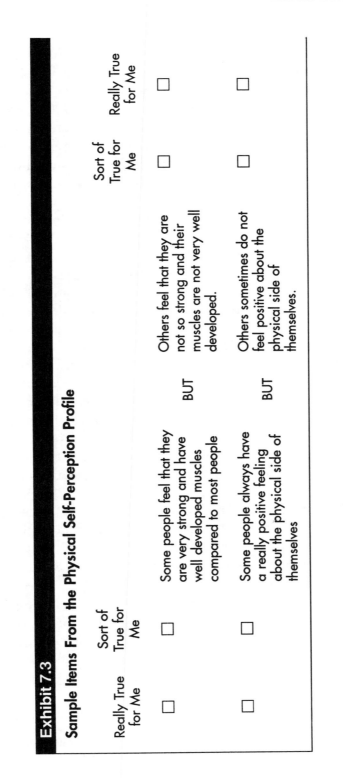

Really True for Me	Sort of True for Me				Sort of True for Me	Really True for Me
☐	☐	Some people feel that they are very strong and have well developed muscles compared to most people	BUT	Others feel that they are not so strong and their muscles are not very well developed.	☐	☐
☐	☐	Some people always have a really positive feeling about the physical side of themselves	BUT	Others sometimes do not feel positive about the physical side of themselves.	☐	☐

process. Stage 1 involved the identification of salient physical self-domains. On the basis of findings from a content validity analysis of open-ended questionnaire responses by 143 college students (63 men and 80 women), Fox and Corbin (1989) determined four subdomains to be salient for the initial profile: perceived body attractiveness, sports competence, physical strength, and exercise and fitness. Stage 2 focused on construction of the PSPP. Paralleling the scale construction work of Harter (see this volume), instrument subscales were formulated, with each comprising six items designed in a four-choice structured-alternative format. This initial version of the PSPP included four physical self-perception subscales, in addition to a global Physical Self-Worth subscale.[2] Finally, in Stage 3, PSPP scores were subjected to a series of item analyses, factor analyses, and psychometric analyses to determine their internal consistency and test–retest reliability estimates; the tendency of PSPP items to evoke socially desirable responding was also tested (see below). On the basis of three independent samples of college students ($n = 151$, $n = 128$, and $n = 90$), findings from these studies guided item modification and led ultimately to a finely tuned PSPP that was subsequently used (a) to generate the normative data and (b) to initiate testing for the construct validity of the instrument.

Psychometric Properties. *Reliability.* On the basis of two independent samples of college students ($N = 234$ and $N = 355$), Fox (1990) reported internal reliability coefficients for each of the five PSPP subscales across gender. For men, coefficient alpha values ranged from .80 (Physical Self-Worth) to .92 (Sports Competence; mean $\alpha = .87$); for women, they ranged from .82 (Physical Strength) to .89 (Sports Competence; mean $\alpha = .86$).[3] Test–retest reliabilities based on a third independent sample have also been reported over 16-day ($n = 40$) and 23-day ($n = 36$) periods. These estimates ranged from .74 (Physical Self-Worth) to .92 (Sports Competence) over 16 days (mean $r = .83$), and from .81 (Physical Strength) to .87 (Body Attractiveness) over 23 days (mean $r = .85$).

The manual provides a modicum of information on the reliability of the PIP scores. Accordingly, Fox (1990) reported correlations between items of the same subscale as ranging from .56 to .84 (no specific information is provided with respect to samples). Test–retest reliability

---

2. Ambiguity associated with items constituting the original Exercise and Fitness subscale led to a revision of three items to reflect physical conditioning rather than fitness; as a consequence, its label was changed to the Physical Condition subscale (Fox & Corbin, 1989).

3. However, Physical Strength yielded the highest alpha estimate for Sample 1.

coefficients ranging from .68 to .83 over a 36-day period were also reported for a sample of 36 university students.

Validity. Although Fox and Corbin (1989) reported no findings related to the concurrent validity of the PSPP (but see Marsh, in press-a; Marsh et al., 1994; Marsh, chapter 6, this volume), they nonetheless provided critically important information bearing on both its predictive and construct validities. Fox and Corbin used discriminant function analysis to test the predictive validity of the PSPP. Based on the interpretation of structure coefficients, findings from this research have provided strong support for the capability of the Physical Strength, Sports Competence, and Physical Condition subscales to discriminate between active and nonactive, as well as between high-active and low-active, adults in a manner that is consistent with both competence motivation theory (Harter, 1978) and previous empirical research (see Fox & Corbin, 1989, p. 427). The Body Attractiveness subscale, however, was found to be less effective in predicting group membership. This finding notwithstanding, Fox and Corbin argued in support of the Body Attractiveness subscale as an important dimension of physical self-esteem. In substantiating their claim, they noted Harter's (1990a) contention that physical appearance remains one of the most dominant aspects of self-esteem throughout life and noted also that in the development of the PSPP, the topic of body attractiveness not only dominated the open-ended responses, but explained the greatest amount of variance in the global Physical Self-Worth construct.

Evidence of construct validity related to the PSPP was derived from both exploratory and confirmatory factor analytic studies. Furthermore, in addition to testing for the factorial validity of the instrument, Fox and Corbin (1989) tested for the validity of its underlying theoretical structure, an extremely vital yet rarely invoked practice in testing for evidence of construct validity related to a measuring instrument.[4] Factor analytic findings from both the exploratory and confirmatory approaches provided strong support for the five-factor structure of the PSPP, whereas results from zero-order factor intercorrelations argued for the validity of its hierarchically structured physical self-concept theoretical underpinning.

Fox and Corbin (1989) further tested for the construct validity of the instrument by examining the convergent validity of its subscales with

---

4. To the best of my knowledge, Marsh, in his development of his three SDQ scales, was the first to implement this sound construct validation practice.

external criteria to which they should be logically linked. As such, they determined that the three subscales found to be most effective in predicting group membership (i.e., Physical Strength, Sports Competence, and Physical Condition) were closely related to a logically related physical activity. For example, high Physical Strength was most closely associated with weight training, as was Sports Competence with involvement in ball sports. For the Body Attractiveness subscale, however, gender appeared to influence its relations with both external criteria and the PSPP's other subscales. For example, whereas the Body Attractiveness subscale appeared to be most closely linked to the Physical Condition subscale and to endurance exercise (mainly aerobic dance and jogging), calisthenics, and dance for women, it was most closely tied to both the Physical Condition and Strength subscales and to weight training and calisthenics for men. These findings led Fox and Corbin to suggest that perhaps this construct might be more effectively studied within the framework of a health belief theoretical model.

Finally, as a check on the susceptibility of the PSPP to evoke socially desirable responding, item and subscale scores were correlated with the short form of the Marlowe–Crowne Social Desirability Scale (Reynolds, 1982). Based on findings of nonsignificant correlations ($p > .05$, except for two items),[5] Fox (1990) concluded that the PSPP seems little affected by this form of response bias.

The only validity information provided on the PIP derives from a principal-components analysis of data representing 175 female and 180 male university students. Although the factor structure was clear and consistent with the hypothesized PIP structure for women, it was substantially less so for men. Specifically, items from the Body Importance and Strength Importance subscales cross-loaded on the Condition Importance factor. On the basis of these findings, Fox (1990) noted that researchers should exercise caution in their interpretation of PIP scores for male university students.

Related Psychometric Research

Findings from two recent studies have provided support for the psychometric adequacy of the PSPP as a measure of physical self-esteem for adults. In a construct validity study on a sample of 260 adults (111 men and 149 women; mean age = 44.1 years), Sonstroem et al. (1992) tested for the factorial and criterion validity of the instrument, as well as its

---

5. Fox and Corbin (1989) did not identify these items.

internal consistency reliability. Whereas principal component analytic findings supported the factorial structure of the PSPP, they also revealed scale overlap between the Body Attractiveness and Physical Self-Worth subscales, thereby supporting the work of Fox and Corbin (1989) with college students. Furthermore, their findings from discriminant function analyses also concurred with Fox and Corbin's research on the PSPP. Sonstroem and colleagues found the instrument to validly discriminate between exercisers and nonexercisers and to predict degree of exercise involvement as determined by a physical activity questionnaire. Finally, internal consistency reliabilities were found to range from .86 (Physical Condition) to .90 (Sports Competence and Physical Strength) for men (mean α = .88) and from .90 (all subscales except Physical Condition) to .91 (Physical Condition) for women (mean α = .90).

In a second study, Sonstroem et al. (1994) used confirmatory factor analytic and structural equation modeling procedures to validate the underlying theoretical structure of the PSPP, as well as to test for evidence of its convergent validity with logically related external criteria. Based on a sample of female aerobic dancers (N = 216; mean age = 38.4 years), findings from this study supported both the validity of the PSPP in measuring multidimensional and hierarchically structured perceptions of physical competence and its association with appropriate aspects of physical activity, as measured by a physical activity participation questionnaire.

Another recent study tested the cross-cultural generalizability of the PSPP. Based on two samples of British college students (n = 132 and n = 117), Page, Ashford, Fox, and Biddle (1993) reported strong evidence in support of the PSPP's factorial structure, its criterion validity, and its internal consistency reliability, with alpha estimates ranging from .74 to .90.

Finally, using the PSPP as a springboard, a group of researchers in England recently initiated work on a modified version of the original instrument for use with children (Biddle et al., 1993). Labeled the PSPP–C, this new instrument has been tested with British children 12 to 15 years of age and found to yield unclear subdomains of Physical Strength, Physical Condition, Body Attractiveness, and Sports Competence. Furthermore, although the instrument demonstrated adequate internal consistency reliability estimates with the younger children, they were less so for the older adolescents. Finally, Biddle et al. reported no association between the PSPP–C and susceptibility to social desirability, as measured by the lie scale of the Junior Eysenck Personality Questionnaire (Eysenck & Eysenck, 1975). Because work on this children's version of the PSPP is in its early stages of development, reported findings must be interpreted with caution.

Evaluation Summary

Designed as a multidimensional measure of physical self-esteem, the PSPP has made a prodigious contribution to the area of self-concept measurement. Not only does it fill a critically important void in our current pool of available instrumentation, but it represents an exceptionally psychometrically sound assessment scale. As with the Self Description Questionnaires, development of the PSPP has been carefully and skillfully tied to an empirically testable theoretical model; in the case of the PSPP, this model represents a multidimensional and hierarchically structured physical self-concept. So, too, testing of the instrument for evidence of various aspects of reliability and validity has been both rigorous and thorough. However, given substantial evidence to date of the instrument's factorial validity, I recommend that henceforth more use be made of confirmatory factor analytic procedures; in particular, use of these procedures within the framework of (a) a second-order factor model for purposes of testing, more rigorously, the hierarchical structure of the hypothesized physical self-concept structure, (b) a multigroup invariance model that enables the simultaneous testing for equality of both item measurements and factorial structure across groups, and (c) an MTMM model to more firmly establish its convergent and discriminant validities. Overall, I concur with Sonstroem et al. (1992) that

> the aegis of the Physical Self-Perception Profile is believed to represent an outstanding advance in the conceptualization of the self-esteem construct, particularly as it relates to perceived competencies in exercise and sport. It provides heuristic opportunities for increased understanding of the physical self. (pp. 219–220)

Source Information

Location: Office for Health Promotion, Northern Illinois University, DeKalb, Illinois 60115

Cost: No charge for manual.

GENERAL SELF-CONCEPT

Rosenberg Self-Esteem Scale

Although the Rosenberg Self-Esteem Scale (SES; Rosenberg, 1965, 1989) was designed to measure unidimensional, global self-esteem for adolescents, substantial use of the instrument with adults over the years has established its appropriateness for this population as well. For this reason, then, it is cited here in chapter 7. For details related to this instrument, however, readers are referred to chapter 6.

Measurement of Multiple Self-Concept Domains

Adult Self-Perception Profile

Description

The Adult Self-Perception Profile (ASPP; Messer & Harter, 1986) was designed to address the need for a psychometrically sound measure that could tap the complexity of multidimensional adult self-concepts. The instrument is firmly grounded in Harter's theoretical conceptualization of self-concept (see, e.g., Harter, 1983, 1985a, 1986) and uses the same structured-alternative item format as both the Self-Perception Profile for Children and the Self-Perception Profile for Adolescents (see chapters 5 and 6, respectively). Messer and Harter noted that in addition to enriching a theoretical understanding of the dimensional structure of adult self-concept, the ASPP can be effectively included in a test battery to be used for clinical assessment. For example, the scale can serve to help clients identify particular domains in their life that are problematic; these areas are identified through the use of discrepancy scores. Likewise, the ASPP can be used as a measure of self-concept change after an intervention program.

In keeping with developmental theory and empirical research related to self-concept (e.g., Harter, 1983; Marsh, 1989; Shavelson et al., 1976), the ASPP considers the adult's perception of self to be more differentiated than is the case for either preadolescents or adolescents. As such, the instrument is designed to measure self-perceptions related to 11 domains of everyday life that may be regarded as salient for most adults. Because it is typically the case that individuals do not perceive themselves as equally capable in all domains of their life, this approach allows for the examination of a profile of self-concepts across these important areas. In addition to the measurement of these specific facets, the ASPP also taps the adult's overall sense of general self-worth. Thus, in measuring global self-worth independent of adequacy and competence judgments, researchers and clinicians are able to examine relations between this global construct of self and domain-specific self-perceptions. As such, the ASPP is theoretically linked to the correlated-factor model of self-concept described in chapter 1.

Target Population
The ASPP was designed for specific use with adults. (Although college students are adults, by legal definition, the measurement of self-concept for this population has been addressed in a separately developed instrument [Neemann & Harter, 1986; see this chapter].)

Scale Structure
The ASPP is a 50-item self-report scale that comprises 12 subscales. Eleven scales are designed to measure self-perceptions in relation to specific domains of one's life, and one scale taps perception of self in general (Global Self-Worth). Each of the specific-domain subscales is composed of 4 items, whereas the Global Self-Worth scale comprises 6. For both sets of subscales, half the items are worded in the positive direction (i.e., reflection of high competency) and half in the negative direction. All items are based on a 4-point structured-alternative format, in an attempt to offset socially desirable responding.

As with the Self-Perception Profiles for preadolescents and adolescents (Harter, 1985b, 1988c, respectively), the Global Self-Worth subscale of the ASPP measures perceptions of self in general, in a sense that is separate and apart from any particular domain of perceived competence or adequacy. In other words, global self-esteem is not considered to be merely a sum or average of responses across a large array of items designed to tap multiple domain areas (e.g., see the Coopersmith, 1967, Self-Esteem Inventory). Rather, it is measured directly and independent of the more specific self-concept facets, which are captured by the following subscales:

- Sociability. Taps perceived behavior in the presence of others. In particular, the items probe the extent to which individuals perceive themselves as fun to be with, liking to meet new people, and at ease with others.
- Job Competence. Measures perceived competence in relation to

one's major occupation. Essentially, items that constitute this scale reflect the extent to which individuals feel productive, competent, and proud of their work.

- Nurturance. Reflects one's adequacy in caring for others. Items in this scale focus on one's ability to foster the growth of others and to care for children as a contribution to the future.
- Athletic Competence. Measures one's sense of athletic prowess. As such, the items tap perceptions of competence and willingness to participate in sports, as well as readiness to try other new physical activities.
- Physical Appearance. Measures the extent to which one is satisfied and happy with his or her overall appearance. In particular, items tap the extent to which individuals feel attractive and are generally content with their facial features and hair.
- Adequate Provider. Reflects one's capability to provide support both for him or herself and significant others. Items in this scale tap the extent to which individuals meet their own material needs, as well as those of the important people in their life.
- Morality. Measures perceptions of one's own behavior in relation to standards of conduct deemed to be socially acceptable. Items focus on the extent to which individuals live up to their own moral standards and perceive their behavior as being ethically sound.
- Household Management. Ascertains one's ability to manage household activities. Items are designed to tap the extent to which one is organized, efficient, and generally capable of keeping the household running smoothly.
- Intimate Relationships. Focuses on the ability to maintain a close, meaningful relationship with one's spouse, lover, or very special friend. Items measure the extent to which a person seeks out close and intimate relationships, and within which she or he feels free to communicate openly.
- Intelligence. Within the context of the ASPP, this construct is defined as the ability to learn and know. Items probe the extent to which one feels smart, is capable of understanding things, and feels intellectually capable.
- Sense of Humor. Focuses on one's ability to see the funny side of things. Items tap the extent to which people can laugh at themselves and various ironies of life and find it easy to joke with friends and colleagues.

A sample item taken from the Sense of Humor subscale of the ASPP is presented in Exhibit 7.4.

The question format of the ASPP parallels that of the other Self-Perception Profiles. As such, the individuals are first presented with a description of two types of people and then asked to identify which one of the two most resembles them. Messer and Harter (1986) contended that the effectiveness of this question format lies in the implication that half of the adults in the world view themselves one way, whereas the other half hold opposing views. In this way, either choice is legitimized. Once the respondents have chosen between these two groups, they then determine whether the behavior described is really true or just sort of true for them.

In keeping with all self-perception scales developed by Harter and colleagues, the manual for the ASPP includes a separate Importance Rating scale designed to tap perceptions of importance in relation to each domain. This scale, for adults, is based on a 4-point Likert-type scale that ranges from *not very important* (1) to *very important* (4) and comprises 11 items, one for each domain-specific self-concept. In addition to these items, respondents are asked to identify the three areas that are most important, and three that are least important, to them.

The Importance Rating scale must be used if one is interested in calculating discrepancy scores. In accordance with Harter's model of self-worth, the discrepancy between a person's perceptions of competence in a particular domain and his or her perceived importance of that domain has implications for the person's level of self-worth. Because adults typically do not feel equally competent in all domains, and because not all domains will be perceived as being equally important, the focus of this model is to identify the discrepancy scores in the salient domains (Messer & Harter, 1986). As such, a discrepancy score represents the difference between the perceived importance and perceived competence scores in all domains that have an importance rating of 4. Discrepancy scores are not obtained for domains that are rated as having lower importance to the person. (For a more extensive discussion of importance and discrepancy scores, readers are referred to chapter 1 of this volume; see also Bogan, 1988; Cronbach & Furby, 1970; Hattie, 1992; Marsh, 1986b, 1993e; Wells & Marwell, 1976; Wylie, 1989.)

Administration and Scoring

In keeping with the administration and scoring of the Self-Perception Profile for Children (Harter, 1985b; chapter 5, this volume) and for

Exhibit 7.4

Sample Item From the Adult Self-Perception Profile

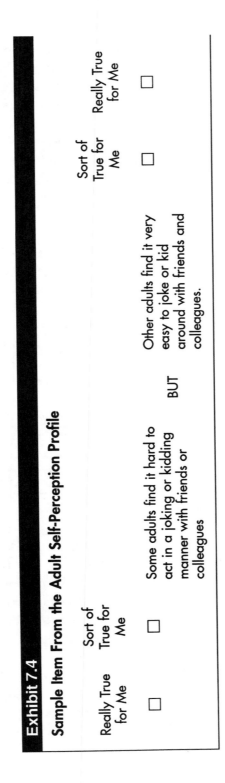

Really True for Me	Sort of True for Me		Sort of True for Me	Really True for Me
☐	☐	Some adults find it hard to act in a joking or kidding manner with friends or colleagues	BUT	Other adults find it very easy to joke or kid around with friends and colleagues.	☐	☐

Adolescents (Harter, 1988c; chapter 6, this volume), the ASPP can be administered either individually or in groups, and the mode of responding and scoring is identical. However, in explaining the question format to adults, the researcher must clarify that for any given item, they must check only one box on either side of the item statement; they do not check both sides. A scoring key and instructions for the computation of discrepancy scores are provided in the manual. Messer and Harter (1986) advised that the instrument typically takes approximately 20 min to complete.

Normative Data

Samples. Norms development for the ASPP was based on two independent samples of adults drawn largely from locations within Colorado. Sample A ($N = 141$) comprised upper-middle-class parents whose ages ranged from 30 to 50 (no mean value provided); all subjects had completed high school, and 95% were White. To determine gender and occupational differences, this sample was subsequently divided into four groups that represented full-time homemakers and mothers ($n = 42$), part-time working women and mothers ($n = 26$), full-time working women and mothers ($n = 29$), and full-time working men and fathers ($n = 44$). Sample B ($N = 215$) was composed of two equal groups of lower- and middle-class mothers with children under 3 years of age; over 90% were married, over 50% had a college education, and over 98% were White. The average age for the lower-class mothers was 22 years; for the middle-class mothers, it was 26 years.

Selection and Refinement of Items. No information is provided regarding this phase of ASPP development.

Psychometric Properties. Reliability. On the basis of each of the two normative samples, Messer and Harter (1986) reported internal consistency reliability coefficients for each of the 11 subscales. Across the four subgroups that constitute Sample A and Sample B, internal consistency reliabilities ranged from .87 to .92 (mean $\alpha = .89$) for Global Self-Worth, from .65 to .75 (mean $\alpha = .71$) for Job Competence, from .75 to .86 (mean $\alpha = .81$) for Intelligence, from .84 to .91 (mean $\alpha = .88$) for Athletic Competence, from .81 to .87 (mean $\alpha = .84$) for Physical Appearance, from .63 to .86 (mean $\alpha = .74$) for Sense of Humor, from .73 to .82 (mean $\alpha = .78$) for Sociability, from .72 to .88 (mean $\alpha = .80$) for Intimate Relationships, from .63 to .88 (mean $\alpha = .77$) for Morality, from .65 to .87 (mean $\alpha = .73$) for Nurturance, from .82 to .90 (mean α = .87) for Household Management, and from .80 to .90 (mean α = .84) for the Adequate Provider subscales.[6]

On the basis of these results, Messer and Harter (1986) concluded that for the most part, the internal consistency reliability of the ASPP is quite acceptable. However, they cautioned that the Adequate Provider subscale may not be appropriate for use with upper-class women who are either full-time homemakers or work part-time; these women did not perceive themselves as providers, and thus, the items were meaningless.

To date, no test–retest reliability estimates have been reported.

Validity. Messer and Harter (1986) reported findings from an exploratory factor analysis of ASPP responses to only the specific domain subscales for Sample B. However, although the authors contended that the sample size ($N = 205$) for this group substantiated such analyses, I consider it to be marginal at best. Indeed, given the strong likelihood of unstable factor-loading estimates, I encourage them to test the factorial validity of the instrument with additional samples that yield a more adequate case/item ratio.

Results from this single factor analysis yielded a clear 10-factor solution; the Job Competence factor could not be defined. For each subscale, Messer and Harter (1986) reported only the average target[7] (across the four items) and nontarget loadings; these ranged from .65 to .89 ($M = .77$) for the former and from .04 to .09 ($M = .07$) for the latter. Although these findings reflect a very strong factor pattern, it would be more beneficial to potential users of the ASPP to review the factor-loading estimates for each item. As noted earlier, the Job Competence subscale was problematic. Because this scale exhibited weak cross-loadings on the Nurturance factor, Messer and Harter pointed to the sample composition as a possible explanation; approximately 50% of the sample were full-time homemakers whose primary job involved child rearing. As a consequence, they anticipate that given a sample in which all subjects are full-time workers, the Job Competence subscale will emerge as a separate factor. Clearly, substantially more research is needed to validate the factorial structure of the ASPP.

Unfortunately, no factor intercorrelations are reported in the man-

---

6. Messer and Harter (1986) noted that owing to their attenuation of the overall estimate, reliability coefficients were not reported for the full-time homemaker (α = .06) and part-time working women (α = .57) subgroups.

7. Loading of the item on the factor it was designed to measure.

ual, and no other construct validity research appears to have been conducted.

Related Psychometric Research

I am aware of no additionally reported psychometric research conducted either by Messer and Harter or by others with respect to the ASPP and its accompanying Importance Rating scale.

Evaluation Summary

The ASPP is a relatively new instrument that is clearly in need of substantial testing to establish both its psychometric properties and its construct validity. However, it is included in this volume because (a) it represents a welcome addition to the currently limited pool of self-concept scales appropriate for use with adult populations; (b) it is a potentially strong assessment measure that is solidly linked to a well-established body of theory; (c) its construction reflects important empirical findings that have shown self-concept to comprise both a separate and independent global self-esteem component (i.e., not a sum or aggregate of more specific self-concept facets), as well as specific multidimensional components that become increasingly differentiated with age; indeed, the ASPP represents the only self-concept instrument, specifically designed for a working adult population, that addresses this multidimensional perspective[8]; and (d) its subscales are designed to tap perceptions of self in relation to viable and salient domains within the context of our current Western lifestyle.

Given that the ASPP has the potential to make a rich and valuable contribution to self-concept assessment, it deserves much greater attention than it has apparently thus far been paid. In particular, and as I have noted elsewhere in this volume with respect to other measures, I encourage the authors, as well as other interested researchers, to use various confirmatory factor analytic strategies in testing for both the validity and invariance of its factorial structure and for evidence of convergent, criterion-related, and discriminant validity. Indeed, this call is facilitated by Messer and Harter's (1986, p. 6) gracious generosity to interested researchers in granting permission to copy the instrument for their own purposes.

---

8. Although the Self Description Questionnaire (Marsh, 1992d) can also be used with an adult population, it was not specifically designed for use with adults who are full-time members of the workforce.

Source Information

Location: Susan Harter, University of Denver, Department of Psychology, 2155 South Race Street, Denver, Colorado 80208-0204

Cost: Manual: $15.00

Self Description Questionnaire III

Description

The Self Description Questionnaire III (SDQ–III; Marsh, 1992d) is designed to measure multiple dimensions of self-concept for college students and other adults. As was the case with the SDQ–II, the SDQ–III evolved from the original SDQ instrument, the SDQ–I. In keeping with its companion scales, the SDQ–III comprises a multidimensional structure that is firmly rooted in the Shavelson et al. (1976) theoretical model of self-concept. It differentiates itself from the other two scales, however, with respect to (a) number of subscales, (b) number of items, and (c) number of response-scale points. More specifically, the SDQ–III is designed to measure self-concepts related to eight nonacademic areas, four academic areas, and a single global perception of self (i.e., general self-concept).

Target Population

The SDQ–III was originally designed for use with late adolescents and young adults (16–25 years of age). Marsh (1992d) cautioned that although the instrument may be suitable for younger respondents, the reading level may be inappropriate; use of either the SDQ–II or SDQ–I may be more appropriate. He also noted that the SDQ–III may be used with adults older than 25. However, users should be aware that the instrument does not tap many important elements of adult lives.

Scale Structure

The SDQ–III is a 136-item self-report scale that comprises 13 subscales: (a) 8 nonacademic (Physical Ability, Physical Appearance, Peer Relations—Same Sex, Peer Relations—Opposite Sex, Parent Relations, Emotional Stability, Honesty/Trustworthiness, and Spiritual Values/Religion); (b) 4 academic (Verbal, Mathematics, Problem Solving, and General—Academic); and (c) 1 that measures overall global self-concept (General—Self). The items are structured on an 8-point Likert-type scale format; some subscales are composed of 10 items, whereas

---

Exhibit 7.5

Sample Item From the Self Description Questionnaire III

1	2	3	4	5	6	7	8
Definitely False	False	Mostly False	More False Than True	More True Than False	Mostly True	True	Definitely True

_____ I am usually pretty calm and relaxed.

---

others are composed of 12. To disrupt acquiescence response biases, half of the items in each subscale are worded negatively. A sample item from the Emotional Stability subscale of the SDQ–III is presented in Exhibit 7.5.

Administration and Scoring

As with its companion scales, the SDQ–III can be administered either individually or in groups. For each statement provided in the question-naire, respondents are asked to identify which one of the eight alter-native responses listed at the top of each page best describes them, by placing the appropriate numeral in the space provided beside each item (see Exhibit 7.5). Marsh (1992d) noted that when the SDQ–III is group-administered, the examiner typically reads the instructions aloud before having the respondents complete the questionnaire. However, he pointed out that for respondents 16 years or older who have an ade-quate command of English, completion of the SDQ–III is self-explan-atory. Marsh reported that most respondents typically complete the questionnaire in less than 20 min.

Responses to the SDQ–III can be scored either manually, by means of the Scoring and Profile Booklet provided, or by computer, by means of the scoring program disk provided. The booklet provides for the calculation of subscale raw scores and total scale raw scores (Nonaca-demic, Academic, and Total Self). Raw scores related to each subscale, as well as the total raw score, may be converted to midinterval percentile ranks and nonnormalized T scores. The norms tables in the manual provide information for each sex separately, by age (<21 years and >21 years), and in combination.

Normative Data

Samples. Norms development and standardization of the SDQ–III were based on a series of research studies in which subjects completed the entire instrument; studies that used only selected scales were excluded. Accordingly, normative data reported in the manual are based on 2,436 sets of responses by Australians between the ages of 13 and 48 years; less than 1% were younger than 16 years, and 7% were older than 26 years. Given that approximately two thirds of the respondents were students, Marsh (1992d) cautioned that this group may be overrepresented. For each of the SDQ–III subscales, as well as the total score, the following information is provided in the norms tables: midinterval percentile, nonnormalized T score, mean, median, standard deviation, and coefficients of skewness and kurtosis.

Selection and Refinement of Items. Marsh (1992d) reported that the initial version of the SDQ–III was structured from the seven scales of the original SDQ–I, with the exception that the Peer Relations subscale was divided into same-sex and opposite-sex components; in addition, the instrument contained a General—Self subscale that was formulated from the Rosenberg (1965, 1979) Self-Esteem Scale and two other scales measuring emotional stability and problem solving/creative thinking. This initial SDQ–III, then, comprised 180 items designed to measure these 11 self-concept dimensions. The instrument was then administered to a sample of university students (sample size not reported) who were asked to identify important areas of daily functioning that they considered should be incorporated. Although both item and factor analyses of the responses supported the initial 11 subscales, a substantial number of respondents suggested that 2 additional subscales be included: Honesty/Trustworthiness and Spiritual Values/Religion; these subscales were subsequently added. Finally, on the basis of findings from both item and factor analyses of the university sample data, selection of the most reliable items resulted in a further reduction of 44 items. The final version of the SDQ–III, therefore, comprises 136 items designed around 13 subscales.

Psychometric Properties. Reliability. Although Marsh (1992d) noted that reliability statistics have typically been reported in all published SDQ–III studies, the information reported here is based on the full set of responses comprising the normative sample ($N = 2,436$), as summarized in the manual. Accordingly, Marsh reported internal consistency reliability coefficients ranging from .76 (Honesty/Trustworthiness) to .95 (Spiritual Values/Religion), with a mean alpha over the 13 subscales of .90; indeed, only the subscale Honesty/Trustworthiness was less than .84. In addition, correlations among item responses in each subscale and the corrected item–scale correlations (i.e., correlation between an item and the summed responses from other items in the same scale) have been reported to range from .24 (Item 121, measuring Honesty/ Trustworthiness) to .89 (Items 41 and 67, measuring Spiritual Values/ Religion), with an overall mean correlation of .65. Although in the face of these summary statistics, the Honesty/Trustworthiness subscale would seem to be the weakest, it nonetheless yielded a very respectable coefficient alpha value of .76. However, given either the deletion or revamping of at least 7 of the 12 items in this subscale (Items 4, 17, 69, 82, 121, 132, and 134), the internal consistency reliability can be expected to increase, thereby making it more in line with the other SDQ–III subscales.

Test–retest reliability related to the SDQ–III is reported in the manual based on a study by Marsh, Richards, and Barnes (1986a, 1986b) in which they examined responses by 361 participants in a 26-day residential Outward Bound program. Subjects completed the SDQ–III at four different time points: 1 month before (T_1), first day of (T_2), last day of (T_3), and 18 months after completion of the program (T_4). Based on the full sample of participants who completed the questionnaire at all four time points ($N = 229$), Marsh et al. (1986a, 1986b) reported stability coefficients over the 1-month control interval to be highest (median $r = .87$) and stability coefficients over the 18-month period to be the lowest (median $r = .74$); nonetheless, given that the ages of these participants ranged from 16 to 25 years and that they frequently reported significant life changes during this period (i.e., getting married, moving out of family home, or starting university), this latter value is remarkably substantial. These indicators of measurement stability provide strong evidence of test–retest reliability in relation to the SDQ–III.

Validity. As noted earlier, given the traditionally poor factor structure associated with most self-concept scales (Marsh, 1992b; Wylie, 1974), most tests of concurrent validity have been based on total scores. A more rigorous test of such validity can be attained, however, when the subscales of both instruments are structured to measure the same constructs. Designed within the framework of an MTMM analysis, two studies have tested the concurrent validity of particular SDQ–III subscales against the matching scales of other well-known self-concept instruments. Whereas the first study (Marsh & Richards, 1988b) focused on the nonacademic subscales of the SDQ–III, the second study (Marsh et al., 1988) focused primarily on the academic subscales but also included the General—Self subscale.

In examining convergent validities between the Tennessee Self-Concept Scale (Fitts, 1965) and nonacademic subscales of the SDQ–III, Marsh and Richards (1988b) reported correlations to be highest for the Physical (Ability $r = .53$, Appearance $r = .71$); Social (Peer Relations—Same Sex $r = .61$, Peer Relations—Opposite Sex $r = .59$); and Parent Relations ($r = .68$) subscales. In the second study, Marsh et al. (1988) examined convergent validities between each of three SDQ–III academic subscales (Verbal, Mathematics, and General—Academic) and matching scales in the Affective Perception Inventory (API; Soares & Soares, 1979) and the Self-Concept of Ability Scale (SCAS; Brookover, 1962)[9]; convergent validity of the SDQ–III General—Self scale was examined with respect to the Rosenberg (1965) Self-Esteem Scale and the Self Concept subscale of the API, a measure of general self-concept. Findings revealed strong convergent validities, with coefficients ranging from .54 (Verbal; SDQ–III/SCAS) to .86 (Mathematics; SDQ–III/API), with a mean r of .69.

In keeping with its companion instruments (SDQ–I and SDQ–II), most validity research related to the SDQ–III has focused on tests of its construct validity. Again, in the light of the volume of research conducted in this regard, I refer readers both to the manual (Marsh, 1992d) and to the important review article previously noted (Marsh, 1990b) for a more in-depth treatment of the various aspects of construct validity tested. Included here is a brief summary of both within- and between-network construct validity research.

Within-network research related to the SDQ–III has been based on item pairs using both exploratory and confirmatory factor analyses,[10] as well as MTMM analyses. Initial tests of its factorial validity were based on samples representing two different Australian student populations: high school girls in Grades 11 and 12 ($N = 296$) and teachers' college/university students ($N = 151$; Marsh & O'Neill, 1984). Results from both samples revealed very strong factor structures, with each of the 13 subscales of the SDQ–III being remarkably clear. For the high school girls, target loadings were consistently high (90% = .50 or higher, with none less than .35),

---

9. The two subject-specific subscales of Verbal and Mathematics were constructed from the original scale, which measures only academic self-concept.

10. As noted previously, this pattern has been used in all testing of the SDQ instruments by Marsh and colleagues. For an elaboration of the rationale, see Marsh (1992c).

nontarget loadings were low (98% = .20 or lower, and none greater than .33), and correlations among the factors were minimal (mean $r = .08$); for the college students, target loadings were reported to be similarly large (median $r = .72$), nontarget loadings to be small (median $r = .02$), and factor correlations ranged from $-.19$ to $.32$ (median $r = .07$).

In a follow-up factor analytic investigation, based on data taken from a previously published study (Marsh, Richards, & Barnes, 1986b), Marsh (1987b) tested the validity of SDQ–III subscale scores for 361 late adolescents and young adults (median age = 21 years) enrolled in an Outward Bound program. A first-order factor analysis clearly identified all 13 self-concept facets purportedly measured by the SDQ–III.

Marsh (1992d) also reported findings from a single factor analytic study of the SDQ–III based on the full normative sample ($N = 2,436$). Not surprisingly, an exceptionally clear 13-factor structure was identified; specifically, (a) target loadings were remarkably high, with values ranging from .44 to .94 ($Md = .71$), (b) nontarget loadings were substantially smaller, with values ranging from $-.17$ to $.25$ ($Md = .02$), and (c) correlations among the factors were modest, with values ranging from $-.06$ to $.36$ ($Md = .10$).

Perhaps the most stringent test of an instrument's factorial structure is the extent to which it is similar across subgroups of a particular population. Marsh (1992d) addressed this issue in relation to the normative sample of 2,436 SDQ–III responses. For these purposes, he divided the data into four groups representing males (<20 years; >20 years) and females (<20 years; >20 years). Findings from four separate factor analytic studies (one for each group) demonstrated strong replicability of the clearly demarcated 13-factor structure found with both the entire normative sample and other reported factor analyses of the SDQ–III. Based on a statistically more rigorous approach to testing for factorial invariance using confirmatory factor analysis procedures, studies have shown the SDQ–III to be factorially invariant across both gender (Marsh, 1987a) and age (Marsh & Hocevar, 1985). Taken together, findings from these multigroup studies have provided strong support for the generalizability of both the SDQ–III factor structure and the validity of its hypothesized structure within the framework of the Shavelson et al. (1976) theoretical model on which it is based.

Between-network research related to the SDQ–III, as with its companion instruments, the SDQ–I and SDQ–II, has examined relations between particular subscales of the instrument and a wide array of other constructs such as gender, age, academic performance, inferred self-concepts (by significant others such as teachers, parents, and peers), family background characteristics, self-attribution, and experimental conditions associated with intervention programs designed to enhance self-concept. In the process of testing these relations, Marsh and colleagues addressed important theoretical issues in self-concept research, such as frame-of-reference effects, causal predominance between academic self-concept and academic achievement, self-attributions for academic success and failure, self–other agreement, and intervention effects. Findings from this research provide exceptionally strong support for the construct validity of the SDQ–III.

Related Psychometric Research

In a study of 898 Grade 11 and Grade 12 Canadian high school students, Byrne (1988a) tested (a) for the factorial validity of three academic subscales of the SDQ–III (Verbal, Mathematics, and General—Academic), as well as the General—Self subscale; and (b) for their invariance across low-track ($n = 285$) and high-track ($n = 613$) students. She reported an exceptionally strong four-factor solution, with all factor loadings and subscale correlations statistically invariant across the two ability levels. Based on a second study of 991 Grade 11 and Grade 12 students, Byrne (1988b) tested the same hypotheses across adolescent boys ($n = 455$) and girls ($n = 446$). Although the same clear factor structure found in the previous study was obtained, tests for invariance revealed two item measurements of general self-concept to be nonequivalent across gender. Overall, however, findings from these two studies provide vigorous support for the factorial validity of the SDQ–III.

Based on a sample of Canadian university students ($N = 941$), Marsh and Byrne (1993) reported the same consistent findings as those summarized above, thereby adding further support for the exceptionally sound structure of the SDQ–III. Indeed, Marsh (1992d) noted that the results from this study—with those from nine other studies that differed systematically in terms of gender, age, socioeconomic status, and student/nonstudent status—exemplify the remarkably strong generalizability of the SDQ–III factor structure.

More recently, Vispoel (1995c) reported on the psychometric properties of the SDQ–III for 831 college students. Although the primary focus of his study was to test the validity of various models that integrated self-perceptions of dance, dramatic art, visual art, and music skills into the Shavelson et al. (1976) model and to assess relations between artistic and other facets of self-concept, tests for the internal consistency reliability of SDQ–III subscale scores are of interest here. Accordingly, Vispoel reported coefficient alpha estimates ranging from .77 (for Honesty/Trustworthiness) to .96 (for Mathematics and Physical Ability, mean α = .90).

Evaluation Summary

The SDQ–III is currently the most extensively validated self-concept measure available for use with adults. Following the same research strategy as that related to the other SDQ scales, this past decade has seen the SDQ–III undergo rigorously extensive testing to establish its psychometric soundness as a measure of self-concept. Thus, I again conclude that researchers, clinicians, counselors, and others interested in the measurement of self-concept can feel confident in the validity of interpretations based on responses to the multidimensionally sensitive items of the SDQ–III. Nonetheless, I suggest here also that information related to the reading level of SDQ–III items be included in the next version of the manual, because such information may be helpful to researchers wishing to test for the validity of SDQ–III responses with samples representative of various exceptional or differential cultural populations.

Source Information

Location: Publication Office, School of Education and Language Studies, University of Western Sydney, P.O. Box 555, Campbelltown, New South Wales 2560, Australia

Cost: Kit: $50.00 (includes SDQ–III, manual, and scoring key)

Self-Perception Profile for College Students

Description

The Self-Perception Profile for College Students (SPPCS; Neemann & Harter, 1986) was designed to fill an important instrument void that has existed between the measurement of adolescent self-concepts and the measurement of adult self-concepts. Indeed, although college students can be regarded as adults in the legal sense, they typically straddle the boundary between adolescence and adulthood. For example, although they often live away from home and thus are free of direct parental control, and have accepted responsibility for their life and educational goals, they are not yet in the full-time workforce and hold no responsibility for the nurturance of others or for the management of a household. To address this obvious need in self-concept measurement, the SPPCS was developed as a multidimensional scale that comprised subscales designed to tap important domains relevant to the lives of a college population.

Construction of the SPPCS drew heavily from the three other Self-Perception Profiles designed to measure preadolescent (Harter, 1985b), adolescent (Harter, 1988c), and adult (Messer & Harter, 1986) self-concepts. Given that college students are integrated into an academic environment, the Scholastic Competence, Athletic Competence, and Social Acceptance subscales were modeled after those that constitute the preadolescent and adolescent assessment scales. Because college students also share much in common with the adult population, the Morality, Intelligence, Physical Appearance, and Sense of Humor subscales for the adult scale were used as a pattern in building similar subscales for the SPPCS. The adolescent scale was also important in contributing three subscales that were more age appropriate than either the preadolescent or adult versions of the Self-Perception Profile battery; these subscales were Close Friendships, Romantic Relationships, and Job Competence. Finally, two additional subscales were created specifically for use with the college population; these are designed to tap perceptions of creativity and relations with parents.

As with the other assessment measures developed by Harter and colleagues, the SPPCS is firmly grounded in Harter's theoretical conceptualization of self-concept (see, e.g., Harter, 1983, 1985a, 1986) and uses the same structured-alternative item format as the Self-Perception Profile for Children (see chapter 5), the Self-Perception Profile for Adolescents (see chapter 6), and the Adult Self-Perception Profile (see earlier section, this chapter). In addition to the measurement of the specific facets noted above, the SPPCS also taps perceptions of an overall sense of global self-worth. However, as emphasized elsewhere, this judgment is measured not as a summative composite of multidimensional self-concepts, but rather as a perception of general esteem that exists separate and apart from perceptions of specific domains in one's everyday life. Thus, global self-worth is measured by means of a separate subscale. The SPPCS is theoretically linked to the correlated-factor model of self-concept described in chapter 1.

Target Population

The SPPCS was designed for specific use with the traditional full-time undergraduate college student (age = 17–23 years). However, Neemann and Harter (1986) noted that the instrument might also be appropriate for use with older, single, full-time undergraduate students, as well as graduate students. For students who are registered on a part-time basis, married, employed in a full- or part-time job, or can for other reasons be regarded as nontraditional college students, the authors suggested that the Adult Self-Perception Profile may be more appropriate.

Scale Structure

The SPPCS is a 54-item self-report scale that comprises 13 subscales. Twelve scales are designed to measure self-perceptions that relate to specific domains of one's life, and 1 scale taps perception of self in general (Global Self-Worth). Each of the specific-domain subscales comprises 4 items, whereas the Global Self-Worth scale comprises 6. For both sets of subscales, half of the items are worded in the positive direction (i.e., reflection of high competency), and half of the items are worded in the negative direction. Neemann and Harter (1986) noted that all items are based on a 4-point structured-alternative format, in an attempt to offset socially desirable responding.

The 12 specific-domain subscales of the SPPCS fall into two categories: those designed to tap self-perceptions of competencies or abilities and those measuring perceptions of one's social relationships. The 5 subscales that focus on competency are as follows: Intellectual Ability, Job Competence, Athletic Competence, Scholastic Competence, and Creativity. Because the first 3 subscales were fully described above for the Adult Self-Perception Profile, only the latter 2 are described below:

- Scholastic Competence. Taps perceived competence in relation to the student's actual school work. Items focus on the extent to which individuals feel competent in their mastery of the coursework undertaken.
- Creativity. Measures perceived ability to be creative and inventive. As such, items tap the extent to which one perceives himself or herself as having a lot of original ideas.

The seven subscales that focus on social relationships are Romantic Relationships, Close Friendships, Physical Appearance, Sense of Humor, Morality, Social Acceptance, and Parent Relationships. The first two subscales are fully described with respect to the Self-Perception Profile for Adolescents (see chapter 6), and the next three subscales are described with respect to the Adult Self-Perception Profile, discussed earlier (this chapter). Thus, only the latter two are described here, as follows:

- Social Acceptance. Reflects satisfaction with one's social skills. In particular, items probe the extent to which individuals find it easy to make friends, interact with other people, and generally feel socially accepted.
- Parent Relationships. Focuses on liking and feeling comfortable with one's interactions with parents. Items measure the degree to which students like and feel natural with the way they act in the presence of their parents, as well as the extent to which they get along with their parents.

A sample item taken from the Creativity subscale of the SPPCS is presented in Exhibit 7.6.

Paralleling those for the Self-Perception Profiles for preadolescents, adolescents, and adults, the manual for the SPPCS includes a separate scale that enables researchers to tap perceptions of importance in relation to each domain; for college students, this rating scale comprises 24 items, 2 related to each specific-domain subscale. However, an additional inclusion in the SPPCS manual is the Social Support scale. Addressing Rosenberg's (1979) contention that it is an individual's perception of what significant others think that is important in the formation of self-conceptions, this scale was designed as a vehicle for measuring the extent to which college students perceive the important people in their life as acknowledging the college students' worth as people. This scale is composed of 20 items, 4 of which load on one of five subscales (Close Friend, Mother, People in Campus Organizations, Father, and Instructors).

Administration and Scoring

In keeping with the administration and scoring of the Self-Perception Profiles for preadolescents (Harter, 1985b; chapter 5), adolescents (Harter, 1988c; chapter 6), and adults (Messer & Harter, 1986; this chapter), the SPPCS can be administered either individually or in groups, and the mode of responding and scoring is identical; likewise, a scoring key and instructions for the computation of discrepancy scores are provided in the manual. (For details related to each of these factors, see the description of the Adult Self-Perception Profile [Messer & Harter, 1986], this chapter.) Neemann and Harter (1986) advised that the instrument typically takes approximately 30 min to complete.

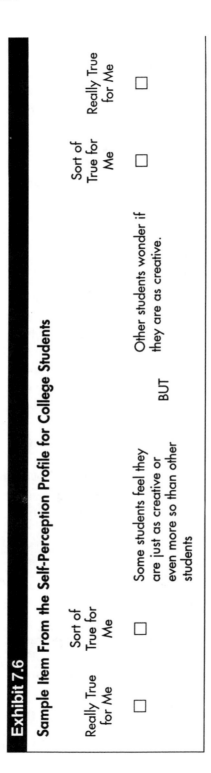

Exhibit 7.6

Sample Item From the Self-Perception Profile for College Students

	Really True for Me	Sort of True for Me			Sort of True for Me	Really True for Me
	☐	☐	Some students feel they are just as creative or even more so than other students	BUT Other students wonder if they are as creative.	☐	☐

Normative Data

Samples. Norms development for the SPPCS was based on one sample of college students ($N = 300$; mean age = 19.8 years) drawn from two universities in Colorado ($n_1 = 182$ and $n_2 = 118$). Of the total sample, 70 subjects were male and 230 female; further decomposition revealed 142 freshmen, 94 sophomores, 41 juniors, and 23 seniors (Neemann & Harter, 1986). Moreover, 93% of the students were White, and 94% had never been married.

Selection and Refinement of Items. Development of the SPPCS began with an initial study of two independent samples of college students. One sample ($N = 134$) represented volunteer subjects who completed and mailed in a preliminary version of the instrument; the second sample ($N = 57$) comprised students from a "subject pool" who were given either a class credit or their own self-perception profile in exchange for their participation in the project. Neemann and Harter (1986), however, provided no additional details regarding (a) the number of items included in the initial draft of the SPPCS, (b) the analyses conducted on these data and the results thereof, (c) the criteria used in the selection of items, and (d) the number of items either deleted or modified.

Psychometric Properties. *Reliability.* Neemann and Harter (1986) reported internal consistency reliability coefficients for each of the 12 subscales, but only as they pertain to the total sample of college students ($N = 300$). These alpha estimates were as follows: Intellectual Ability ($\alpha = .86$), Job Competence ($\alpha = .76$), Athletic Competence ($\alpha = .92$), Scholastic Competence ($\alpha = .84$), Creativity ($\alpha = .89$), Romantic Relationships ($\alpha = .88$), Close Friendships ($\alpha = .82$), Physical Appearance ($\alpha = .85$), Sense of Humor ($\alpha = .80$), Morality ($\alpha = .86$), Social Acceptance ($\alpha = .80$), and Parent Relationships ($\alpha = .88$).

Validity. Neemann and Harter (1986) reported findings from a principal components analysis of SPPCS responses based only on the specific-domain subscales. Component loadings are shown in the manual to range from a mean (across the four items) of .69 (Intellectual Ability) to .89 (Athletic Competence), and the authors reported that no cross-loadings were greater than .35.[11] On the basis of the values reported in the manual, it seems clear that SPPCS responses for this normative sample are appropriately described by a 12-factor structure. However, without reported information on at least the substantial cross-loadings, it is difficult for the reader to determine the clarity with which

---

11. In my view, however, this value is excessively high for a cross-loading.

each factor is defined. Moreover, given the known problem of inflated loadings, as well as other widely recognized limitations associated with principal components analyses (e.g., Gorsuch, 1990; Hubbard & Allen, 1987; Snook & Gorsuch, 1989), these findings should be interpreted with caution.

Results are also reported for intercorrelations among both the specific-domain and Global Self-Worth factors. Interestingly, these findings were consonant with responses by both preadolescents (Harter, 1985b) and adolescents (Harter, 1988c) to their specific Self-Perception Profiles, in demonstrating global self-worth to be most highly related to Physical Appearance.[12]

Finally, with respect to the Importance Rating scale, Neemann and Harter (1986) have reported internal consistency reliability estimates ranging from .53 (Social Acceptance Importance) to .84 (Athletic Competence Importance, mean α = .73). Also reported are correlations between each Importance Rating subscale and Global Self-Worth. These coefficients ranged from .19 (Athletic Competence Importance) to .86 (Physical Appearance Importance, mean r = .44).

Related Psychometric Research

I am aware of only one study that has sought to examine the psychometric properties and validity of SPPCS responses, albeit only 5 of the 13 subscales were put to the test. Based on responses from a sample of 323 undergraduate university students (126 men and 197 women; mean age = 20.8 years), Crocker and Ellsworth (1990) tested the factorial validity of, and the internal consistency reliability related to, 5 subscales: Scholastic Competence, Athletic Competence, Social Acceptance, Physical Appearance, and Global Self-Worth. Findings from a principal-axis factor analysis with varimax rotation yielded a strong and clearly defined five-factor solution, with target factor loadings ranging from .43 to .83. Internal consistency reliability coefficients were reported as ranging from .74 (Scholastic Competence) to .90 (Athletic Competence), with a mean coefficient alpha of .82.

Evaluation Summary

As was the case for the Adult Self-Perception Profile (reviewed earlier in this chapter), the SPPCS is a relatively new instrument that is clearly in need of substantial testing to establish both its psychometric prop-

---

12. Although Neemann and Harter (1986) also cited Messer and Harter's (1986) work with adults as demonstrating a similar finding, I was unable to locate this information.

erties and its construct validity. However, like its companion instrument, the SPPCS represents a welcome addition to the currently limited pool of self-concept scales appropriate for use with college students (see also R. D. Brown, 1992; Davis, 1992). So too is it solidly linked to a well-established body of theory, and its construction reflects important empirical findings that demonstrate an individual's global self-esteem to coexist with multiple domain-specific facets but also to represent a separate and independent facet in its own right.

Because the SPPCS has the potential to make a rich and valuable contribution to self-concept assessment for the traditional college student population, it can benefit substantially from rigorous construct validity research conducted within the framework of covariance structure models. In particular, I encourage the authors, as well as other interested researchers, to use various confirmatory factor analytic strategies in testing for both the validity and invariance of its factorial structure and for evidence of convergent, criterion-related, and discriminant validity. As noted above with respect to the adult scale, this task has been facilitated by Neemann and Harter's (1986, p. 4) considerate generosity to interested researchers in granting permission to copy the instrument for their own purposes.

Source Information

Location: Susan Harter, University of Denver, Department of Psychology, 2155 South Race Street, Denver, Colorado 80208-0204

Cost: Manual: $15.00

Tennessee Self-Concept Scale

Description

The Tennessee Self-Concept Scale (TSCS; Roid & Fitts, 1988/1994) is designed to measure multiple content-dependent dimensions of self-concept for adults, as well as for adolescents. Given its development, which is based primarily on a clinical perspective, it can be used for a variety of purposes: counseling, clinical assessment and diagnosis, research in the behavioral sciences, and personnel selection. For details related to this instrument, readers are referred to chapter 6.

SENIOR ADULTHOOD (65+ YEARS)

From my search of the self-concept literature in general, and the self-concept psychometric literature in particular, I had no difficulty in determining this period of the life span to be the most poorly served by adequate assessment measures (see also Breytspraak & George, 1979, 1982; Hattie, 1992). The Tennessee Self-Concept Scale notwithstanding (see chapter 6), not only was I able to find only one reference to a self-report measure designed specifically for use with this age group (Eden, 1981), but also I was unable to locate any other study that addressed psychometric issues related to any assessment instrument intended for this population. Furthermore, a search of the literature relative to the three instruments recommended by Breytspraak and George (1979), and specific instruments cited by the same authors (1982), yielded no positive results. Overall, albeit more than a decade later, my findings regarding the status of self-concept measurement for the senior population concur with those of others (Breytspraak & George, 1979, 1982; Seltzer, 1975; Wylie, 1989) in revealing instruments that have rarely been used more than once and that demonstrate little to no evidence of psychometric research having been conducted on them.

One self-concept instrument that has received a modicum of use in studies that focused on substantive gerontological issues has been the Twenty Statements Test (TST; Kuhn & McPartland, 1954).[13] In contrast to structured measures which—according to some (e.g., W. J. McGuire & Padawer-Singer, 1976)—inhibit expression of a "true" self-concept, this instrument uses an open-ended nondirective format that purports to tap one's spontaneous self-concept despite little evidence to support this claim (McCrae & Costa, 1988). More specifically, the respondent is asked to give 20 answers to the question "Who am I?" with the number of dimensions being established a priori by the researcher. Given the multiplicity of environmental and personal factors that can impinge on the self-conceptions of the 65+ population, this approach to their measurement might seem like a reasonable alternative. One potentially serious limitation of the TST, however, relates to its structure, coding, and scoring system. For example, with researchers establishing their own self-concept dimensionality and criteria for coding and scoring, it becomes virtually impossible to establish any data regarding the instru-

---

13. My own literature search, however, did not find this to be the case.

ment's psychometric properties. Furthermore, as noted by Wylie (1979), there is no guidance provided by the developers regarding the handling of widely discrepant numbers of responses by subjects, despite the request for only 20.

Although the general notion of using an open-ended response procedure with elderly subjects is intuitively appealing, use of the TST for this purpose seems ill-advised for several reasons: (a) Despite its 30-year existence, there is still a void of information related to its construct validity and psychometric properties; (b) there appears to be no known pattern of findings, as derived from the elderly populations over the years; and (c) somewhat related to the previous point, there has been no established systematic effort to build an inventory of findings over replicated testings of the same populations.

Noteworthy, however, is another assessment strategy that in contrast to the TST, has built up a voluminous pool of self-concept findings in relation to the elderly. Although this measurement approach is also based on an open-ended response format, and because there is no standardized self-report measure of self-concept specifically designed for the elderly of which I am aware, I consider it important to at least make readers aware of this alternative strategy.[14] Indeed, based on a strong record of systematic replication research, this instrument would seem to provide a variable alternative to the TST for those interested in measuring the self-concept of persons 65 years of age and older. We turn now to this alternative assessment strategy.

The Self-Perception Genesis Method

Description

The Self-Perception Genesis Method (*Genese des Perceptions de Soi* [GPS]; L'Ecuyer, 1978) is a self-report method for measuring self-concept that was developed from Bugental and Zelen's (1950) "Who Are You?" (WAY) technique, a precursor of the Twenty Statements Test (TST). Whereas the WAY method required that subjects describe themselves in three statements, the TST extended this criterion to 20 statements. Both methods necessarily restrict (a) the number of ways by which individuals can describe themselves and (b) the extent to which the multiplicity of self-concept facets and their structure can be evaluated for each indi-

---

14. Although the Tennessee Self-Concept Scale is appropriate for use with individuals 65 years and older, it was designed for use with a wide span of age groups, ranging from 13 to over 65 years.

vidual. To address these limitations, L'Ecuyer developed the GPS method. Although he retained the question "Who are you?" individuals being assessed by means of the GPS method are given complete freedom to describe themselves in any way they wish. These descriptions are then coded according to a standardized and quantifiable format.

The GPS method is solidly linked to L'Ecuyer's (1992) experiential–developmental model of self-concept. Both have been the product of continuous and systematic study of the self-concept by L'Ecuyer and his colleagues over the past 27 years. Because the primary purpose of this longitudinal research strategy has been to study the structure of self-concept for nonclinical populations across the life span, it was critical to develop an assessment instrument that could be used with equivalent appropriateness with all age groups. After a multitude of studies and years of refinement, the present (and final) form of the GPS method evolved. As a consequence of this ongoing program of research, there is now a wealth of self-concept findings relative to individuals ranging in age from 3 to 100 years (see, e.g., L'Ecuyer, 1989, 1992, 1994). For purposes of this volume, however, the review presented here is limited to application with the senior adult population.

Target Population

As noted above, the GPS method is appropriate for use with all age groups.

Scale Structure

The GPS method represents a self-report strategy that allows the subjects to describe themselves freely. More specifically, they are asked three questions, each of which is taken here from L'Ecuyer (1992). First, they are asked to "describe yourself in the most complete way you can, no matter what others think" (p. 113). Second, as a check on the extent to which the central perceptions identified in the quantification of the first question corresponded to what the individual considered to be important, subjects are then asked, "Within all you said in answering the first question, what is the most important to you?" (L'Ecuyer, 1992, p. 113). Finally, as a check on the completeness of the reported perceptions of self, subjects are asked a series of questions related to a broad spectrum of specific self-concept dimensions. For example, the interviewer might say, "Some individuals of your age speak about things like . . . their body. Do you have something to say about yourself concerning this topic?" In this regard, the GPS method is distinctly different from both the WAY and TST approaches to the open-ended format. More important, it addresses Yardley's (1987) concern that subjects be actively involved in "making sense of both the research event and their own responses within that event" (p. 213).

The theoretical framework to which all self-reported descriptions are linked comprises 43 dimensions of self-concept that are organized within a three-tier hierarchical structure. These three strata are termed *structures, substructures,* and *categories.* L'Ecuyer (1992) referred to this framework as representing an experiential–developmental model, because it allows for changes in the hierarchical network at various stages of the life span. In other words, the importance assigned by an individual to particular aspects of the self (e.g., somatic self) varies across his or her life span as a consequence of both experiential and developmental factors. The significance of this theoretical structure is that it can accommodate descriptions tapped by the GPS method at any stage of the life cycle. A summary of this experiential–developmental model is presented in Table 7.1.

Administration and Scoring

L'Ecuyer (1992) provided several caveats that need to be taken into account when the GPS method is used with the elderly population. In particular, the difficulty lies not with the subjects' understanding of the question "Who are you?" but, rather, with their ability to limit their responses to a succinct description of themselves and not their "whole-life review" (L'Ecuyer, 1992, p. 105). Thus, L'Ecuyer (1992) suggested that in lieu of having elders provide an oral description, have them complete a written description. Nonetheless, he proposed that an even sounder strategy to keep the divulgence of information on track would be to have the interviewer offer to record the information for the subject, while reminding him or her to speak very slowly. L'Ecuyer noted that when the latter approach is used, subjects are more inclined to perceive the interview as being for a scientific purpose.

A critical aspect of the GPS method is that the coding of self-perceptions must reflect the meaning intended by the respondent, not a psychological interpretation assigned to it by the interviewer (see, e.g., Yardley, 1987). Thus, the individual meaning is determined from the sentence itself and from the general protocol into which it is expressed, because it may take on a completely different focus when considered external to its contextual framework. As such, each description is coded in accordance with the conceptual framework presented in Table 7.1

Table 7.1

Experiential–Developmental Model of the Self Concept

Structures	Sub-Structures	Categories
MATERIAL SELF (SM)	Somatic Self (SSo)	Physical appearance and traits (tra) Physical condition (cph)
	Possessive Self (SPo)	Possession of objects (obj) Possession of persons (per) Aspirations (asp) Activities (listing) (ena)
PERSONAL SELF (SP)	Self Image (ImS)	Feelings and emotions (sem) Interests (int) Capacities and aptitudes (apt) Qualities and failings (def) Simple denominations (nom) Role and status (rol)
	Self Identity (IdS)	Consistency (con) Ideology (ide) Abstract identity (ida)
ADAPTATIVE SELF (SA)	Self Esteem (VaS)	Competency (com) Personal value (vap) Adaptative strategies (sta) Autonomy (aut)
	Self Activities (AcS)	Ambivalence (amb) Dependency (dep) Actualization (act) Lifestyle (sty) Receptivity (rec)
SOCIAL SELF (SS)	Social Attitudes (PaS)	Domination (dom) Altruism (alt)
	References to Sexuality (RaS)	Simple references (res) Sexual attractiveness + experiences (sex)
SELF–NON-SELF (SN)	References to Others (ReA) Opinions of Others (OpA)	

Note. From "An experiential–developmental framework and methodology to study the transformations of the self-concept from infancy to old age," by R. L'Ecuyer, 1992. In T. M. Brinthaupt & R. P. Lipka (Eds.), *The self: Definitional and methodological issues.* Albany: State University of New York Press. Reprinted with permission of the State University of New York Press.

and then quantified. This quantification process begins by first counting the number of sentences coded in each of the categories (i.e, 3rd column of the model shown in Table 7.1), thereby yielding the number of subjects with at least one response coded in a given category. The pro-

Table 7.2

Quantification of the Number of Subjects With Responses on Some Dimensions of the Self

Structures	Sub-Structures	Categories	
MATERIAL SELF #1, 2, 3, 4, 5, 6, 7 8, 9, 10, 12, 14, 15 N=13	Somatic Self #1, 2, 6, 7, 9, 12, 14, 15 N=8	Physical traits #6, 12 Physical cond. #1, 2, 6 7, 9, 14, 15	N=2 N=7
	Possessive Self #1, 2, 3, 4, 5, 6, 7, 8, 9, 10, 14, 15 N=12	Objects #1, 2, 3, 4, 5, 6, 7, 8, 9, 10 Persons #1, 3, 5, 7, 14, 15	N=10 N=6

Note. From "An experiential–developmental framework and methodology to study the transformations of the self-concept from infancy to old age," by R. L'Ecuyer, 1992. In T. M. Brinthaupt & R. P. Lipka (Eds.), The self: Definitional and methodological issues. Albany: State University of New York Press. Reprinted with permission of the State University of New York Press.

cess proceeds next with quantification of the substructures; as such, the number of subjects having at least one response coded for an underlying category of a given substructure is tabulated. Finally, quantification of the higher order level of the structures yields the number of subjects having a response in at least one of the substructures. To better conceptualize this quantification process, an example extrapolated from the full experiential–developmental model and taken from L'Ecuyer (1992, p. 115) is presented in Table 7.2.

Normative Data

Samples. During his work with the GPS over the past 27 years, L'Ecuyer has conducted 2,655 interviews, which have yielded self-concept descriptions from a total of 857 subjects ranging in age from 3 to 100 years; of these, 1,060 interviews have been conducted with 262 people who were 65 years or older (R. L'Ecuyer, personal communication, December 5, 1994). Pertinent to this latter population, he has reported findings related to seven study groups; these represent the ages of 65–69, 70–74, 75–79, 80–84, 85–90, 90–94, and 95–100 (L'Ecuyer, 1991).

Selection and Refinement of Items. As noted above, development and refinement of the GPS method have been continuous over the past 27 years. Specifically, to take into account, more appropriately, the wide diversification of self-reported content inherent in measurements derived from the many age groups across the life span, L'Ecuyer (1992) reported a need to expand both the structures and substructures of his original model (see Table 7.1).

Psychometric Properties. Reliability. To establish test–retest reliability estimates for the GPS method, L'Ecuyer (1992) assessed the extent to which subjects' responses on the first question (i.e., "Who are you?"; see above) were identical to those given at the retest session (i.e., second testing stage; see above). Although estimates were computed for all 43 dimensions, L'Ecuyer cautioned that interpretations based on 3 may be problematic for occasional groups; these were the structure somatic self, its physical condition category and its social attitudes substructure. Information related to these reliability estimates are reported elsewhere in French (see L'Ecuyer, in press). I am aware of no other reliability information that has been reported in English.

Validity. L'Ecuyer (1992) reported on what he termed "experiential validity" (p. 116). This phenomenon is obtained through the implementation of four steps. First, the interviewer makes an initial coding of the responses. Second, the interviewer meets with the respondent and asks for a more detailed explanation of exactly what he or she meant by the particular self-description. Third, concomitant with this reiterated explanation, the interviewer recodes the responses. Finally, the two sets of coded responses are compared. Given findings of no substantial differences between the two codifications, L'Ecuyer concluded that the coded data truly represented the subject's perceptions of self. It is in this sense, then, that L'Ecuyer would argue for evidence of experiential validity. In this regard, he reported that differences had been found only 17 times out of 34,091 (L'Ecuyer, 1992, p. 116).[15]

Related Psychometric Research

I am not aware of any additional psychometric research that has been conducted on the GPS method and reported in English.

Evaluation Summary

The GPS method represents a unique approach to the measurement of self-concept for the elderly. Although it is based on the open-ended response format, it is apparent that L'Ecuyer has gone to great lengths

---

15. The total number of possibilities (34,091) represents the number of subjects interviewed (3–100 years of age) times the number of self-concept dimensions (43).

to overcome the limitations typically associated with this assessment strategy. Of particular note is that a mechanism for testing both the reliability and validity of the GPS approach has been incorporated into the actual assessment process. In this regard, the GPS method clearly stands apart from other extant adaptations of the open-ended response approach to self-concept measurement. Indeed, L'Ecuyer is to be commended for his persistent and dedicated pursuit, over the past quarter of a century, of a psychometrically sound approach to the measurement of self-concept!

Source Information

Location: Rene L'Ecuyer, 539 rue Meilleur, Sherbrooke, Quebec, Canada J1J 2P4

Cost: Dr. L'Ecuyer recommended that interested readers write to him for updated information on the GPS method.

8 Measures of Self-Concept for Special Populations

In structuring the contents of this volume, one of my strongest wishes was to include one chapter devoted to self-concept measures that had been designed specifically for use with special populations. I had hoped to provide information bearing on the selection of instruments for appropriate use with at least two (educable and trainable) mentally retarded populations, as well as with various physically disabled populations. My aspiration in this regard arose from my observations, over the years, that in measuring self-concepts for these various special populations, most researchers used assessment scales that were normed on normal populations.

Unfortunately, my search of the literature revealed such instrumentation to be disappointingly sparse and serves to highlight this critical void in the availability of self-concept measures for special populations. As a consequence of this search, I am able to provide readers with information related only to instruments appropriate for use with persons having learning disabilities and hearing impairments. Although each of the instruments described below is still in need of substantial research to establish more firmly the psychometric soundness of its scores with the intended populations, they nonetheless stand as valuable self-concept measures in this area of research.

The first scale, developed by Boersma and Chapman (1992), is designed to measure multidimensional components of the more specific academic self-concept. Although originally constructed for use with normally achieving children, this instrument has been tested extensively with various learning-disabled (LD) populations; for this reason, in ad-

221

dition to its academically oriented focus, it is also included here. The second measure, designed by Renick and Harter (1988), was specifically designed for use with LD children and measures multiple domain-specific self-concepts, as well as overall global self-worth. This is a multifaceted approach that taps self-perceptions across different domains. The third instrument, developed by Oblowitz, Green, and Heyns (1991), is designed to measure the multiple self-concepts of children with hearing impairments across important domains in their lives. Although this unique instrument is still in the early stages of psychometric testing and norms development, its potential as a valuable measure of self-concept for this population would seem to be enormous; it is therefore included in this chapter. Finally, I summarize findings from a recent validity study of a revised form of the Tennessee Self-Concept Scale for use with children having hearing impairments (Gibson-Harman & Austin, 1985). We turn now to a review of these four instruments.

INDIVIDUALS WITH LEARNING DISABILITIES

Perception of Ability Scale for Students

The Perception of Ability Scale for Students (PASS; Boersma & Chapman, 1992) is a 70-item dichotomously scaled measure of academic self-concept that was originally designed for use with normally achieving children in Grades 3 to 6. The instrument is fully described for this population in chapter 5. However, over at least the past two decades, the authors have also gathered substantial evidence supporting the validity of PASS scores for LD children as well (for reviews, see Boersma & Chapman, 1992; Chapman, 1988a; Chapman & Boersma, 1991).[1] Although Boersma and Chapman reported no construct validity research findings in relation to this population, they did report on the discriminatory power of the PASS in differentiating between LD and non-LD children. Given the volume of this literature, and because researchers interested in measuring the self-concepts of LD children may wish to tailor their investigation specifically to academic self-concepts, I considered it important to include mention of the PASS in this chapter. Summarized below, then, is a review of findings from research that demonstrates the capability of this scale to discriminate between LD and

---

1. Boersma and Chapman (1992) also reported evidence in support of its use with other exceptional populations (educable mentally retarded and gifted).

non-LD children.[2] For a full description of the PASS, however, see chapter 5.

Chapman and Boersma (1980) tested for differences in PASS full scale and subscale scores for 81 LD and 81 non-LD children from two suburban elementary schools (Grades 3–6). Whereas all LD children were receiving part-time resource room assistance, the non-LD children were randomly selected from the regular school classes; all had normal-range group-test IQ scores, albeit those for the LD group were slightly lower than those for the normally achieving group. Findings revealed a statistically significant difference between the two groups on the full scale, with LD children reporting substantially lower scores. The same findings were found with respect to all subscale scores, except those for Penmanship and Neatness. Exactly the same findings were reported by Hiebert, Wong, and Hunter (1982) in their study of 30 LD and 46 non-LD students in Grades 8 and 10. Furthermore, as a follow-up to their previous work, Cullen, Boersma, and Chapman (1981) reported similar findings for Grade 3 LD ($n = 70$) and non-LD ($n = 73$) children in which IQ (on the basis of the Wechsler Intelligence Scale for Children—Revised [WISC–R; Wechsler, 1974]), age, and socioeconomic status were controlled. In this case, however, scores for LD children were substantially lower than they were for non-LD children for the full scale, as well as for all subscales.

Based on a sample of LD ($n = 25$) and non-LD ($n = 211$) children in Grades 4 to 6, Janzen, Boersma, Fisk, and Chapman (1983) also reported findings of lower full scale PASS scores, as well as lower subscale scores for all except the Confidence scale. Likewise, in a comparison of mildly LD ($n = 162$) and non-LD ($n = 50$) children in Grades 3 through 6, A. Thomas and Pashley (1982) found that before an attribution-based intervention program, the LD students had significantly lower full scale PASS scores.

Finally, Chapman and Wilkinson (1988) reported findings from a longitudinal study in which the academic self-concepts of LD and non-LD students were tracked over a 5-year period. During the first phase, the study followed 78 LD and 71 non-LD students from the start of Grade 6 through the end of Grade 7. Results revealed significant differences between the two groups of students on all PASS subscales except Penmanship and Neatness. In the second phase of the study, 51

---

2. Studies conducted before 1988 were based on an earlier version of the instrument, entitled the Student's Perception of Ability Scale.

LD and 53 non-LD students were assessed in the middle of Grade 10. Findings yielded the same pattern of differences between the two groups of students.

Taken together, results from these studies provide strong evidence that the PASS can effectively discriminate between LD and non-LD children. Indeed, after a meta-analytic study of LD self-concept research, Chapman (1988a) reported a mean effect size of −.92, which can be interpreted as indicating that 85% of LD students had full scale PASS scores that were lower than the average PASS score for non-LD students.

On the face of these reviewed studies, then, it would appear that the PASS can be used appropriately with both LD and non-LD children, a fact that clearly increases its value as a measure of self-concept. This is particularly so in research where comparisons of LD and non-LD children may be of interest. What is needed now, however, is a well-organized program of construct validation and other psychometric research that tests, more rigorously, the appropriateness of using the PASS with LD children.

Self-Perception Profile for Learning Disabled Students

The Self-Perception Profile for Learning Disabled Students (SPPLD; Renick & Harter, 1988) is a self-report measure of self-concept designed for use with LD children. Harter (1990b) defined this population as children "within the normal range of intelligence who have specific deficits in the area of information processing, reading, writing, and the manipulation of symbols" (p. 307). Development of the SPPLD evolved from Renick's (1985, 1988) investigations of self-concept dimensionality for special populations of children. On the basis of responses from Harter's (1985b) Self-Perception Profile for Children (SPPC; see chapter 5) and earlier versions thereof, Renick determined that self-concept structure was somewhat different for LD children (Grades 3–8) than it was for normally achieving children. This difference related to perceptions of competency and adequacy in particular domains. Although both groups of children were able to clearly distinguish among each of the five specific domains being tapped by the SPPC (scholastic competence, athletic competence, social acceptance, physical appearance, and behavioral conduct), the LD children went beyond these a priori dimensional boundaries and made still further distinctions within the scholastic competence domain. This distinction revealed the salience of two specific self-concept facets not found with normally achieving children. The first facet represented LD children's perceptions of their general intellectual ability (e.g., being smart); the second facet related to their perceived competence in specific academic tasks (e.g., reading, writing, spelling, and mathematics; Harter, 1990b).

As a consequence of these revelations, Renick and Harter (1988) considered it important to construct a new instrument capable of tapping, more appropriately, the self-concepts of LD children. Because these children were able to distinguish among the five specific domains measured by the SPPC, the authors used this instrument as the springboard for building the SPPLD. As such, the SPPC was adapted to accommodate the measurement of five additional domains: intellectual ability and the more specific academic competencies of reading, writing, spelling, and mathematics. Renick and Harter described and rationalized these subscale domains as follows:

- General Intellectual Ability. This domain reflects the extent to which LD children perceive themselves as being smart, bright, and good learners in school. It was included as a subscale in the SPPLD for two reasons. First, given that research has shown LD children to differentiate between perceptions of their intellectual ability and their academic performance, failure to take this distinction into account would mask important information. Second, in the light of these findings, with the fact that LD children have average or above average intelligence, it would seem useful to have an instrument that permits the researcher to measure their perceived intellectual ability independent from their perceived competencies in specific academic subject areas. Thus, inclusion of the General Intellectual Ability subscale, in addition to the other academic-specific subscales facilitates this important issue.

- Reading, Spelling, Writing, and Mathematics Competencies. These four separate subscales measure the extent to which LD children perceive themselves as proficient in each of these subject areas. Renick and Harter (1988) chose these specific self-concept dimensions for inclusion in the SPPLD on the basis of the literature that has shown these academic areas to be the ones with which most LD children experience difficulty; in addition, they represent the building blocks of learning. Because the LD population is known to be quite heterogeneous with respect to these academic competencies, the provision of their separate subscales enables researchers to examine differences, as well as similarities, across the four academic domains. As noted above also, it permits the assessment of relations between perceived academic competencies and general intellectual ability. Items within the Reading Competence scale tap the notions of being able to read most books and stories quite easily, as well as the speed with which they can be read. The Spelling Competence subscale measures the extent to which children perceive themselves as being able to spell, and are at ease in spelling, most words that they encounter. Items constituting the Writing Competence subscale focus on perception of selves as good writers; specifically, the scale measures the extent to which LD children view their ability to write sentences and paragraphs well enough to create a good story. Finally, the Mathematics Competence items tap the extent to which LD children perceive themselves as good at mathematics and able to understand basic mathematical concepts.

Taken together, then, the SPPLD is composed of 10 subscales as follows: (a) Social Acceptance, Athletic Competence, Physical Appearance; Behavioral Conduct (taken from the SPPC); (b) General Intellectual Ability; (c) Reading, Spelling, Writing, and Mathematics Competencies; and (d) Global Self-Worth (taken from the SPPC). In keeping with the other Self-Perception Profiles developed by Harter and associates, the SPPLD is grounded in the same theoretical perspective that self-concept is a multidimensional construct that reflects domain-specific evaluations, as well as overall judgments of self-worth (Harter, 1990b). Of critical importance is the fact that this global judgment of self-worth is measured not indirectly, as a summative composite of multidimensional self-concepts, but, rather, directly, as a separate and independent construct in its own right. Thus, the SPPLD is theoretically linked to the correlated-factor model of self-concept described in chapter 1.

Target Population

Although the SPPLD was originally designed for use with LD children in Grades 3 through 8 (ages 8–12 years), Renick and Harter (1988) provided psychometric evidence that substantiates its use with normally achieving children as well. Thus, in addition to research that addresses issues relevant to LD children, the instrument can also be used appropriately with normally achieving children in research for which self-perceptions of specific academic areas may be of interest. Of course, in the light of its appropriateness with both groups of children, another valuable use of the SPPLD is in research that focuses on the comparison of self-perceptions of LD and those of normally achieving children.

Scale Structure

The SPPLD is a 46-item self-report scale that comprises 10 subscales. Nine scales are designed to measure self-perceptions in relation to specific domains of one's life (Athletic Competence, Social Acceptance, Physical Appearance, Behavioral Conduct, General Intellectual Ability, Reading Competence, Spelling Competence, Writing Competence, and Mathematics Competence), and one is designed to measure perception of self in general (Global Self-Worth). The academic competence subscales (Reading Competence, Spelling Competence, Writing Competence, and Mathematics Competence) are each composed of four items; all others are composed of five. As with the other self-perception instruments developed by Harter and colleagues, the items are counterbalanced so that within each subscale, either two or three items are worded in the positive direction, and the remainder are worded in the negative direction. All items are presented in a 4-point structured-alternative format intended to offset the tendency for children to respond in a socially desirable manner. One sample item from the General Intellectual Ability subscale of the SPPLD is presented in Exhibit 8.1.

As was true for the SPPC (as well as the other SPP scales), the manual for the SPPLD includes a separate scale that enables researchers to tap perceptions of importance in relation to each domain. This rating scale, for LD children, is composed of 18 items, 2 for each domain-specific subscale.

Administration and Scoring

In keeping with the SPPC, described in chapter 5, the SPPLD can be administered either individually or in groups, and the mode of responding and scoring is identical. Likewise, a scoring key and instructions for the computation of discrepancy scores are provided in the manual. (For details related to each of these factors, readers are referred to chapter 5.)

Renick and Harter (1988) issued an additional administration caveat, however, when the SPPLD is used with LD children. Given that by definition, these children experience reading difficulties, Renick and Harter highly recommended that each item be read aloud during its administration, unless the administrator is certain that each child can read and comprehend the items in a competent manner. The authors

Exhibit 8.1

Sample Item From the Self-Perception Profile for Learning Disabled Students

Really True for Me	Sort of True for Me			Sort of True for Me	Really True for Me
☐	☐	Some kids feel that they are just as smart as others their age	BUT	Other kids *aren't so sure* and wonder if they are as smart.	☐	☐

also suggested that the children be encouraged to use an index card to cover items to which they are not responding. To facilitate this practice, the administrator may ask children to cover all items, except the first one, with an index card. After completion of the first item, children are then asked to move the card to the second item, and so on. This careful administrative procedure can be helpful in maintaining LD children's attention to the task at hand.

Normative Data

Samples. Standardization of the SPPLD for LD children was based on two independent samples of Colorado children in Grades 4 through 8 who had been identified for inclusion in an LD program on the basis of the state criteria. Sample A ($N = 90$) comprised children attending public school resource rooms, and Sample B ($N = 111$) comprised children attending a private school for LD children and adolescents. The two samples were comparable to one another in terms of socioeconomic status (middle to upper-middle class), location within the community (suburban), and ethnicity (97% White).

Children in Sample A (public school) worked for 1 to 2 hr per day in a small group setting and attended regular classes for the remainder of the day. Renick and Harter (1988) reported that each of these children demonstrated (a) a full scale WISC–R (Wechsler, 1974) IQ score of at least 80; (b) at least a 40% discrepancy score between academic ability and achievement, as measured by the Woodcock–Johnson Psychoeducational Battery (Woodcock, 1978); and (c) a significant impairment in one or more areas of information processing. No child showed evidence of behavioral or emotional difficulties as his or her primary handicapping condition.

Children in Sample B (private school) were members of classes consisting of only 10 to 12 other LD children, who were taught by one teacher specialist in the area of learning disabilities, along with at least one teaching assistant. In lieu of designating classes by grade, this private school categorized them in one of four divisions; only students enrolled in the lower school (age = 9–14 years; Grade = 3–6) and junior high (age = 11–16 years; Grade = 7–8) divisions were included in this sample (Renick & Harter, 1988).[3] Renick and Harter (1988) reported that for these children, (a) IQ scores ranged from 80 to 128, as measured by either the WISC–R (Wechsler, 1974), the Stanford–Binet In-

---

3. Although there is overlap across age and grade, the authors noted that substantial effort is made to group together children who are academically and socially similar.

telligence Scale (Forms L or M; Thorndike, Hagen, & Sattler, 1986), or the Slossen Intelligence Test (Slossen, 1963); (b) discrepancy scores between academic ability and achievement were significant on private school entry;[4] and (c) the majority of students had been previously identified as LD by their home school district.

Selection and Refinement of Items. No information related to these issues is provided in the SPPLD manual.

Psychometric Properties. Reliability. Across the two samples of LD children, Renick and Harter (1988) reported mean internal consistency reliability coefficients for each of the 10 subscales; these are as follows: General Intellectual Ability (α = .81), Reading Competence (α = .86), Spelling Competence (α = .89), Writing Competence (α = .78), Mathematics Competence (α = .88), Social Acceptance (α = .81), Athletic Competence (α = .82), Physical Appearance (α = .82), Behavioral Conduct (α = .83), and Global Self-Worth (α = .83). On the basis of these results, Renick and Harter concluded that internal consistency reliability estimates for the SPPLD were adequate. No other reliability information is reported in the manual for this population of LD children.

Validity. The only validity research reported in the SPPLD manual relates to exploratory factor analytic findings on the basis of the combined sample of LD children; only the domain-specific subscales were included in the analysis.[5] Overall, results revealed a relatively clear nine-factor solution, with all target loadings greater than .34, and most (35/40) greater than .51; only two cross-loadings greater than .20 (.22) were reported. Findings from this analysis led Renick and Harter (1988) to conclude that

> not only do the original subscales taken from the Self-Perception Profile for Children form independent factors when used with a learning disabled population, but the additional subscales of General Intellectual Ability, Reading Competence, Spelling Competence, Writing Competence, and Math Competence are equally clear and interpretable. (p. 16)

Both reliability and factor analytic results based on SPPLD responses for normally achieving children are also reported in the manual. However, given our focus on the LD population, and in the interest of space, these findings are not reported here. Finally, although the

4. The term *significant* is not defined in the manual, and the measuring instrument is not identified.

5. There is no indication whether these results derived from principal components or principal-axis factor analyses.

authors reported their use of oblique rotation in the analyses described above, they did not report correlational values among the subscale factors, nor did they report any other validity research findings.

Related Psychometric Research

I am aware of no additionally reported psychometric research conducted on the SPPLD, either by Renick and Harter or by others.

Evaluation Summary

In view of the fact that the SPPLD was developed from the SPPC, which itself was carefully and systematically modeled from an earlier version of the instrument (the Perceived Competence Scale for Children [Harter, 1982]) and on the basis of the reliability and validity findings reported to date, the SPPLD holds a great deal of promise as an important measure of self-concept for this population. However, substantially more research is needed to more fully establish its psychometric soundness. As has been the case for its companion instruments described in this volume, for which I have also called for more psychometric and construct validity research to be conducted, the SPPLD is included here because of its strong theoretical foundation and because of the critical need for self-concept measures appropriate for use with the LD population.

It is hoped that if this potentially valuable instrument becomes better known to a wide community of researchers, the SPPLD will soon accrue a valuable body of important construct validity information. In particular, the SPPLD could benefit substantially from rigorous construct validity work based on the analysis of covariance structures. More specifically, it would be of interest (a) to test for the validity and invariance of its factorial structure using a confirmatory factor analytic model (b) to test for evidence of convergent and discriminant validity based on an MTMM model, and (c) bearing in mind the difficulty of developmental factors, to test for the stability of its factorial structures across reasonable time periods. Indeed, in the light of Renick and Harter's (1988, p. 4) gracious generosity in granting permission to copy the instrument, thereby facilitating the process, the authors have shown their support and encouragement for such research to be conducted.

Source Information

Location: Susan Harter, University of Denver, Department of Psychology, 2155 South Race Street, Denver, Colorado 80208-0204

Cost: Manual: $15.00

INDIVIDUALS WITH HEARING IMPAIRMENTS

Self-Concept Scale for the Hearing-Impaired

Description

The Self-Concept Scale for the Hearing-Impaired (SSHI; Oblowitz, Green, & Heyns, 1991) is a 40-item self-report measure of self-concept designed for use with hearing-impaired children. The instrument was designed, in part, to address the limitations of previous self-concept research related to this population, in which the instruments used had been initially developed for use with normal-hearing children. For example, both the Piers–Harris Children's Self-Concept Scale (Piers, 1984) and the Tennessee Self-Concept Scale (Roid & Fitts, 1988/1994) have been used with the hearing-impaired (Gibson-Harman & Austin, 1985; Koelle & Convey, 1982; Loeb & Sarigiani, 1986; Yachnick, 1986); findings from these studies pointed to potential difficulties in the interpretation of test scores for hearing-impaired children and adolescents. Essentially, the problem revolves around a limited understanding of the language (Garrison & Tesch, 1978; Koelle & Convey, 1982) and a low level of test-taking skills (Yachnick, 1986) for this population of children. It was with these limitations in mind, then, that Oblowitz and colleagues were stimulated to develop the SSHI.

Although the authors do not explicitly link the SSHI to a particular model of self-concept, I consider it to be most closely affiliated with the nomothetic model described in chapter 1.

Target Population

The SSHI has been uniquely designed for use with hearing-impaired children. Although the targeted age range is not specifically stated, it would appear by the ages of the normative samples that it is appropriate for use with children 11 through 19 years of age.

Scale Structure

The SSHI is a 40-item gender-specific self-report scale that comprises four subscales, with the number of items varying across scales. Specifically, the instrument measures Personal Self-Concept (4 items; e.g., "I want to wear my hearing aids"); Physical Self-Concept (4 items; e.g., "I like the way I look"); Academic Self-Concept (8 items; e.g., "I do well at schoolwork"); and Social Self-Concept (24 items). The latter scale, however, can be decomposed into four subcomponents; these are as follows: Teachers (4 items; e.g., "My teacher understands me"); Family

(4 items; e.g., "My brothers and sisters like me"); Peers (6 items; e.g., "I feel different from most boys and girls"); and Hearing Peers and Society (10 items; e.g., "I can go to the same places as hearing boys and girls"). In addition to these separate dimensions of self-concept, Oblowitz et al. (1991) suggested that general self-concept could be measured by considering the separate dimensions' sum across domains (but see arguments by Harter and others, as noted throughout this volume, against this procedure).

For each item, the respondent is presented with three pictures of the same young girl (or boy), albeit the facial expression is different (happy, neutral, or sad). In an effort to offset response bias, the order of these differential representations varies for each item. In other words, no two consecutive items display pictures in the same order. Accompanying each picture is a statement enclosed within a balloon caption. Oblowitz et al. (1991) noted that in this way, the pictures serve to focus the task nonverbally, whereas the statements ensure specificity. Because the instrument was designed to be gender specific, there is one for use with girls (i.e., all picture portrayals are girls) and one for use with boys (i.e., all picture portrayals are boys). A sample item representing the Hearing Peers and Society component of the Social Self-Concept subscale of the SSHI is presented in Figure 8.1.

Administration and Scoring

Written instructions on the first page of the SSHI (i.e., a sample page) describe three steps to follow in completing the questionnaire; each is accompanied by instructions to the administrator to clearly demonstrate each step. These three steps identify the fact that (a) there are three girls (in the case of the female version)—one is very happy, one is very sad, and one is not so sad or happy; (b) each girl is saying something, and they are to read what she is saying; and (c) they are to determine which girl is most like them and then mark their choice by placing a tick in the block appearing below that figure.

Because hearing-impaired respondents are subject to various types of errors, Oblowitz et al. (1991) emphasized that it is critical that administrators use a total communication approach in conveying both the test instructions and the meaning of any items that are not understood. They further suggested that for students who may have weaker language proficiency skills, the SSHI be administered one item at a time. Completion of the instrument should take approximately 30 min.

The pictorial item format represents a 3-point scale that renders

Figure 8.1

Sample item from the Hearing Peers and Society component of the Social Self-Concept subscale of the Self-Concept Scale for the Hearing-Impaired. Copyright by Neil Oblowitz. Reprinted with permission.

assignments of negative, neutral, and positive self-perceptions to scores of 1, 2, or 3, respectively. Subscale SSHI scores can then be easily computed through a simple summation of the appropriate items.

Normative Data

Samples. Standardization of the SSHI was based on a sample of 253 hearing-impaired students from three different special schools; ages ranged from 11 to 19 years. Under the supervision of a psychologist, class teachers administered the test to small groups of not more than 10 students.

Selection and Refinement of Items. The original pool of SSHI items was derived from reviews of both the self-concept and hearing-impaired literatures and an examination of several self-concept scales. This process yielded 80 items that represented both newly constructed items and items selected from four self-concept instruments that were modified to ensure simplicity of language and minimization of conceptual com-

plexity (Oblowitz et al., 1991).[6] Initial testing of this 80-item SSHI involved a small sample of hearing-impaired children who ranged in age
from 11 to 18 years.[7] Data were subsequently examined by professionals
who work with the hearing-impaired, to determine the extent to which
each item met the following criteria: (a) importance with respect to the
particular perception of self being measured, as determined by empirical as well as theoretical research; (b) appropriateness in terms of age
range and specific domain being measured; (c) simplicity of language;
(d) pupil interest and motivation, as determined by respondent comments and professional observations; and (e) the extent to which the
item directly represented the self-perception being tapped (Oblowitz
et al., 1991).

Psychometric Properties. Reliability. On the basis of complete data
from 198 students out of the original sample of 253, over intervals of
28 to 34 days, Oblowitz et al. (1991) reported test–retest reliability coefficients of .49, .62, .67, and .68 for the SSHI Physical Self-Concept,
Personal Self-Concept, Social Self-Concept, and Academic Self-Concept
subscales, respectively; a reliability coefficient of .70 was reported for
the total scale. Additionally, the authors reported test–retest reliability
information in relation to the total scale, with particular group factors
taken into account as follows: (a) Across degree of hearing loss, the
estimates were .68 (profound), .66 (moderate), and .87 (mild); (b)
across the level of language and communication, they were .62 (poor),
.67 (average), and .81 (good); and (c) across age, they were .76 (11–
13 years of age), .64 (14–16 years of age), and .75 (17–19 years of age).
No significant differences were found between the two gender-specific
versions of the instrument. No other reliability information was
reported.

Validity. Given the lack of other self-concept measures for use with
hearing-impaired adolescents—in addition to the fact that relations between self-concept and personality traits, social adjustment, and manifest behavior have not yet been established—Oblowitz et al. (1991) reported some difficulty in testing for the validity of SSHI scores. As a
consequence of these obstacles, they resorted to more unconventional
methods in their attempt to establish some evidence of validity; these
included correlations between SSHI total scale scores and (a) ratings of

---

6. The instruments were the Canadian Self-Esteem Inventory (Battle, 1977), the Bledsoe Self-
Esteem Scale (Bledsoe, 1964), the Lipsitt Self-Concept Scale (Lipsitt, 1958), and the
Piers–Harris Children's Self-Concept Scale (Piers & Harris, 1964).

7. Sample size is not specified.

inferred self-concept, based on a short form of the instrument by three professionals who knew the student well, and (b) total scale scores on the Coopersmith (1967) Self-Esteem Inventory for 42 hearing adolescents for whom the items had been modified accordingly. Although relations between the hearing-impaired student and professional rating scores were low (mean r across schools = .31), those between the two self-concept total scores for the hearing-impaired sample and the hearing sample were fairly high (.81).

Finally, although Oblowitz et al. (1991) reported a summary of relations between extracted factors on an exploratory analysis of the SSHI and its hypothesized dimensions, these findings are very unclear and are inconsistent with the structure of the instrument; although no factor loadings were reported, the authors indicated that 31 factor loadings were greater than .50.[8]

Related Psychometric Research

I am aware of no additionally reported psychometric research conducted on the SSHI.

Evaluation Summary

As the first self-concept instrument to be specifically designed for use with hearing-impaired adolescents, the SSHI clearly fills a very important void in this area of psychological assessment. However, based on the theoretical perspective of Harter (e.g., 1988a) and others (e.g., Marsh, 1986b), which argues for a separate global self-worth facet, I would caution against making any interpretations based on the SSHI total score; the most valuable aspect of this instrument lies with its separate subscales. On the basis of recent theoretical and empirical developments in self-concept research, I encourage the authors to consider the development of a separate global self-concept subscale in lieu of a simple summation of scores across domains.

Although the SSHI is still in its infancy, findings from the limited psychometric research reported to date suggest that the instrument holds great potential as a valuable self-concept measure for this population. As noted earlier, however, substantially more work is needed to firmly establish both its construct validity and its other psychometric properties. In keeping with my recommendations stated elsewhere in this volume, I believe that the SSHI would benefit substantially from

---

8. It is presumed that the authors meant 31 out of the 40 loadings expected to load on the dimensions they were designed to measure.

rigorous construct validity work based on the analysis of covariance structures. More specifically, it would be of interest to test for the validity and invariance of its factorial structure using a confirmatory factor analytic model.

Source Information

Location: Neil Oblowitz, MEd, Chartered Psychologist, Via P. Sotto-corno 52, 20129 Milano, Italy

Cost: The manual and scale are presently available in draft form only. Interested users may write to Mr. Oblowitz for updated information.

Tennessee Self-Concept Scale—Revised

In the interest of completeness, and because the information may be useful to readers searching for self-concept measures for use with the hearing-impaired, I include here a summary of information bearing on the development of a revised form of the Tennessee Self-Concept Scale (TSCS–R; Gibson-Harman & Austin, 1985) for use with these populations. In particular, the revision takes into account vocabulary and sentence length, as well as the use of idioms and references to social issues that are relevant to a population of early adolescents and older (e.g., "I am popular with men"; Gibson-Harman & Austin, 1985).

Based on a sample of 179 individuals (12–21 years of age) that included normal-hearing persons ($n = 77$), deaf persons ($n = 75$), and hard-of-hearing persons ($n = 27$), Gibson-Harman and Austin (1985) began the first in a series of steps to establish norms for the TSCS–R. Initially, revision of the scale involved a reduction in the required reading level. This was accomplished by simplifying language structure, shortening sentences, and reducing the number of syllables per 100 words (i.e., lowering the vocabulary level), while concomitantly retaining the scale's suitability for the original target age groups (adolescence through adulthood). By means of information derived from a pilot study, subscale analysis, and informal investigation, 79 of the original 100 TSCS test items were revised. The authors reported a Dale–Chall (Dale & Chall, 1948) estimated readability level of Grade 3.5 for the TSCS–R (Gibson-Harman & Austin, 1985).

Results from this research yielded a correlation of .85 between the total scores of the original and TSCS–R scales. Test–retest reliability estimates, based on the total TSCS–R score over a 2- to 4-week interval was reported to be .82 for all hearing-impaired participants ($n = 102$), .76 for deaf respondents, and .90 for hard-of-hearing respondents. Based on these findings, Gibson-Harman and Austin (1985) felt confident that with further research and revision, the TSCS–R could prove useful as a measure of self-concept for hearing-impaired persons.

Self-Concept Measurement: State of the Art and Future Directions

STATE OF THE ART OF SELF-CONCEPT MEASUREMENT

Undoubtedly as a consequence of the landmark critiques of self-concept research in general (Wylie, 1968, 1979), and self-concept measurement, in particular (Shavelson et al., 1976; Wylie, 1974, 1989), the present state of the art appears to be healthier than it has ever been before. Indeed, given the slow but steady growth of construct validity research addressing diverse self-concept measurement issues over the past 18 years, it seems apparent that the caveats issued by these authors have not gone unheeded. This observation can be evidenced from a number of improvements in the area of self-concept measurement. Regardless of this promising trend, however, there still remain a few weak areas in need of attention. These positive and negative aspects of the present state of the art of self-concept measurement are now summarized. We turn first to the positive factors.

Advances in Self-Concept Measurement

Over the past decade, several improvements in the measurement of self-concept have taken place. First, most recently developed scales have been designed to measure multiple dimensions of self-concept, with each dimension bearing on an important domain in one's daily life (e.g., academic, social, physical, and emotional domains). Lately, however, there has been a movement to develop multidimensional scales that are specific to a particular domain (e.g., physical self-concept scale, with each subscale tapping one facet of physical self-concept). Second, whereas some older, well-established instruments provided for the indirect measurement of global self-concept through the summation of scores across multidimensional subscales, the inability of this practice to yield an appropriate score is now widely recognized. As a consequence, most recently developed multidimensionally structured instruments interested in tapping global self-concept do so directly by means of a separate subscale. Third, in developing self-concept measures, increasingly more researchers are cognizant of the importance of linking the instrument to a strong body of theory, thereby making it possible to test for its construct validity. As a case in point, note that several test developers have built their instruments within the framework of the Shavelson et al. (1976) hierarchical model of self-concept. Finally, the extended rigor with which self-concept measures have been tested over the past 8 to 10 years is very encouraging. Increasingly, more researchers are using analyses of covariance structures to test various construct validity issues related to their instruments. In particular, they are using confirmatory factor analytic procedures to test for (a) the validity and invariance of hypothesized factorial structures within and across groups, respectively, and (b) evidence of convergent and discriminant validity within the framework of MTMM models.

Weaknesses in Self-Concept Measurement

Turning now to the other side of the coin, my review revealed several weaknesses still prevalent in the area of self-concept measurement. In broad terms, these shortcomings relate to nonoptimal methodological strategies, absence of instrumentation with respect to particular populations, and inattention to the influence of cross-cultural factors. A brief elaboration of each follows.

Nonoptimal Methodological Strategies

Although many test developers have paid close attention to calls from Wylie (1974, 1989) and Shavelson et al. (1976) for more rigorous construct validity research in the construction and testing of self-concept measures, many others remain content to rely on weak and simplistic methodological procedures; at least four are noteworthy here. First, many instruments have been developed and normed on only one or two excessively small samples, with no attempt to replicate findings across either the same or other populations. In the rare instance where replication work has been conducted, there has been no attempt to test for the invariance of item measurement and factorial structure across groups using rigorous statistical procedures. Second, use of confirmatory factor analyses in testing for the validity of test scores from established instruments is still a rare practice; more common is the use of exploratory factor analysis. These applications are limited in at least two ways. (a) Most purported factor analyses are not in fact factor analyses at all but, rather, are principal components analyses. Given the known limitations associated with this procedure (see, e.g., Borgatta, Kercher, & Stull, 1986; Gorsuch, 1990; Hubbard & Allen, 1987; Snook & Gorsuch, 1989), interpretations based on findings must be made cautiously. (b) Despite evidence of correlated factors, many researchers still proceed in using varimax, rather than oblique rotational procedures. Third, despite urgent pleas by both Shavelson et al. (1976) and Wylie (1974, 1989) for the use of MTMM analyses, this procedure is rarely used; it is used even more rarely within the framework of covariance structure analysis, which has addressed many of the prominent limitations associated with the original Campbell and Fiske (1959) approach (see, e.g., Byrne & Goffin, 1993). Finally, researchers fail to conduct and report adequate information related to both the reliability and validity of test scores derived from the self-concept instrument under study.

Absence of Instrumentation

My review of self-concept measures revealed a serious void in the availability of self-report (or other) self-concept measures appropriate for use with the elderly (65 years and older; see also Hattie, 1992); adults other than college students; and diverse mentally and physically handicapped populations. I consider lack of instrumentation in relation to the elderly and the handicapped to be more critical. Indeed, given the thrust of current social policies in addressing the mental health needs of both the elderly and the handicapped, I strongly encourage researchers to consider the development of self-concept measures that can be used appropriately with these populations.

One major difficulty common to all three populations in the development of useful and meaningful self-concept measures is the number of context-specific situations to be addressed. The elderly population, for example, comprises individuals whose lifestyles are widely discrepant: those dependent on full-time nursing home or family care; those living independently in either their own or a senior citizen home; those still actively employed in the workforce either on a full-time or part-time basis; those retired from the workforce who actively participate in community work, sports, and travel, or follow the sun to warmer climates during the cold months of the year; and so on. Given the vast diversity of domains inherent in each of these contexts, it seems unlikely that any one instrument could adequately and appropriately measure self-concepts across this broad collage of senior citizens. Rather, instrument development may need to be specific to particular environmental contexts.

Similarly, for adults younger than 65, there are those actively engaged in the workforce and those who are unemployed either by choice or otherwise. For those who are employed, a self-concept measure specific to their particular profession or job category may be most meaningful. Although there is evidence of some interest in the development of instruments to measure self-perceptions related to one's work, this area of research is very new, and construction efforts are only in the initial stages. Two examples of work-related self-concept measures are the Dimensions of Self-Concept (Form W; Crowder & Michael, 1989a, 1989b, 1991; McNeely Foraker & Michael, 1994) and the Work Self-Concept Scale (Hines, Durham, & Geoghegan, 1991).

Consistent with the contextual diversity noted for the two previous populations, the problem is no less dramatic for the handicapped populations. However, the development of appropriate self-concept instrumentation may be somewhat eased in this instance by the more or less clear delineation of one handicapping condition from another. Nonetheless, there is a very distinct and critical need for self-concept measures relative to this wide diversity of populations.

Inattention to Cross-Cultural Factors

This limitation in the area of self-concept measurement pertains to two different, albeit related, aspects of construct validity. The first of these bears on the widespread failure to validate scores from a particular self-concept scale across other ethnic or racial groups when all scores are derived from the same English (and original) version of the instrument. In the light of increasing evidence in the substantive literature that reveals a strong interest in testing for mean differences across diverse cultural and racial groups, it is surprising that so few researchers have actually tested for the cross-cultural equivalence of both the measurement and structure of their selected self-concept instruments.

The second point relates to the development and use of self-concept measures that have been adapted into another language for use with a cultural group that differs from the one on which the instrument was originally normed. Of course, as noted in chapter 2 and as stated in the *Standards for Educational and Psychological Testing* (1985), any adaptation of a measuring instrument essentially renders it a new instrument, thereby requiring the establishment of new norms based on the cultural group of interest. Furthermore, the reliability and validity of its scores based on this new population must also be determined.

Unfortunately, this important caveat has largely gone unheeded in self-concept research. Most typically, researchers have merely translated an instrument from one language to another and then proceeded to address their substantive questions of interest. Not only is the straight translation of a measuring instrument an inadequate and dubious practice (see Hambleton, 1994; Spielberger, 1992), but it is highly unlikely that the factorial structure of the adapted instrument will be identical to that of the original normative group. Thus, if the interpretation of scores from translated tests is to be meaningful, it is critical that the researcher establish new norms and evidence of construct validity based on data from the population of interest.

FUTURE DIRECTIONS IN SELF-CONCEPT MEASUREMENT

A number of interesting and exciting perspectives regarding self-concept measurement are currently under way. First, there is an interest in the development of instruments designed to measure multifaceted dimensions of domain-specific self-concepts (e.g., academic, physical, and social). Second, several researchers have sought alternative approaches to the open-ended question format in their efforts to address the various limitations associated with self-report pencil-and-paper questionnaires. Finally, consonant with the rapidly growing interest in the use of computer-based testing procedures, there is some indication that this testing strategy may soon become a reality in the measurement of self-concept. Each of these innovative trends is now reviewed.

We turn first to a description of three extremely interesting and potentially valuable new self-report measures. Although each is still in its infancy and, thus, in need of substantially more construct validity research, there is clear evidence that this rigorous process is now well under way.

Recently Developed Self-Report Measures

Arts Self-Perception Inventory

The Arts Self-Perception Inventory (ASPI; Vispoel, 1992) is designed to measure self-perceptions of one's competence in relation to four major arts-related domains: music, visual arts, dance, and dramatic arts. This self-report scale is modeled after the Self Description Questionnaires (Marsh, 1992c, 1992d) and, thus, is closely linked to the Shavelson et al. (1976) model of self-concept (see Vispoel, 1993a, 1995c). At present, there are two versions of the ASPI: one for use with junior and senior high school students and another for use with college students and other adults. We turn now to a brief description of these two new instruments.

Adolescent Scale

The adolescent version of the ASPI is composed of 40 items, each of which is based on a 6-point Likert-type scale (i.e., *false, mostly false, more false than true, more true than false, mostly true,* or *true*). Ten items constitute each of the four subscales; 5 are worded positively, and 5 are worded negatively. The initial testing of this instrument was based on responses from 205 seventh-grade students (mean age = 12 years). Results from this study yielded strong evidence of internal consistency reliability (all αs = .92), a clear four-factor simple structure, theoretically reasonable correlations among the four self-concept dimensions that the ASPI was designed to measure, and a substantively reasonable pattern of correlations between these constructs and external criteria to which they should be logically linked (i.e., interests, self-ratings of ability, reported course grades, nonartistic dimensions of self-concept, and school subject areas; Vispoel, 1993a).

College/Adult Scale

The adult version of the ASPI is composed of 48 items, each of which is based on an 8-point scale (i.e., *definitely false, mostly false, moderately false, more false than true, more true than false, moderately true, mostly true,* or *definitely true).* Twelve items constitute each subscale; half are worded positively, and half negatively. In a recent study designed to test the validity of an extended version of the Shavelson et al. (1976) model that included self-perceptions of dance, dramatic art, visual art, and music skills, Vispoel (1995c) reported important construct validity and psychometric findings that bear directly on the adult ASPI scale. On the basis of test scores from 831 college students (mean age = 24 years), he reported the four arts-related self-concepts to be clearly defined, albeit best described by a higher order artistic domain factor (Artistic Self-Concept). However, in light of the fact that these analyses were based on a composite of items from both the ASPI and the Self Description Questionnaire III, conclusions of clear factorial structure, on the basis of these data, need to be interpreted cautiously. Internal consistency reliability estimates for each of these first-order factors were extremely high; except for the drama facet ($\alpha = .95$), all others yielded alpha coefficients of .96.[1]

More recently, Vispoel (1995a) tested for the validity and invariance of the adult version of the ASPI across two samples of college students ($n_1 = 175$ and $n_2 = 258$). Findings from this study again revealed internal consistency reliabilities to be high ($\alpha s > .95$), a clear four-factor structure that replicated across samples, and subscale scores that formed a logically consistent correlational pattern with a wide variety of external criterion measures. In keeping with Marsh's (1992d) construct validity research with the Self Description Questionnaire III, Vispoel (1995a) based all analyses on ASPI item pairs. Given this methodological strategy, it would be interesting to determine whether the same factor analytic findings held when analyses were based on single, rather than paired, items.

The ASPI shows great promise as a potentially valuable measure of self-concept in relation to the fine arts. Vispoel is currently in the process of validating a computerized version of the ASPI (W. P. Vispoel, personal communication, April 11, 1995). Although the development of a manual is currently under way, it is not yet available for distribution. In the interim, interested readers may obtain updated information related to the ASPI by writing to the author as follows: Walter P. Vispoel, College of Education, Psychological and Quantitative Foundations, University of Iowa, 361 Lindquist Center, Iowa City, Iowa 52242.

---

1. All analyses were based on item clusters of three or four items, rather than on single items, which likely contributed to these exceptionally high values (see Vispoel, 1995c).

Music Self-Perception Inventory

The Music Self-Perception Inventory (MUSPI; Vispoel, 1993b) represents an extension of the Music subscale of the Arts Self-Perception Inventory (ASPI) described in the previous section. As such, it focuses solely on the music domain. In particular, the MUSPI taps self-concepts in relation to six domain-specific dimensions of music (singing, instrument playing, reading music, composing music, listening skill, and creating dance movements), and one general dimension of music ability (overall music skills).[2] In keeping with the development of the ASPI, the MUSPI is firmly tied to the Shavelson et al. (1976) model of self-concept.

As with the ASPI, the MUSPI has both a junior/senior high school and a college/adult version. Although both forms of the instrument are composed of 84 items, the high school version is based on a 6-point Likert-type scale, whereas the college/adult version is based on an 8-point scale format. For both instruments, the 12 items that constitute each subscale are balanced between positive and negative wording. Although construct validity research is currently in progress, Vispoel (1995b) reported internal consistency reliability coefficients ranging from .95 to .96, strong evidence of a clear factorial structure and substantively meaningful relations among subscale scores themselves, as well as with other logically related external criteria.

Although this instrument is still very new, it bears watching closely. As noted for the ASPI, Vispoel is currently in the process of validating a computerized version of the MUSPI. Indeed, the stage already seems set for a systematic program of sound construct validity research to be conducted. Readers interested in following up on findings from further research bearing on the MUSPI are advised to contact the author as follows: Walter P. Vispoel, College of Education, Psychological and Quantitative Foundations, University of Iowa, 361 Lindquist Center, Iowa City, Iowa 52242.

Reading Self-Concept Scale

The Reading Self-Concept Scale (RSCS; Chapman & Tunmer, 1992) is a 30-item self-report scale designed to measure self-perceptions of reading ability for young children (ages 5–10 years). More specifically, the instrument assesses three aspects of perceived reading ability: competence in reading, difficulty in reading, and attitude toward reading.

---

2. The General Music Self-Concept subscale is common to both the MUSPI and the ASPI.

Ten items constitute each subscale. The response format of the RSCS is structured as a 5-point scale, ranging from *yes, always* to *yes, usually* to *undecided or unsure* to *no, not usually* to *no, never*. To ensure that children thoroughly understand how to respond to each item, Chapman and Tunmer included 10 practice items in the scale and, in addition, recommended that the administrator demonstrate the response process by means of three or four examples.

In the light of the recognized importance of reading as a central learning activity of young children, impetus for construction of the RSCS arose from the authors' perceived need for an instrument capable of assessing children's self-concepts relative to specific dimensions of their reading ability. Chapman and Tunmer (1992) noted that existing self-concept instruments were limited in that they were either (a) very task-specific in terms of particular events or activities or (b) too general in terms of tapping a range of school subjects and activities. Based on an initial pool of 50 items, constructed in consultation with reading specialists and teachers of young primary school children, Chapman and Tunmer (1992) conducted item analyses of RSCS responses for two independent samples of children ($N = 787$; age = 5–7 years). Findings from these studies subsequently led to the final 30-item scale.

The psychometric soundness of the 30-item RSCS has been tested on data from two independent samples of children ($n_1 = 444$; age = 5–7 years; $n_2 = 771$; age = 5–10 years). On the basis of results from these studies, Chapman and Tunmer (1992) have reported mean alpha coefficients for the separate subscales of .72 (Reading Competence), .75 (Reading Difficulty), and .77 (Reading Attitude), and for the full scale of .85. Based on both exploratory and confirmatory factor analytic procedures, the test authors also reported a well-defined three-factor reading self-concept structure.

Given that children's self-concepts can vary across the three components of reading competence tapped by the RSCS (Chapman & Tunmer, 1995), this instrument would appear to be a potentially valuable instrument in gathering more precise profiles on their reading abilities. In particular, this instrument seems ideally suited for use with remedial programs where it may be of interest to assess a child's self-perception of reading competency before and after intervention. Readers interested in obtaining further information on the RSCS are advised to contact the first author as follows: James W. Chapman, Education Department, Massey University, Private Bag 11222, Palmerston North, New Zealand.

New and Recently Adapted Self-Report Methodologies

In my reviews of the self-concept literature, I have become interested in three relatively new approaches to measuring perceptions of self, each of which represents an adaptation of the open-ended response format. Although each represents a form of self-reporting, the methodology used in tapping this information differs substantially from the typical pencil-and-paper questionnaire format. My original intent in writing this section was to provide an extensive description of each of these procedures. Unfortunately, however, letters to each of the authors requesting further information yielded no response. As a consequence, I can provide only a brief description of each measurement approach. As was the case for the three previously described measuring instruments, these measurement approaches require substantial construct validity research to be conducted.

A Projective Technique

The first procedure of note involves the development of a projective technique for measuring the self-esteem of kindergarten children. This measure, entitled Faces and Feelings, is designed to tap information related to important significant others, as well as feelings about home and school activities (Juhasz & Munshi, 1990). Interestingly, this instrument was designed and constructed by a group of 47 kindergarten children, under the guidance of, as well as in collaboration with, their teacher, over a period of 3 weeks. After a teaching unit on feelings, children were actively involved in a discussion of what things and people made them feel good about themselves, feel important, and able to do well and the negative counterparts of these perceptions. Additionally, children were asked to tell how they felt in different situations and how they thought other people would feel about them and their behavior in different situations. From this pool of words, children chose the words *happy, sad,* and *okay* to best represent feelings that (a) "I am worthwhile and feel good about myself," (b) "I am no good and feel bad about myself," and (c) "I am good enough, am satisfied, but don't feel really great or really bad about myself," respectively (Juhasz & Munshi, 1990, p. 694).

After completion of the response format for the Faces and Feelings instrument, the children next identified and reached a consensus on the five people who most influenced their feelings about themselves.

These were "Mum, Dad, Teacher, Family, and Friend" (Juhasz & Munshi, 1990, p. 694). Furthermore, they identified common places and activities that made them feel able or not able to do well; these were Home, School, Vacation, Freetime, Mathematics, and Reading. Under the children's direction, the teacher next drew faces to correspond to each of the three response alternatives. Finally, the instrument was pilot tested with each child.

In summary, the Faces and Feelings self-esteem measure uses a combination of stimulus–response options. As such, the child is asked to (a) draw six pictures representing people who are important and significant in her or his life; (b) draw six pictures of situations that are important in his or her life; (c) draw three faces on precut circles, representing happy, sad, and okay emotions; and (d) match a face to each picture, showing how a particular person or situation makes her or him feel about herself or himself. As such, this instrument uses less structured stimuli than is typically the case for projective-type measures.

Juhasz and Munshi (1990) reported that the Faces and Feelings measure is effective in eliminating the most pervasive problems associated with self-concept measurement and in identifying self-concepts relative to different domains (see, e.g., Hughes, 1984; chapter 1, this volume); it can also yield important information bearing on significant others in a young child's life. The fact that the concept to be interpreted was represented by a child's drawing, rather than a preestablished model provided by an adult researcher, quite likely contributed to the effectiveness of this instrument. As such, it eliminates the need to teach the child the meaning of these representations, because he or she already "owns" his or her pictures through the process of drawing them (Juhasz & Munshi, 1990).

An Interview Technique

The second methodological approach of interest represents an adaptation of the Who Are You? technique (Bugental & Zelen, 1950) noted in chapter 8. The present version, entitled "Tell Me About Yourself," is an interview procedure for use with children in kindergarten through Grade 12 (Brinthaupt & Erwin, 1992; Brinthaupt & Lipka, 1985). Adult interviewers are trained in the format. Children are first informed that they will be asked to tell the interviewer about themselves and that although everything they say will be recorded, this information will not be given to parents, teachers, or others. The interviewer records as accurately as possible all phrases and statements made by the child in response to the request, "Tell me about yourself." After the child is finished with his or her self-description, the interviewer then repeats each of his or her statements and asks the child if there is something that should be changed.

Scoring of the interview data follows a three-step process. As such, the statements are evaluated first for evidence of self-concept content (i.e., descriptions of self), and second for evidence of self-esteem (i.e., whether the child wished to maintain or change the self-concept content). Coding for the latter uses the plus/minus system of coding (see Brinthaupt & Lipka, 1985). Finally, the statements are assessed with respect to their relative positions in the protocol (i.e., the point in the interview at which the statements were made).

Brinthaupt and Lipka (1985) argued that this form of self-reporting has several advantages over the usual pencil-and-paper questionnaire. First, it provides for the simultaneous acquisition of information relevant to both a child's self-concept and self-esteem. Because this approach allows for discrimination between how children describe themselves and the extent to which they are satisfied with their self-descriptions, it provides a more detailed profile of their self-perceptions. Second, the examination of position effects relative to each statement made by the child during the interview can be interpreted as indicators of salience, with early statements being regarded as more salient. Finally, Brinthaupt and Lipka suggested that this interview approach may be less likely to elicit socially desirable and acquiescent responses than is the case for the self-report approach to self-concept measurement where response formats are typically used. As such, the respondent has the opportunity to react in a patterned manner that may be irrelevant to his or her perceptions of self. Relatedly, Brinthaupt and Erwin (1992) suggested that "such effects are likely to be magnified to the extent that accurate self-reports are seen as less important than is socially desirable responding" (p. 152).

The Notion of Possible Selves

The third interesting area of research is not so much a methodological strategy as it is a broadening of the investigative horizon to take into account social and temporal contextual frameworks in studying the self-concept (see, e.g., Yardley, 1987). Of import here is the work of Markus and associates (Markus, Cross, & Wurf, 1990; Markus & Nurius, 1986,

1987) and their studies of *possible selves*. The notion of possible selves represents individuals' ideals of what they might become, what they would like to become, and what they are afraid of becoming. Markus and Nurius (1987) reasoned that these possible selves serve as the cognitive representations of enduring goals, aspirations, motives, fears, and threats and, as such, they formulate a conceptual bridge between the self-concept and motivation.

Another aspect of this research perspective is the notion of the *working self-concept*. This concept requires a change in one's view of the self-concept as a typically stable phenomenon to one that is fluid and readily molded by particular social contexts. For example, consider an 8-year-old boy who is a star hockey player and highly regarded by both his coach and teammates; within this context, his self-esteem is likely to be very positive. Within the context of school, however, where his academic performance is poor and he is unpopular with his classmates, his self-esteem is likely to be very low. The working self-concept, then, represents a continually active, albeit shifting, array of self-knowledge that is not all available at any one time (Markus & Nurius, 1987). Rather, it is triggered by a number of different circumstances, such as, for example, the immediate social milieu within which the individual is functioning. It thus becomes clear that because each of us views himself or herself from a multiplicity of perspectives, we necessarily harbor a host of possible selves. To facilitate any meaningful study of these possible selves, then, it becomes necessary to think in terms of the working (or active), rather than the usual latent (stable), self-concept.

Markus and Nurius (1986, 1987) empirically tested for the validity of possible selves with data derived from survey, experimental, and clinical studies. To assess possible selves, the researchers used two approaches: (a) Participants were asked to generate their own list of possible selves, and (b) participants were provided with a list of possible selves. In each case, participants were subsequently asked to indicate: (a) whether the item had described them in the past, (b) whether the item was ever considered as a possible self, (c) how probable the possible self was for them, and (d) how much they would like the item to be true for them. On the basis of their samples, Markus and Nurius found that all individuals possessed many possible selves. Furthermore, they were willing to fully describe the negative as well as the positive selves.[3]

---

3. Although Wylie (1989) noted that a detailed coding sheet is available from these researchers, I was not successful in my attempt to obtain one.

Computer-Based Testing

As we all know, only too well, the impact of computers on our everyday lives over the past 15 years or so has been nothing short of phenomenal. Indeed, within the educational system alone, the U.S. Department of Education reported an increase in the use of computers in schools from 18% in 1981 to 97% in 1990 (Educational Testing Service, 1993)! The past 5 years, in particular, have witnessed dramatic growth in the use of computers for testing purposes. Although most work to date has focused on achievement testing, endeavors are rapidly moving toward the inclusion of psychological testing as well. In this regard, the Buros–Nebraska Institute of Mental Measurements recently reported an increase in computerized psychological assessment measures from 4 to 400 between 1965 and 1990, a hundredfold increase (C. W. Conoley, Plake, & Kemmerer, 1991).

The term *computer-based testing* embraces three aspects of the testing enterprise: test administration, test scoring, and test interpretation (Butcher, Keller, & Bacon, 1985; Cohen et al., 1988). Of the three, computerized test scoring and interpretation have had the longest life span.[4] Note that these services are available to the test user for many self-concept measures described in the present volume. In contrast, use of computers for test administration purposes is relatively new and opens up endless possibilities for improving on the traditional paper-and-pencil format. Indeed, the advantages of computer-administered testing procedures would appear to outweigh, by far, the disadvantages. In the light of its newness and its potential for substantial impact on the administration of self-concept self-report measures, I limit my discussion here to the administration aspect of computerized testing. We turn now to a review of (a) the related advantages and disadvantages of this procedure, (b) responsibilities inherent in the use of computerized tests, and (c) existing computer-based versions of self-concept measures.

Advantages of Computer-Based Test Administration

The positive aspects of using computers in the administration of self-concept measures extend to the test developer, the test user, and the test taker.

---

4. Sweetland and Keyser (1991) listed close to 1,000 computer-scorable tests in psychology, education, and industrial/organizational development, with multiple scoring and interpretive services available for many of these tests. Furthermore, Wetzler and Marlowe (1994) noted that approximately 25% of clinical psychologists regularly use computer-scoring and interpretive services in their practice.

The Test Developer

Although the number of ramifications for the development of self-concept self-report instruments would appear to be boundless at this point, five of the most salient are noted here. First, computerized item stimulus displays can provide a very interesting and motivating alternative to the standard paper-and-pencil format. Second, given the possibility of item branching (the capability of the computer to tailor both the content and order of test items in accordance with preceding responses), the test developer can provide a wide range of questions that become progressively more specific in relation to particular variables of interest. For example, within the context of self-perceptions bearing on social competence with peers, these might include the more specific variables of classmates, friends in the same school, other students in the same school, friends in other schools, friends outside of the school, and the like. Third, item branching further allows for matching the reading level and language of the test taker to the content wording of the questionnaire. Fourth, given the wide range of available graphic and auditory software, the test developer has the capacity to simulate real-life situations and voice-activated responses. This particular feature of computer-based testing is expected to be especially fruitful in the development of self-concept measures for various exceptional populations, such as the hearing-impaired, visually impaired, and mentally handicapped. Finally, computer-based testing provides the test developer with almost limitless control over the duration of interitem response intervals.

The Test User

Aside from the obvious savings in time and cost in the computerized administration of tests (Butcher et al., 1985; Rogers, 1995), the test user can benefit from many other features. First, the computer is as patient and as unbiased as it is programmed to be, and material is always presented in exactly the same way with every administration of a particular test (Cohen et al., 1988; Wetzler & Marlowe, 1994). As a consequence, test bias arising from leniency and halo effects is expected to be virtually eliminated. Second, given the impartiality of both the administrator (the computer) and the test scorer (the computer), some (e.g., Mazzeo & Harvey, 1988) have speculated that the incidence of response bias should decrease substantially, particularly as it relates to social desirability. However, Finegan and Allen (1994), based on data from three independent samples of college students, reported findings of a slight increase in social desirability for respondents having little or no computer experience. Also, Butcher et al. (1985) raised the possibility of a new breed of response-set biases. Third, within the same context, some have predicted the possibility that the purposefulness of examinees' responses can be monitored. For example, presented with indicators that a test taker is responding in an inconsistent fashion, or is faking, the computer can be programmed to admonish him or her to be more careful or to prevent further responses until a purposeful one is given (Butcher et al., 1985; Cohen et al., 1988; Space, 1981). Finally, the test user can derive the benefits of speedier access to test scores, conversion of raw scores to standardized scores, and analyses of the data. Furthermore, because the examinee interacts directly with the computer, errors are necessarily reduced through the elimination of the intermediary data-entry step, and missing data are minimized as a consequence of the forced-response process.

The Test Taker

In general, the overall positive effects of computerized psychological questionnaires to the test taker are threefold. First, he or she is offered the opportunity to complete the questionnaire in a more comfortable setting that can include fewer people than would be the case with the administration of a traditional paper-and-pencil scale. Second, aside from the testing of students, for whom testing is typically administered in time-regulated periods within the academic institution, computerized tests can allow for more flexibility in terms of individual testing times and dates. Finally, reported findings from the use of psychological tests with examinees in both nonclinical (e.g., Elwood & Clark, 1978; Reardon & Loughead, 1988; Skinner & Allen, 1983) and clinical (e.g., Burda, Starkey, & Dominguez, 1991; Plutchik & Karasu, 1991) settings have indicated a preference for computer-administered rather than person-administered tests. This has been found to be particularly so when test takers are asked to respond to personally sensitive items (Plutchik & Karasu, 1991). Moreover, as noted by Simola and Holden (1992), this may be particularly advantageous when working with children who are often disinterested in completing traditional paper-and-pencil tests.

Disadvantages of Computer-Based Test Administration

Issues related to fairness in testing practices have precipitated a number of concerns with respect to computer-based tests. First, of prime concern has been the question of whether individuals who are computer literate have an unfair advantage over those who are unfamiliar with the use of a computer. However, findings from field studies conducted throughout the United States have demonstrated no significant difference in scores between computer-literate and computer-nonliterate test takers (Educational Testing Service, 1993). Indeed, these researchers argued that with a well-developed introductory tutorial, it is possible to teach individuals all that they need to know in several minutes. Furthermore, comparisons between performance scores based on a computer-administered test and a standard paper-and-pencil version of the same test yielded no significant differences (Educational Testing Service, 1993).

Second, there has been concern that computerized testing may be unfair to persons with physical disabilities that perhaps impede their ability to respond (e.g., defective motor skills or impaired hearing or vision). However, as noted earlier, the extensive graphic and auditory capabilities of computers can be programmed to accommodate these deficiencies (see, e.g., Butcher et al., 1985).

Finally, some have expressed concern that the computerized administration of tests may be perceived by test takers as a somewhat dehumanizing experience (Rogers, 1995). However, research findings to date have indicated precisely the opposite reaction. Indeed, as noted earlier, respondents have reported the completion of computerized self-report measures to be more interesting and relaxing than traditional paper-and-pencil versions. As noted by Wetzler and Marlowe (1994), "Computers never pass judgement, blush, retaliate or reject. Like the proverbial blank screen, they simply record" (p. 56). Herein may lie the clue to their growing appeal.

Responsibilities in the Use of Computer-Based Tests

Of course, these advantages and disputed disadvantages of computerized testing notwithstanding, both the test developer and test user must accept their responsibilities in validating these adapted instruments (see *Standards*, 1985). I now address these responsibilities.

Of particular import in the use of computerized tests, as with all adapted tests, is that the equivalency of their scores with those from a paper-and-pencil version of the same test cannot be assumed a priori; rigorous testing of this equality assumption must be conducted (Butcher et al., 1985; C. W. Conoley et al., 1991; Simola & Holden, 1992). Such construct validity research entails at least two modes of inquiry. First, in accordance with the *Standards for Educational and Psychological Testing*

(1985), any adaptation of a test to the computer automatically implies the development of a new test. As such, scores from this test must be validated in the same manner as would be required for a test that was translated into another language. Second, because of possible interaction effects between the medium of administration and the psychological construct being assessed, equivalence between computerized and paper-and-pencil versions of the same measuring instrument must be tested statistically. For example, Rogers (1995) noted that preliminary research in this area suggests that individuals tend to be more honest in their responses to a computer than to an interviewer. Such findings imply that scores from computerized versions of tests may differ from those based on traditional formats, thereby indicating nonequivalent measures of the same construct. In the face of such evidence, the onus is on both the test developer and the test user to establish either separate norms for each version of the test or a statistical correction (i.e., weighting) formula for scores for one of the two versions of the instrument (Cohen et al., 1988).

Computer-Based Self-Concept Measures

Computerized versions of self-concept instruments, until very recently, have been virtually nonexistent. Indeed, I am aware of only one well-established instrument (the Piers–Harris Children's Self-Concept Scale; Piers, 1984) for which computer-based administration has been made available. Accordingly, findings from a recent study of equivalency across the computerized and standard paper-and-pencil versions of the instrument for 279 children (8–17 years) demonstrated negligible administration-mode effects (Simola & Holden, 1992). These researchers concluded that computerized administration of the Piers–Harris scale did not affect its psychometric properties and, thus, that the two versions of the instrument may be regarded as equivalent.

More recently, as noted earlier in this chapter, Vispoel (1992, 1993b) is currently engaged in research that tests both the validity of scores derived from computerized versions of the Arts Self-Perception Inventory and the Music Self-Perception Inventory and their equivalence across the computerized and standard paper-and-pencil modes of administration. Although this form of self-concept measurement is presently sparse, my expectation is that owing to the boundless flexibility offered by this approach to self-concept measurement, we shall soon witness a flurry of activity in this direction.

In summary, these four innovative approaches to the study of self-concept offer alternatives that may be of great interest to many readers. Critically needed at this point, however, is a systematic program of research that tests for the construct validity and psychometric soundness of these methodologies and postulated self-concepts.

References

Anastasi, A. (1986). Evolving concepts of test validation. *Annual Review of Psychology, 37,* 1–15.

Anastasi, A. (1988). *Psychological testing.* New York: Macmillan.

Archambault, F. X., Jr. (1992). [Review of the Tennessee Self-Concept Scale (Revised)]. In J. J. Kramer & J. C. Conoley (Eds.), *The eleventh mental measurements yearbook* (pp. 931–933). Lincoln, NE: Buros Institute of Mental Measurements.

Arellano, O. R., & Chapman, J. W. (1992). Academic self-concepts among English- and Spanish-speaking Mexican-American students. *School Psychology International, 13,* 271–281.

Bandura, A. (1977). *Social learning theory.* New York: McGraw-Hill.

Bandura, A. (1982). Self-efficacy mechanisms in human agency. *American Psychologist, 37,* 122–147.

Bandura, A. (1986). *Social foundations of thought and action: A social cognitive theory.* Englewood Cliffs, NJ: Prentice Hall.

Bardos, A. N. (1991). *Relationship between the Multidimensional Self Concept Scale, Draw A Person: Screening Procedure for Emotional Disturbance, and the Emotional and Behavioral Problem Scale for a sample of emotionally/behaviorally disturbed children.* Manuscript submitted for publication.

Battle, J. (1977). Test–retest reliability of the Canadian Self-Esteem Inventory for Children. *Psychological Reports, 38,* 1343–1345.

Battle, J. (1979). Self-esteem of students in regular and special classes. *Psychological Reports, 44,* 212–214.

Battle, J. (1981). *Culture-free self-esteem inventories.* Austin, TX: Pro-Ed.

Benson, J., & Hocevar, D. (1985). The impact of item phrasing on the validity of attitude scales for elementary school children. *Journal of Educational Measurement, 22,* 231–240.

Benson, J., & Rentsch, J. (1988). Testing the dimensionality of the Piers–Harris Children's Self-Concept Scale. *Educational and Psychological Measurement, 48,* 615–626.

Bentler, P. M. (1972a). [Review of the Piers–Harris Children's Self-Concept Scale]. In O. K. Buros (Ed.), *The seventh mental measurements yearbook* (pp. 306–307). Highland Park, NJ: Gryphon Press.

Bentler, P. M. (1972b). [Review of the Tennessee Self Concept Scale]. In O. K. Buros (Ed.), *The seventh mental measurements yearbook* (pp. 366–367). Highland Park, NJ: Gryphon Press.

Bentler, P. M. (1978). The interdependence of theory, methodology, and empirical data: Causal modeling as an approach to construct validity. In D. B. Kandel (Ed.), *Longitudinal research on drug use: Empirical findings and methodological issues* (pp. 267–302). New York: Wiley.

Biddle, S., Page, A., Ashford, B., Jennings, D., Brooke, R., & Fox, K. (1993). Assessment of children's physical self-perception. *International Journal of Adolescence and Youth, 4,* 93–109.

Bills, R. E. (1975). *A system for assessing affectivity.* University, AL: University of Alabama Press.

Blascovich, J., & Tomaka, J. (1991). Measures of self-esteem. In J. P. Robinson, P. R. Shaver, & L. S. Wrightsman (Eds.), *Measures of personality and social psychological attitudes* (pp. 115–160). San Diego: Academic Press.

Bledsoe, J. C. (1964). Self concepts of children and their intelligence, achievement, interests, and anxiety. *Journal of Individual Psychology, 20,* 55–58.

Bloom, B. S. (1976). *Human characteristics and school learning.* New York: McGraw-Hill.

Boersma, F. J., & Chapman, J. W. (1979). *The Student's Perception of Ability Scale: Manual.* Edmonton, Alberta, Canada: University of Alberta.

Boersma, F. J., & Chapman, J. W. (1984). *The Student's Perception of Ability Scale: Revised manual.* Edmonton, Alberta, Canada: University of Alberta.

Boersma, F. J., & Chapman, J. W. (1992). *Perception of Ability Scale for Students: Manual.* Los Angeles: Western Psychological Services.

Bogan, J. (1988). The assessment of self-esteem: A cautionary note. *Australian Psychologist, 23,* 383–389.

Boggs, S. R., & Eyberg, S. (1990). Interview techniques and establishing rapport. In A. M. La Greca (Ed.), *Through the eyes of the child: Obtaining self-reports from children and adolescents* (pp. 85–108). Boston: Allyn & Bacon.

Bolea, A. S., Felker, D. W., & Barnes, M. (1971). A pictorial self-concept scale for children in K–4. *Journal of Educational Measurement, 8,* 223–224.

Bollen, K. A. (1989). *Structural equations with latent variables.* New York: Wiley.

Borgatta, E. F., Kercher, K., & Stull, D. E. (1986). A cautionary note on the use of principal components analysis. *Sociological Methods & Research, 15,* 160–168.

Bracken, B. A. (1992). *Multidimensional Self Concept Scale.* Austin, TX: Pro-Ed.

Bracken, B. A., Bunch, S., & Keith, T. Z. (1992, August). *Factor analysis of five self-concept scales.* Paper presented at the American Psychological Association Annual Meeting, Washington, DC.

Bracken, B. A., & Howell, K. K. (1991). Multidimensional self-concept validation: A three-instrument investigation. *Journal of Psychoeducational Assessment, 9,* 319–328.

Bracken, B. A., & Kelley, P. (in press). *Assessment of interpersonal relations.* Austin, TX: Pro-Ed.

Bracken, B. A., & Mills, B. C. (1994). School counselor's assessment of self-concept: A comprehensive review of 10 instruments. *The School Counselor, 42,* 14–31.

Breytspraak, L. M., & George, L. K. (1979). Measurement of self-concept and self-esteem in older people: State of the art. *Experimental Aging Research, 5,* 137–148.

Breytspraak, L. M., & George, L. K. (1982). Self-concept and self-esteem. In D. J. Mangen & W. A. Peterson (Eds.), *Research instruments in social gerontology: Vol. 1. Clinical and social psychology* (pp. 241–302). Minneapolis: University of Minnesota Press.

Brinthaupt, T. M., & Erwin, L. J. (1992). Reporting about the self: Issues and implications. In T. M. Brinthaupt & R. P. Lipka (Eds.), *The self: Definitional and methodological issues* (pp. 137–171). Albany: State University of New York Press.

Brinthaupt, T. M., & Lipka, R. P. (1985). Developmental differences in self-concept and self-esteem among kindergarten through twelfth grade students. *Child Study Journal, 15,* 207–221.

Brookover, W. B. (1962). *Self-Concept of Ability Scale*. East Lansing, MI: Education Publication Services.

Brown, L., & Alexander, J. (1991). *Self-Esteem Index: Examiner's manual*. Austin, TX: Pro-Ed.

Brown, R. D. (1992). [Review of the Self-Perception Profile for College Students]. In J. J. Kramer & J. C. Conoley (Eds.), *The eleventh mental measurements yearbook* (pp. 813–815). Lincoln, NE: Buros Institute of Mental Measurements.

Bugental, J. F. T., & Zelen, S. L. (1950). Investigations into the self-concept: The W-A-Y technique. *Journal of Personality, 18*, 483–498.

Burda, P. C., Starkey, T. W., & Dominguez, F. (1991). Computer administered treatment of psychiatric in-patients. *Computers in Human Behavior, 7*, 1–5.

Burns, R. B. (1979). *The self-concept: Theory, measurement, development, and behavior*. New York: Longman.

Buros, O. K. (Ed.). (1972). *The seventh mental measurements yearbook*. Highland Park, NJ: Gryphon Press.

Buros, O. K. (Ed.). (1978). *The eighth mental measurements yearbook*. Highland Park, NJ: Gryphon Press.

Butcher, J. N., Keller, L. S., & Bacon, S. F. (1985). Current developments and future directions in computerized personality assessment. *Journal of Consulting and Clinical Psychology, 53*, 803–815.

Byrne, B. M. (1983). Investigating measures of self-concept. *Measurement and Evaluation in Guidance, 16*, 115–126.

Byrne, B. M. (1984). The general/academic self-concept nomological network: A review of construct validation research. *Review of Educational Research, 54*, 427–456.

Byrne, B. M. (1986). Self-concept/academic achievement relations: An investigation of dimensionality, stability, and causality. *Canadian Journal of Behavioural Science, 18*, 173–186.

Byrne, B. M. (1988a). Measuring adolescent self-concept: Factorial validity and equivalency of the SDQ III across gender. *Multivariate Behavioral Research, 23*, 361–375.

Byrne, B. M. (1988b). The Self Description Questionnaire III: Testing for equivalent factorial validity across ability. *Educational and Psychological Measurement, 48*, 397–406.

Byrne, B. M. (1989). *A primer of LISREL: Basic applications and programming for confirmatory factor analytic models*. New York: Springer-Verlag.

Byrne, B. M. (1990). Methodological approaches to the validation of academic self-concept: The construct and its measures. *Applied Measurement in Education, 3*, 185–207.

Byrne, B. M. (1994). *Structural equation modeling with EQS and EQS/Windows: Basic concepts, applications, and programming*. Newbury Park, CA: Sage.

Byrne, B. M. (1996). Academic self-concept: Its structure, measurement, and relation with academic achievement. In B. A. Bracken (Ed.), *Handbook of self-concept: Developmental, social, and clinical considerations*. New York: Wiley.

Byrne, B. M., & Bazana, P. G. (in press). Testing for the construct validity of social and academic competencies for early/late preadolescents and adolescents: A multitrait–multimethod analysis. *Applied Measurement in Education*.

Byrne, B. M., & Goffin, R. D. (1993). Modeling MTMM data from additive and multiplicative covariance structures: An audit of construct validity concordance. *Multivariate Behavioral Research, 28*, 67–96.

Byrne, B. M., & Schneider, B. H. (1988). Perceived Competence Scale for Children: Testing for factorial validity and invariance across age and ability. *Applied Measurement in Education, 1*, 171–187.

Byrne, B. M., & Shavelson, R. J. (1986). On the structure of adolescent self-concept. *Journal of Educational Psychology, 78,* 474–481.

Byrne, B. M., & Shavelson, R. J. (1987). Adolescent self-concept: Testing the assumption of equivalent structure across gender. *American Educational Research Journal, 24,* 365–385.

Byrne, B. M., & Shavelson, R. J. (in press). On the structure of social self-concept for pre-, early, and late adolescents: A test of the Shavelson et al. (1976) model. *Journal of Personality and Social Psychology.*

Byrne, B. M., & Worth Gavin, D. A. (in press). *The Shavelson model revisited: Testing for the structure of academic self-concept across pre-, early, and late adolescents. Journal of Educational Psychology.*

Campbell, D. T., & Fiske, D. W. (1959). Convergent and discriminant validation by the multitrait–multimethod matrix. *Psychological Bulletin, 56,* 81–105.

Caracosta, R., & Michael, W. B. (1986). The construct and concurrent validity of a measure of academic self-concept and one of locus of control for a sample of university students. *Educational and Psychological Measurement, 46,* 735–744.

Carmines, E. G., & Zeller, R. A. (1979). *Reliability and validity assessment.* Beverly Hills, CA: Sage.

Chapman, J. W. (1988a). [Longitudinal cohort study of cognitive–motivational, affective, and achievement variables for students from Form 1 through Form 5]. Unpublished data.

Chapman, J. W. (1988b). Learning disabled children's self-concepts. *Review of Educational Research, 58,* 347–371.

Chapman, J. W. (1989, March). *The Perception of Ability Scale for Students: Results from accumulated research.* Paper presented at the American Educational Research Association Annual Meeting, San Francisco.

Chapman, J. W., & Boersma, F. J. (1980). *Affective correlates of learning disabilities.* Lisse, The Netherlands: Swets & Zeitlinger.

Chapman, J. W., & Boersma, F. J. (1991). Assessment of learning disabled students' academic self-concepts with the PASS: Findings from 15 years of research. *Developmental Disabilities Bulletin, 19,* 81–104.

Chapman, J. W., Boersma, F. J., & Maguire, T. O. (1977, June). *Some preliminary findings with the Student's Perception of Ability Scale: Implications for research with learning disabled children.* Paper presented at the Canadian Psychological Association Annual Meeting, Vancouver, British Columbia, Canada.

Chapman, J. W., & Tunmer, W. E. (1992). *Reading Self-Concept Scale.* Unpublished scale. Palmerston North, New Zealand: Educational Research & Development Centre, Massey University.

Chapman, J. W., & Tunmer, W. E. (1995). Development of young children's reading self-concepts: An examination of emerging subcomponents and their relationship with reading achievement. *Journal of Educational Psychology, 87,* 154–167.

Chapman, J. W., & Wilkinson, L. (1988). *Self-concept, identity status and emotional status of Form 5 learning disabled students: A longitudinal study of intermediate school predictors* (Department of Education Research Contract No. 47–17–151). Palmerston North, New Zealand: Massey University.

Chiu, L.-H. (1988). Measures of self-esteem for school-age children. *Journal of Counseling and Development, 66,* 298–301.

Cohen, R. J., Montague, P., Nathanson, L. S., & Swerdlik, M. E. (1988). *Psychological testing: An introduction to tests and measurements.* Mountainview, CA: Mayfield.

Collins, L. C., Kafer, N., & Shea, J. D. (1985). The Piers–Harris Children's Self-Concept Scale: An Australian study. *Australian Psychologist, 20,* 177–193.

Conoley, C. W., Plake, B. S., & Kemmerer, B. E. (1991). Issues in computer-based test interpretive systems. *Computers in Human Behavior, 7*, 97–101.

Conoley, J. C., & Kramer, J. J. (Eds.). (1989). *The tenth mental measurements yearbook.* Lincoln, NE: Buros Institute of Mental Measurements.

Cooley, E., & Ayres, R. (1988). Cluster scores for the Piers–Harris Children's Self-Concept Scale: Reliability and independence. *Educational and Psychological Measurement, 48*, 1019–1024.

Coopersmith, S. (1967). *The antecedents of self-esteem.* San Franciso: Freeman.

Cosden, M. (1984). [Review of the Piers–Harris Children's Self-Concept Scale]. In D. J. Keyser & R. C. Sweetland (Eds.), *Test critiques* (Vol. 1, pp. 511–521). Kansas City, MO: Test Corporation of America.

Cowan, R., Altmann, H., & Pysh, F. (1978). A validity study of selected self-concept instruments. *Measurement and Evaluation in Guidance, 10*, 211–221.

Crandall, R. (1973). The measurement of self-esteem and related constructs. In J. P. Robinson & P. R. Shaver (Eds.), *Measures of social psychological attitudes* (pp. 45–167). Ann Arbor: Institute for Social Research, University of Michigan.

Crocker, L., & Algina, J. (1986). *Introduction to classical and modern test theory.* Chicago: Holt, Rinehart & Winston.

Crocker, P. R. E., & Ellsworth, J. P. (1990). Perceptions of competence in physical education students. *Canadian Journal of Sport Sciences, 15*, 262–266.

Cronbach, L. J. (1951). Coefficient alpha and the internal structure of tests. *Psychometrika, 16*, 297–334.

Cronbach, L. J., & Furby, L. (1970). How should we measure "change"—Or should we? *Psychological Bulletin, 74*, 68–80.

Cronbach, L. J., & Meehl, P. E. (1955). Construct validity in psychological tests. *Psychological Bulletin, 52*, 281–302.

Crowder, B., & Michael, W. B. (1989a). The construct validity of a revised form of self-concept measure for employees in a work setting. *Educational and Psychological Measurement, 49*, 421–428.

Crowder, B., & Michael, W. B. (1989b). The measurement of self-concept in an employment setting. *Educational and Psychological Measurement, 49*, 19–31.

Crowder, B., & Michael, W. B. (1991). The development and validation of a short form of a multidimensional self-concept measure for high technology employees. *Educational and Psychological Measurement, 51*, 447–454.

Cullen, J. L., Boersma, F. J., & Chapman, J. W. (1981). Cognitive and affective characteristics of Grade Three learning disabled children. *Learning Disability Quarterly, 4*, 224–230.

Dale, E., & Chall, J. S. (1948). A formula for predicting readability: Instructions. *Educational Research Bulletin, 27*, 37–54.

Damon, W., & Hart, D. (1982). The development of self-understanding from infancy through adolescence. *Child Development, 53*, 841–864.

Davis, S. F. (1992). [Review of the Self-Perception Profile for College Students]. In J. J. Kramer & J. C. Conoley (Eds.), *The eleventh mental measurements yearbook* (pp. 815–816). Lincoln, NE: Buros Institute of Mental Measurements.

Delugach, R. R., Bracken, B. A., Bracken, M. J., & Schicke, M. C. (1992). Self-concept: Multidimensional construct exploration. *Psychology in the Schools, 29*, 213–223.

Demo, D. H. (1985). The measurement of self-esteem: Refining our methods. *Journal of Personality and Social Psychology, 48*, 1490–1502.

Dhawan, N., & Roseman, I. J. (1988, August). *Self-concepts across two cultures: India and the United States.* Paper presented at the 9th Conference of the International Association of Cross-Cultural Psychology, Newcastle, Australia.

Dobson, C., Goudy, W. J., Keoth, P. M., & Powers, E. (1979). Further analysis of Rosenberg's Self-Esteem Scale. *Psychological Reports, 44,* 639–641.

Dowd, E. T. (1992). [Review of the Tennessee Self-Concept Scale (Revised)]. In J. J. Kramer & J. C. Conoley (Eds.), *The eleventh mental measurements yearbook* (p. 933). Lincoln, NE: Buros Institute of Mental Measurements.

Eden, E. (1981). Factor analysis of a self-concept instrument for older adults. *Experimental Aging Research, 7,* 159–168.

Educational Testing Service. (1991). *The ETS test collection catalog: Volume 5. Attitude tests.* Phoenix, AZ: Oryx Press.

Educational Testing Service. (1992). *The ETS test collection catalog: Volume 6: Affective measures and personality tests.* Phoenix, AZ: Oryx Press.

Educational Testing Service. (1993). *Computer-based tests: Can they be fair to everyone?* (ETS Board of Trustees' public accountability report). Princeton, NJ: Author.

Ellis, B. B. (1989). Differential item functioning: Implications for test translations. *Journal of Applied Psychology, 74,* 912–921.

Elwood, D. L., & Clark, C. L. (1978). Computer administration of the Peabody Picture Vocabulary Test to young children. *Behavior Research Methods & Instrumentation, 10,* 43–46.

Epstein, J. H. (1985). [Review of the Piers–Harris Children's Self-Concept Scale]. In J. V. Mitchell (Ed.), *The ninth mental measurements yearbook* (Vol. 2, pp. 1168–1169). Lincoln, NE: Buros Institute of Mental Measurements.

Epstein, S. (1973). The self-concept revisited or a theory of a theory. *American Psychologist, 28,* 405–416.

Eysenck, H. J., & Eysenck, S. B. G. (1975). *Manual of the Eysenck Personality Questionnaire.* London: Hodder & Sloughton.

Fenigstein, A., Scheier, M., & Buss, A. (1975). Public and private self-consciousness: Assessment and theory. *Journal of Consulting and Clinical Psychology, 43,* 522–527.

Finegan, J. E., & Allen, N. J. (1994). Computerized and written questionnaires: Are they equivalent? *Computers in Human Behavior, 10,* 483–496.

Fitts, W. H. (1965). *Tennessee Self-Concept Scale: Manual.* Los Angeles: Western Psychological Services.

Flanery, R. C. (1990). Methodological and psychometric considerations in child reports. In A. M. La Greca (Ed.), *Through the eyes of the child: Obtaining self-reports from children and adolescents* (pp. 57–82). Boston: Allyn & Bacon.

Fleming, J. S., & Courtney, B. E. (1984). The dimensionality of self-esteem: II. Hierarchical facet model for revised measurement scales. *Journal of Personality and Social Psychology, 46,* 404–421.

Fox, K. R. (1990). *The Physical Self-Perception Profile manual.* DeKalb: Northern Illinois University, Office of Health Promotion.

Fox, K. R., & Corbin, C. B. (1989). The Physical Self-Perception Profile: Development and preliminary validation. *Journal of Sport and Exercise Psychology, 11,* 408–430.

Franzoi, S. L. (1994). Further evidence of the reliability and validity of the Body Esteem Scale. *Journal of Clinical Psychology, 1,* 237–239.

Franzoi, S. L., & Herzog, M. E. (1986). The Body Esteem Scale: A convergent and discriminant validity study. *Journal of Personality Assessment, 50,* 24–31.

Franzoi, S. L., & Shields, S. A. (1984). The Body Esteem Scale: Multidimensional structure and sex differences in a college population. *Journal of Personality Assessment, 48,* 173–178.

Freeman, R., Thomas, C., Solyom, L., & Hunter, M. (1984). A modified video camera for measuring body image distortion: Technical description and reliability. *Psychological Medicine, 14,* 411–416.

Friedman, A. G. (1992). [Review of Self-Perception Profile for Children]. In D. J. Keyser & R. C. Sweetland (Eds.), *Test critiques* (Vol. 9, pp. 472–479). Austin, TX: Pro-Ed.

Garner, D., Olmstead, M., & Polivy, J. (1983). Development and validation of a multidimensional eating disorder inventory for anorexia nervosa and bulimia. *International Journal of Eating Disorders, 2,* 15–34.

Garrison, W. M., & Tesch, S. (1978). Self-concept and deafness: A review of research literature. *The Volta Review, 80,* 457–466.

Gerken, K. C. (1985). [Review of Joseph Pre-School and Primary Self-Concept Screening Test]. In J. V. Mitchell (Ed.), *The ninth mental measurements yearbook* (Vol. 1, pp. 764–765). Lincoln, NE: Buros Institute of Mental Measurements.

Gibson-Harman, K., & Austin, G. F. (1985). A revised form of the Tennessee Self-Concept Scale for use with deaf and hard of hearing persons. *American Annals of the Deaf, 130,* 218–225.

Gill, D. (1993). Competitiveness and competitive orientation in sport. In R. N. Singer, M. Murphey, & L. K. Tennant (Eds.), *Handbook of research on sport psychology* (pp. 314–327). New York: Macmillan.

Goldman, B. A., & Osborne, W. L. (1985). *Directory of unpublished experimental mental measures* (Vol. 4). New York: Human Sciences Press.

Goldsmith, R. E. (1986). Dimensionality of the Rosenberg Self-Esteem Scale. *Journal of Social Behavior and Personality, 2,* 253–264.

Gorsuch, R. L. (1983). *Factor analysis.* Hillsdale, NJ: Erlbaum.

Gorsuch, R. L. (1990). Common factor analysis versus component analysis: Some well and little known facts. *Multivariate Behavioral Research, 25,* 33–39.

Gray, C. A. (1986). [Review of Joseph Pre-School and Primary Self-Concept Screening Test]. In D. J. Keyser & R. C. Sweetland (Eds.), *Test critiques* (Vol. 5, pp. 230–236). Kansas City, MO: Test Corporation of America.

Greenwald, A. G., Bellezza, F. S., & Banaji, M. R. (1988). Is self-esteem a central ingredient of the self-concept? *Personality and Social Psychology Bulletin, 14,* 34–45.

Guilford, J. P. (1969). *The nature of human intelligence.* New York: McGraw-Hill.

Guilford, J. P. (1985). The structure-of-intellect model. In B. B. Wolman (Ed.), *Handbook of intelligence* (pp. 225–266). New York: Wiley.

Halote, B., & Michael, W. B. (1984). The construct and concurrent validity of two college-level academic self-concept scales for a sample of primarily Hispanic community college students. *Educational and Psychological Measurement, 44,* 993–1007.

Hambleton, R. K. (1994). Guidelines for adapting educational and psychological tests: A progress report. *Bulletin of the International Test Commission* published in the *European Journal of Psychological Assessment, 10,* 229–244.

Hammill, D. D., Brown, L., & Byrant, B. R. (1992). *A consumer's guide to tests in print.* Austin, TX: Pro-Ed.

Hansford, B. C., & Hattie, J. A. (1982). Self measures and achievement: Comparing a traditional review of the literature with a meta-analysis. *Australian Journal of Education, 26,* 71–75.

Harrington, R. G., & Follett, G. M. (1984). The readability of child personality assessment instruments. *Journal of Psychoeducational Assessment, 2,* 37–48.

Hart, D. (1988). The adolescent self-concept in social context. In D. K. Lapsley & F. C. Power (Eds.), *Self, ego, and identity: Integrative approaches* (pp. 71–90). New York: Springer-Verlag.

Hart, D., & Edelstein, W. (1992). Self-understanding development in cross-cultural perspective. In T. M. Brinthaupt & R. P. Lipka (Eds.), *The self: Definitional and methodological issues* (pp. 291–322). Albany: State University of New York Press.

Harter, S. (1978). Effectance motivation reconsidered: Toward a developmental model. *Human Development, 1*, 34–64.

Harter, S. (1982). The Perceived Competence Scale for Children. *Child Development, 53*, 87–97.

Harter, S. (1983). The development of the self-system. In M. Hetherington (Ed.), *Handbook of child psychology: Social and personality development* (Vol. 4, pp. 275–385). New York: Wiley.

Harter, S. (1985a). Competence as a dimension of self-evaluation: Toward a comprehensive model of self-worth. In R. L. Leahy (Ed.), *The development of the self* (pp. 55–122). Orlando, FL: Academic Press.

Harter, S. (1985b). *Manual for the Self-Perception Profile for Children.* Denver, CO: University of Denver.

Harter, S. (1986). Processes underlying the formation, maintenance, and enhancement of the self-concept. In J. Suls & A. Greenwald (Eds.), *Psychological perspectives on the self* (Vol. 3, pp. 137–181). Hillsdale, NJ: Erlbaum.

Harter, S. (1988a). The construction and conservation of the self: James and Cooley revisited. In D. K. Lapsley & F. C. Power (Eds.), *Self, ego, and identity: Integrative approaches* (pp. 43–70). New York: Springer-Verlag.

Harter, S. (1988b). Developmental processes in the construction of self. In T. D. Yawkey & J. E. Johnson (Eds.), *Integrative processes and socialization: Early to middle childhood* (pp. 45–78). Hillsdale, NJ: Erlbaum.

Harter, S. (1988c). *Manual for the Self-Perception Profile for Adolescents.* Denver, CO: University of Denver.

Harter, S. (1990a). Causes, correlates, and the functional role of global self-worth: A life-span perspective. In R. J. Sternberg & J. J. Kolligian, Jr. (Eds.), *Competence considered* (pp. 67–97). New Haven, CT: Yale University Press.

Harter, S. (1990b). Issues in the assessment of the self-concept of children and adolescents. In A. M. La Greca (Ed.), *Through the eyes of the child: Obtaining self-reports from children and adolescents* (pp. 292–325). Boston: Allyn & Bacon.

Harter, S. (1990c). Processes underlying adolescent self-concept formation. In R. Montemayor, G. R. Adams, & T. P. Gullotta (Eds.), *From childhood to adolescence: A transitional period?* Newbury Park, CA: Sage.

Harter, S., & Pike, R. (1983). *The Pictorial Scale of Perceived Competence and Social Acceptance for Young Children* [procedural manual]. Denver, CO: University of Denver.

Harter, S., & Pike, R. (1984). The Pictorial Perceived Competence Scale for Young Children. *Child Development, 55*, 1969–1982.

Hattie, J. (1992). *Self-concept.* Hillsdale, NJ: Erlbaum.

Heilbrun, F. B. (1985). [Review of Dimensions of Self-Concept (DOSC)]. In J. V. Mitchell (Ed.), *The ninth mental measurements yearbook* (Vol. 1, pp. 507–508). Lincoln, NE: Buros Institute of Mental Measurements.

Heise, D. R., & Bohrnstedt, G. W. (1970). Validity, invalidity, and reliability. In E. F. Borgatta & G. W. Bohrnstedt (Eds.), *Sociological methododology 1970.* San Francisco: Jossey-Bass.

Hensley, W. E. (1977). Differences between males and females on the Rosenberg Scale of Self-Esteem. *Psychological Reports, 41*, 829–830.

Hensley, W. E., & Roberts, M. K. (1976). Dimensions of Rosenberg's Scale of Self-Esteem. *Psychological Reports, 38*, 583–584.

Hiebert, B., Wong, B., & Hunter, M. (1982). Affective influences on learning disabled adolescents. *Learning Disability Quarterly, 5*, 334–343.

Hines, L. L., Durham, T. W., & Geoghegan, G. R. (1991). Work self-concept: The development of a scale. *Journal of Social Behavior and Personality, 6*, 815–832.

Hogan, R., & Nicholson, R. A. (1988). The meaning of personality test scores. *American Psychologist, 43*, 621–626.

Howard, G. S. (1990). On the construct validity of self-reports: What do the data say? *American Psychologist, 45*, 292–294.

Hubbard, R., & Allen, S. J. (1987). A cautionary note on the use of principal components analysis: Supportive empirical evidence. *Sociological Methods & Research, 16*, 301–318.

Hughes, H. M. (1984). Measures of self-concept and self-esteem for children ages 3–12 years: A review and recommendations. *Clinical Psychology Review, 4*, 657–692.

Jackson, S., & Marsh, H. W. (1986). Athletic or antisocial: The female sport experience. *Journal of Sport Psychology, 8*, 198–211.

James, W. (1890/1963). *The principles of psychology.* New York: Holt, Rinehart & Winston.

Janzen, H. L., Boersma, F. J., Fisk, R., & Chapman, J. W. (1983). Diagnosis and predictability of learning disabilities. *School Psychology International, 4*, 129–140.

Jersild, A. T. (1952). *In search of self.* New York: Teachers College Bureau of Publications.

Jewell, D. A. (1989). Cultural and ethnic issues. In S. Wetzler & M. M. Katz (Eds.), *Contemporary approaches to psychological assessment* (pp. 299–309). New York: Brunner/Mazel.

Joseph, J. (1979). *Joseph Pre-School and Primary Self-Concept Screening Test.* Wood Dale, IL: Stoelting.

Joseph, J. (1986). Predictive validity study of the Joseph Pre-School and Primary Self-Concept Screening Test. In *Proceedings of the National Association of School Psychologists' Conference* (pp. 213–214). Hollywood, FL: NASP.

Juhasz, A. M. (1985). Measuring self-esteem in early adolescents. *Adolescence, 20*, 877–887.

Juhasz, A. M., & Munshi, N. (1990). "Faces and Feelings": A projective technique for measuring young children's self-esteem. *Perceptual and Motor Skills, 70*, 691–702.

Kaplan, H. B., & Pokorny, A. D. (1969). Self-derogation and psychosocial adjustment. *Journal of Nervous and Mental Disease, 149*, 421–434.

Kaplan, H. E., & Moon, R. L. (1987). Perceived competence and self-worth to emotionally disturbed children [Letter to the editor]. *Journal of American Academy of Child and Adolescent Psychiatry, 26*, 811.

Kelly, G. A. (1955). *The psychology of personal constructs.* New York: Norton.

Keyser, D. J., & Sweetland, R. C. (Eds.). (1992). *Test critiques* (Vol. 9). Austin, TX: Pro-Ed.

Koelle, H. W., & Convey, J. J. (1982). The prediction of the achievement of deaf adolescents from self-concept and locus of control measures. *American Annals of the Deaf, 127*, 769–778.

Kohn, M. L. (1969). *Class and conformity: A study in values.* Homewood, IL: Dorsey.

Kramer, J. J., & Conoley, J. C. (Eds.). (1992). *The eleventh mental measurements yearbook.* Lincoln, NE: Buros Institute of Mental Measurements.

Kugle, C. L., Clements, R. O., & Powell, P. M. (1983). Level and stability of self-esteem in relation to academic behavior of second graders. *Journal of Personality and Social Psychology, 44*, 201–207.

Kuhn, M. H., & McPartland, T. S. (1954). An empirical investigation of self-attitudes. *American Sociological Review, 19*, 68–76.

La Greca, A. M. (1990). Issues and perspectives on the child assessment process. In A. M. La Greca (Ed.), *Through the eyes of the child: Obtaining self-reports from children and adolescents* (pp. 3–17). Boston: Allyn & Bacon.

Larocque, L. (1996). *Preadolescent self-concept: Investigating the invariance of multidimen-*

sional-hierarchical covariance and mean structures across gender. Unpublished doctoral dissertation, University of Ottawa, Ottawa, Ontario, Canada.

Lawton, M. P., & Storandt, M. (1984). Clinical and functional approaches to the assessment of older people. In P. McReynolds & G. J. Chelune (Eds.), *Advances in psychological assessment* (pp. 236–276). San Francisco: Jossey-Bass.

L'Ecuyer, R. (1978). *Le concept de soi [The self-concept].* Paris: Presses Universitaires de France.

L'Ecuyer, R. (1981). The development of the self-concept through the lifespan. In M. D. Lynch, A. A. Norem-Hebeisen, & K. J. Gergen (Eds.), *Self-concept: Advances in theory and research* (pp. 203–218). Cambridge, MA: Ballinger.

L'Ecuyer, R. (1989, July). *Ages and stages in the development of the self-concept across the life span.* Paper presented at the 10th Biennial Meeting of the International Society for the Study of Behavioral Development, Jyväskylä, Finland.

L'Ecuyer, R. (1991, October). *The transformations of the self concept in elders aged 60 to 100.* An invited address presented for the Howard McClusky Symposium at the 40th Annual Adult Education Conference of the American Association for Adult and Continuing Education, Montreal, Quebec, Canada.

L'Ecuyer, R. (1992). An experiential–developmental framework and methodology to study the transformations of the self-concept from infancy to old age. In T. M. Brinthaupt & R. P. Lipka (Eds.), *The self: Definitional and methodological issues* (pp. 96–134). Albany: State University of New York Press.

L'Ecuyer, R. (1994, January). *The modifications of the hierarchical organizations of the self-concept from ages 3 to 100.* Paper presented at the NATO Advanced Research Workshop: "The self in European and North American culture: Development and processes," Crete.

L'Ecuyer, R. (in press). *Methodologie de l'analyse developpementale de contenu: Methode GPS et concept de soi [Method for analyzing developmental content: GPS method and self-concept].* Quebec City, Quebec: Presses de l'Universite du Quebec.

Lipsitt, L. P. (1958). A self-concept scale for children and its relation to the Children's Form of the Manifest Anxiety Scale. *Child Development, 29,* 463–472.

Loeb, R., & Sarigiani, P. (1986). The impact of hearing impairment on self-perceptions of children. *The Volta Review, 88,* 89–101.

Markus, H., Cross, S., & Wurf, E. (1990). The role of the self-system in competence. In R. J. Sternberg & J. J. Kolligian (Eds.), *Competence considered* (pp. 205–226). New Haven, CT: Yale University Press.

Markus, H. R., & Kitayama, S. (1991). Cultural variation in the self-concept. In J. Strauss & G. R. Goethals (Eds.), *The self: Interdisciplinary approaches* (pp. 18–48). New York: Springer-Verlag.

Markus, H., & Nurius, P. (1986). Possible selves. *American Psychologist, 41,* 954–969.

Markus, H., & Nurius, P. (1987). Possible selves: The interface between motivation and the self-concept. In K. Yardley & T. Honess (Eds.), *Self and identity: Psychosocial perspectives* (pp. 157–172). London: Routledge & Kegan Paul.

Markus, H., & Wurf, E. (1987). The dynamic self-concept: A social psychological perspective. *Annual Review of Psychology, 38,* 299–337.

Marsh, H. W. (1986a). The bias of negatively worded items in rating scales for young children: A cognitive–developmental phenomenon. *Developmental Psychology, 22,* 37–49.

Marsh, H. W. (1986b). Global self-esteem: Its relation to weighted averages of specific facets of self-concept and their importance. *Journal of Personality and Social Psychology, 51,* 1224–1236.

Marsh, H. W. (1986c). Negative item bias in ratings for preadolescent children: A cognitive–developmental phenomenon. *Developmental Psychology, 22*, 37–49.

Marsh, H. W. (1986d). Verbal and math self-concepts: An internal/external frame of reference model. *American Educational Research Journal, 23*, 129–149.

Marsh, H. W. (1987a). The factorial invariance of responses by males and females to a multidimensional self-concept instrument: Substantive and methodological issues. *Multivariate Behavioral Research, 22*, 457–480.

Marsh, H. W. (1987b). The hierarchical structure of self-concept and the application of hierarchical confirmatory factor analysis. *Journal of Educational Measurement, 24*, 17–39.

Marsh, H. W. (1989). Age and sex effects in multiple dimensions of self-concept: Preadolescence to adulthood. *Journal of Educational Psychology, 81*, 417–430.

Marsh, H. W. (1990a). The influence of internal and external frames of reference on the formation of math and English self-concepts. *Journal of Educational Psychology, 82*, 107–116.

Marsh, H. W. (1990b). A multidimensional, hierarchical model of self-concept: Theoretical and empirical justification. *Educational Psychology Review, 2*, 77–172.

Marsh, H. W. (1990c). The structure of academic self-concept: The Marsh/Shavelson model. *Journal of Educational Psychology, 82*, 623–636.

Marsh, H. W. (1992a). Content specificity of relations between academic achievement and academic self-concept. *Journal of Educational Psychology, 84*, 35–42.

Marsh, H. W. (1992b). *Self Description Questionnaire (SDQ) I: A theoretical and empirical basis for the measurement of multiple dimensions of preadolescent self-concept. A test manual and research monograph.* Macarthur, New South Wales, Australia: University of Western Sydney, Faculty of Education.

Marsh, H. W. (1992c). *Self Description Questionnaire (SDQ) II: A theoretical and empirical basis for the measurement of multiple dimensions of adolescent self-concept. An interim test manual and research monograph.* Macarthur, New South Wales, Australia: University of Western Sydney, Faculty of Education.

Marsh, H. W. (1992d). *Self Description Questionnaire (SDQ) III: A theoretical and empirical basis for the measurement of multiple dimensions of late adolescent self-concept. An interim test manual and research monograph.* Macarthur, New South Wales, Australia: University of Western Sydney, Faculty of Education.

Marsh, H. W. (1993a). Academic self-concept: Theory, measurement, and research. In J. Suls (Ed.), *Psychological perspectives on the self: The self in social perspective* (Vol. 4, pp. 59–98). Hillsdale, NJ: Erlbaum.

Marsh, H. W. (1993b). The multidimensional structure of physical fitness: Invariance over gender and age. *Research Quarterly for Exercise and Sport, 64*, 256–273.

Marsh, H. W. (1993c). Physical fitness self-concept: Relations to field and technical indicators of physical fitness for boys and girls aged 9–15. *Journal of Sport and Exercise Psychology, 15*, 184–206.

Marsh, H. W. (1993d). *Physical Self Description Questionnaire.* Macarthur, New South Wales, Australia: University of Western Sydney, Faculty of Education.

Marsh, H. W. (1993e). Relations between global and specific domains of self: The importance of individual importance, certainty, and ideals. *Journal of Personality and Social Psychology, 65*, 975–992.

Marsh, H. W. (1994a). The importance of being important: Theoretical models and relations between specific and global components of physical self-concept. *Journal of Sport and Exercise Psychology, 16*, 306–325.

Marsh, H. W. (1994b). Using the national longitudinal study of 1988 to evaluate theoretical models of self-concept: The Self-Description Questionnaire. *Journal of Educational Psychology, 86,* 439–456.

Marsh, H. W. (in press-a). The measurement of physical self-concept: A construct validation approach. In K. R. Fox (Ed.), *The physical self: From motivation to well-being.* Champaign, IL: Human Kinetics.

Marsh, H. W. (in press-b). Sport motivation orientations: Beware of jingle–jangle fallacies. *Journal of Sport and Exercise Psychology.*

Marsh, H. W., & Byrne, B. M. (1993). Do we see ourselves as others infer: A comparison of self–other agreement on multiple dimensions of self-concept from two continents. *Australian Journal of Psychology, 45,* 49–58.

Marsh, H. W., Byrne, B. M., & Shavelson, R. J. (1988). A multifaceted academic self-concept: Its hierarchical structure and its relation to academic achievement. *Journal of Educational Psychology, 80,* 366–380.

Marsh, H. W., Craven, R. G., & Debus, R. (1991). Self-concepts of young children 5 to 8 years of age: Measurement and multidimensional structure. *Journal of Educational Psychology, 83,* 377–392.

Marsh, H. W., & Gouvernet, P. (1989). Multidimensional self-concepts and perceptions of control: Construct validation of responses by children. *Educational Psychology, 81,* 57–69.

Marsh, H. W., & Hattie, J. (1996). Theoretical perspectives on the structure of self-concept. In B. A. Bracken (Ed.), *Handbook of self-concept: Developmental, social, and clinical considerations.* New York: Wiley.

Marsh, H. W., & Hocevar, D. (1985). The application of confirmatory factor analysis to the study of self-concept: First and higher-order factor structures and their invariance across age groups. *Psychological Bulletin, 97,* 562–582.

Marsh, H. W., & Holmes, I. W. M. (1990). Multidimensional self-concepts: Construct validation of responses by children. *American Educational Research Journal, 27,* 89–117.

Marsh, H. W., & O'Neill, R. (1984). Self Description Questionnaire III: The construct validity of multidimensional self-concept ratings by late adolescents. *Journal of Educational Measurement, 21,* 153–174.

Marsh, H. W., Parker, J., & Barnes, J. (1985). Multidimensional adolescent self-concepts: Their relationship to age, sex, and academic measures. *American Educational Research Journal, 22,* 422–444.

Marsh, H. W., & Peart, N. D. (1988). Competitive and cooperative physical fitness training programs for girls: Effects on physical fitness and on multidimensional self-concepts. *Journal of Sport Psychology, 10,* 390–407.

Marsh, H. W., & Redmayne, R. S. (1994). A multidimensional physical self-concept and its relations to multiple components of physical fitness. *Journal of Sport and Exercise Psychology, 16,* 43–55.

Marsh, H. W., & Richards, G. E. (1988a). The Outward Bound Bridging Course for low-achieving high school males: Effect on academic achievement and multidimensional self-concepts. *Australian Journal of Psychology, 40,* 281–298.

Marsh, H. W., & Richards, G. E. (1988b). The Tennessee Self-Concept Scales: Reliability, internal structure, and construct validity. *Journal of Personality and Social Psychology, 55,* 612–624.

Marsh, H. W., Richards, G. E., & Barnes, J. (1986a). Multidimensional self-concepts: A longterm followup of the effect of participation in an Outward Bound program. *Personality and Social Psychology Bulletin, 12,* 475–492.

Marsh, H. W., Richards, G. E., & Barnes, J. (1986b). Multidimensional self-concepts:

The effect of participation in an Outward Bound program. *Journal of Personality and Social Psychology, 45*, 173–187.

Marsh, H. W., Richards, G. E., Johnson, S., Roche, L., & Tremayne, P. (1994). Physical Self-Description Questionnaire: Psychometric properties and a multitrait–multimethod analysis of relations to existing instruments. *Journal of Sport and Exercise Psychology, 16*, 270–305.

Marsh, H. W., & Shavelson, R. J. (1985). Self-concept: Its multifaceted, hierarchical structure. *Educational Psychologist, 20*, 107–125.

Marsh, H. W., Walker, R., & Debus, R. (1991). Subject-specific components of academic self-concept and self-efficacy. *Contemporary Educational Psychology, 16*, 331–345.

Marx, R. W., & Winne, P. H. (1978). Construct interpretations of three self-concept inventories. *American Educational Research Journal, 15*, 99–108.

Marx, R. W., & Winne, P. H. (1980). Self-concept validation research: Some current complexities. *Measurement and Evaluation in Guidance, 13*, 72–82.

Mazzeo, J., & Harvey, A. L. (1988). *The equivalence of scores from automated and conventional educational and psychological tests: A review of the literature* (College Board Rep. No. 88–8). Princeton, NJ: Educational Testing Service.

McCrae, R. R., & Costa, P. T. (1988). Age, personality, and spontaneous self-concept. *Journal of Gerontology, 43*, S177–S185.

McGuire, B., & Tinsley, H. E. A. (1981). A contribution to the construct validity of the Tennessee Self-Concept Scale: A confirmatory factor analysis. *Applied Psychological Measurement, 5*, 449–457.

McGuire, W. J., & McGuire, C. V. (1982). Significant others in self-space: Sex differences and developmental trends in the social self. In J. Suls (Ed.), *Psychological perspectives on the self: The self in social perspective* (Vol. 1, pp. 71–96). Hillsdale, NJ: Erlbaum.

McGuire, W. J., & Padawer-Singer, A. (1976). Trait salience in the spontaneous self-concept. *Journal of Personality and Social Psychology, 33*, 743–754.

McNeely Foraker, B., & Michael, W. B. (1994). Reliability and construct validity of the Dimensions of Self-Concept (DOSC)–Form W measure for an Air Force sample. *Educational and Psychological Measurement, 54*, 409–416.

Messer, B., & Harter, S. (1986). *Manual for the Adult Self-Perception Profile.* Denver, CO: University of Denver.

Michael, W. B. (1992). [Review of the Pictorial Scale of Perceived Competence and Social Acceptance]. In J. J. Kramer & J. C. Conoley (Eds.), *The eleventh mental measurements yearbook* (pp. 671–672). Lincoln, NE: Buros Institute of Mental Measurements.

Michael, W. B., Denny, B., Ireland-Galman, M., & Michael, J. J. (1986–1987). The factorial validity of a college-level form of an academic self-concept scale. *Educational Research Quarterly, 11*, 34–39.

Michael, W. B., Denny, B., Knapp-Lee, L., & Michael, J. J. (1984). The development and validation of a preliminary research form of an academic self-concept measure for college students. *Educational and Psychological Measurement, 44*, 373–381.

Michael, W. B., & Smith, R. A. (1976). The development and preliminary validation of three forms of a self-concept measure emphasizing school-related activities. *Educational and Psychological Measurement, 36*, 521–528.

Michael, W. B., Smith, R. A., & Michael, J. J. (1975). The factorial validity of the Piers–Harris Children's Self-Concept Scale for each of three samples of elementary, junior high, and senior high students in a large metropolitan high school district. *Educational and Psychological Measurement, 35*, 405–414.

Michael, W. B., Smith, R. A., & Michael, J. J. (1978). Further development and validation of a self-concept measure involving school-related activities. *Educational and Psychological Measurement, 38,* 527–535.

Michael, W. B., Smith, R. A., & Michael, J. J. (1989). *Dimensions of Self-Concept (DOSC): A self-report inventory of five school-related factors of self-concept. Forms E, S, and H.* San Diego: Edits.

Miller, L. C., Murphy, R., & Buss, A. H. (1981). Consciousness of body: Private and public. *Journal of Personality and Social Psychology, 41,* 397–406.

Mischel, W., Zeiss, R., & Zeiss, A. (1974). Internal–external control and persistence: Validation and implications of the Stanford Preschool Internal–External Scale. *Journal of Personality and Social Psychology, 29,* 265–278.

Mitchell, J. V., Jr. (Ed.). (1983). *Tests in print: III.* Lincoln, NE: Buros Institute of Mental Measurements.

Mitchell, J. V., Jr. (Ed.). (1985). *The ninth mental measurements yearbook.* Lincoln, NE: Buros Institute of Mental Measurements.

Moskowitz, D. S. (1986). Comparison of self-reports, reports by knowledgeable informants, and behavioral observation data. *Journal of Personality, 54,* 294–317.

Mueller, J. H., Johnson, W. C., Dandoy, A., & Keller, T. (1992). Trait distinctiveness and age specificity in the self-concept. In R. P. Lipka & T. M. Brinthaupt (Eds.), *Self- perspectives across the life span* (pp. 223–255). Albany: State University of New York Press.

Neemann, J., & Harter, S. (1986). *Manual for the Self-Perception Profile for College Students.* Denver, CO: University of Denver.

Norwich, B. (1987). Self-efficacy and mathematics achievement: A study of their relation. *Journal of Educational Psychology, 79,* 384–387.

Nunnally, J. C. (1978). *Psychometric theory.* New York: McGraw- Hill.

Oblowitz, N., Green, L., & Heyns, I. de V. (1991). A self-concept scale for the hearing-impaired. *The Volta Review, 93,* 19–29.

O'Brien, E. J. (1985). Global self-esteem: Unidimensional or multidimensional? *Psychological Reports, 57,* 383–389.

Orme, J. G., Reis, J., & Herz, E. J. (1986). Factorial and discriminant validity of the Center for Epidemiological Studies Depression (CES–D) Scale. *Journal of Clinical Psychology, 42,* 28–33.

Oyserman, D., & Markus, H. R. (1993). The sociocultural self. In J. Suls (Ed.), *Psychological perspectives on the self: The self in social perspective* (pp. 187–220). Hillsdale, NJ: Erlbaum.

Page, A., Ashford, B., Fox, K., & Biddle, S. (1993). Evidence of cross-cultural validity for the Physical Self-Perception Profile. *Personality and Individual Differences, 14,* 585–590.

Pajares, F., & Miller, M. D. (1994). Role of self-efficacy and self-concept beliefs in mathematical problem solving: A path analysis. *Journal of Educational Psychology, 86,* 193–203.

Parish, T. S., & Rankin, C. I. (1982). The Nonsexist Personal Attribute Inventory for Children: A report on its validity and reliability as a self-concept scale. *Educational and Psychological Measurement, 42,* 339–344.

Parish, T. S., & Taylor, C. I. (1978). The Personal Attribute Inventory for Children: A report on its validity and reliability as a self-concept scale. *Educational and Psychological Measurement, 38,* 565–569.

Paulhus, D. L. (1991). Measurement control of response bias. In J. P. Robinson, P. R. Shaver, & L. S. Wrightsman (Eds.), *Measures of social psychological attitudes: Vol. 1: Measures of personality and social psychological attitudes* (pp. 17–59). San Diego: Academic Press.

Pelham, B. W., & Swann, W. B. (1989). From self-conceptions to self-worth: On the sources and structure of global self-esteem. *Journal of Personality and Social Psychology, 57*, 672–680.

Piers, E. V. (1963). [Factor analysis for the Piers–Harris Children's Self-Concept Scale]. Unpublished raw data.

Piers, E. V. (1973). [The Piers–Harris Children's Self-Concept Scale]. Unpublished raw data.

Piers, E. V. (1984). *Piers–Harris Children's Self-Concept Scale: Revised manual.* Los Angeles: Western Psychological Services.

Piers, E. V., & Harris, D. (1964). Age and other correlates of self-concept in children. *Journal of Educational Psychology, 55*, 91–95.

Plutchik, R., & Karasu, T. B. (1991). Computers and psychotherapy: An overview. *Computers in Human Behavior, 7*, 33–44.

Poortinga, Y. H. (1995). Use of tests across cultures. In T. Oakland & R. K. Hambleton (Eds.), *International perspectives on academic assessment.* Boston: Kluwer Academic.

Prout, H. T., & Chizik, R. (1988). Readability of child and adolescent self-reporting measures. *Journal of Consulting and Clinical Psychology, 56*, 152–154.

Reardon, R., & Loughead, T. (1988). Comparison of paper-and-pencil and computer versions of Self-Directed Search. *Journal of Counseling and Development, 67*, 249–252.

Renick, M. J. (1985). *The development of learning disabled children's self-perceptions.* Unpublished master's thesis, University of Denver, Denver, CO.

Renick, M. J. (1988). *Examining the self-perceptions of learning disabled children and adolescents: Issues of measurement and a model of global self-worth.* Unpublished doctoral dissertation, University of Denver, Denver, CO.

Renick, M. J., & Harter, S. (1988). *Manual for the Self-Perception Profile for Learning Disabled Students.* Denver, CO: University of Denver.

Reynolds, W. M. (1982). Development of reliable and short forms of the Marlowe–Crowne Social Desirability Scale. *Journal of Clinical Psychology, 38*, 119–125.

Richards, G. E. (1988). *Physical Self-Concept Scale.* Sydney, New South Wales, Australia: Australian Outward Bound Foundation.

Roberts, G. C. (1993). Motivation in sport: Understanding and enhancing the motivation and achievement of children. In R. N. Singer, M. Murphey, & L. K. Tennant (Eds.), *Handbook of research on sport psychology* (pp. 314–327). New York: Macmillan.

Rogers, T. B. (1995). *The psychological testing enterprise: An introduction.* Pacific Grove, CA: Brooks/Cole.

Roid, G. H., & Fitts, W. H. (1988). *Tennessee Self-Concept Scale* [revised manual]. Los Angeles: Western Psychological Services.

Roid, G. H., & Fitts, W. H. (1994). *Tennessee Self-Concept Scale* [revised manual]. Los Angeles: Western Psychological Services.

Rosenberg, M. (1965). *Society and the adolescent self-image.* Princeton, NJ: Princeton University Press.

Rosenberg, M. (1979). *Conceiving the self.* New York: Basic Books.

Rosenberg, M. (1989). *Society and the adolescent self-image* (rev. ed.). Middletown, CT: Wesleyan University Press.

Roth, D. L., Snyder, C. R., & Pace, L. M. (1986). Dimensions of favorable self-presentation. *Journal of Personality and Social Psychology, 51*, 867–874.

Savin-Williams, R. C., & Jaquish, G. A. (1981). The assessment of adolescent self-esteem: A comparison of methods. *Journal of Personality, 49*, 324–336.

Schmitt, N., & Bedeian, A. G. (1982). A comparison of LISREL and two-stage least squares analysis of a hypothesized life–job satisfaction reciprocal relationship. *Journal of Applied Psychology, 67,* 806–817.

Schmitt, N., & Stults, D. M. (1985). Factors defined by negatively keyed items: The result of careless respondents? *Applied Psychological Measurement, 9,* 367–373.

Schmitt, N., & Stults, D. M. (1986). Methodology review: Analysis of multitrait–multimethod matrices. *Applied Psychological Measurement, 10,* 1–22.

Schunk, D. H. (1985). Self-efficacy and classroom learning. *Psychology in the Schools, 22,* 208–223.

Sears, P. S. (1966). *Memorandum with respect to the use of the Sears Self-Concept Inventory.* Stanford, CA: Stanford Center for Research and Development in Teaching.

Secord, P. F., & Jourard, S. M. (1953). The appraisal of body-cathexis: Body-cathexis and self. *Journal of Consulting Psychology, 17,* 343–347.

Seeman, J. (1966). Personality integration in college women. *Journal of Personality and Social Psychology, 4,* 91–93.

Seltzer, M. (1975). The quality of research is strained. *The Gerontologist, 15,* 503–507.

Shahani, C., Dipboye, R. L., & Phillips, A. P. (1990). Global self-esteem as a correlate of work-related attitudes: A question of dimensionality. *Journal of Personality Assessment, 54,* 276–288.

Shavelson, R. J., & Bolus, R. (1982). Self-concept: The interplay of theory and methods. *Journal of Educational Psychology, 74,* 3–17.

Shavelson, R. J., Bolus, R., & Keesling, J. W. (1983). Self-concept: Recent developments in theory and method. *New Directions for Testing and Measurement, 7,* 25–43.

Shavelson, R. J., Hubner, J. J., & Stanton, G. C. (1976). Self-concept: Validation of construct interpretations. *Review of Educational Research, 46,* 407–441.

Shavelson, R. J., & Stuart, K. R. (1981). Application of causal modeling to the validation of self-concept interpretation of test scores. In M. D. Lynch, K. Gregan, & A. A. Norem-Hebelson (Eds.), *Self-concept: Advances in theory and research* (pp. 223–235). Cambridge, MA: Ballinger.

Shepard, L. A. (1979). Self-acceptance: The evaluative component of the self-concept construct. *American Educational Research Journal, 16,* 139–160.

Sheridan, S. M. (1992). [Review of the Pictorial Scale of Perceived Competence and Social Acceptance]. In J. J. Kramer & J. C. Conoley (Eds.), *The eleventh mental measurements yearbook* (pp. 672–673). Lincoln, NE: Buros Institute of Mental Measurements.

Silber, E., & Tippett, J. (1965). Self-esteem: Clinical assessment and measurement validation. *Psychological Reports, 16,* 1017–1071.

Simola, S. K., & Holden, R. R. (1992). Equivalence of computerized and standard administration of the Piers–Harris Children's Self-Concept Scale. *Journal of Personality Assessment, 58,* 287–294.

Skaalvik, E. M., & Rankin, R. J. (1995). A test of the internal/external frame of reference model at different levels of math and verbal self-perception. *American Educational Research Journal, 32,* 161–184.

Skinner, H. A., & Allen, B. A. (1983). Does the computer make a difference? Computerized versus self-report assessment of alcohol, drug, and tobacco use. *Journal of Consulting and Clinical Psychology, 51,* 267–275.

Slosson, R. L. (1963). *Slosson Intelligence Test (SIT) for children and adults.* New York: Slosson Educational Publications.

Snook, S. C., & Gorsuch, R. L. (1989). Component analysis versus common factor analysis: A Monte Carlo study. *Psychological Bulletin, 106,* 148–154.

Soares, A. T., & Soares, L. M. (1979). *The Affective Perception Inventory.* Trumbell, CT: Soares Associates.

Soares, A. T., & Soares, L. M. (1980). *Test manual: The Affective Perception Inventory.* Trumbell, CT: Soares Associates.

Soares, L. M., & Soares, A. T. (1983, April). *Components of students' self-related cognitions.* Paper presented at the American Educational Research Association Annual Meeting, Montreal. (ERIC Document Reproduction Service No. ED 228 317)

Soares, L. M., & Soares, A. T. (1986, April). *Construct validity of self-perceptions with international implications.* Paper presented at the American Educational Research Association Annual Meeting, San Francisco.

Song, I. S., & Hattie, J. A. (1984). Home environment, self-concept, and academic achievement: A causal modeling approach. *Journal of Educational Psychology, 76,* 1269–1281.

Sonstroem, R. J., Harlow, L. L., & Josephs, L. (1994). Exercise and self-esteem: Validity of model expansion and exercise associations. *Journal of Sport and Exercise Psychology, 16,* 29–42.

Sonstroem, R. J., Speliotis, E. D., & Fava, J. L. (1992). Perceived physical competence in adults: Examination of the Physical Self-Perception Profile. *Journal of Sport and Exercise Psychology, 14,* 207–221.

Space, L. G. (1981). The computer as psychometrician. *Behavior Research Methods and Instrumentation, 13,* 595–606.

Spielberger, C. D. (1992). Critical issues in psychological assessment. *Bulletin of the International Test Commission, 19,* 59–64.

Spielberger, C. D. (1995, July). *The need for guidelines for adapting psychological and educational tests.* Paper presented at the IV European Congress of Psychology, Athens, Greece.

SPSS, Inc. (1988). *SPSS-X User's guide.* Chicago: Author.

Standards for educational and psychological testing. (1985). Washington, DC: American Psychological Association.

Stanwyck, D. J., & Garrison, W. M. (1982). Detection of faking on the Tennessee Self-Concept Scale. *Journal of Personality Assessment, 46,* 426–431.

Stone, W. L., & Lemanek, K. L. (1990). Developmental issues in children's self-reports. In A. M. La Greca (Ed.), *Through the eyes of the child: Obtaining self-reports from children and adolescents* (pp. 18–56). Boston: Allyn & Bacon.

Strein, W. (1993). Advances in research on academic self-concept: Implications for school psychology. *School Psychology Review, 22,* 273–284.

Stunkard, A., Sorenson, T., & Schulsinger, F. (1983). Use of the Danish Adoption Register for the study of obesity and thinness. In S. Kety, L. Rowland, R. Sidman, & S. Matthysse (Eds.), *The genetics of neurological and psychiatric disorders* (pp. 115–120). New York: Raven Press.

Suls, J., & Mullen, B. (1982). From the cradle to the grave: Comparison and self-evaluation across the life-span. In J. Suls (Ed.), *Psychological perspectives on the self: The self in social perspective* (Vol. 1, pp. 97–125). Hillsdale, NJ: Erlbaum.

Sweetland, R. C., & Keyser, D. J. (1986). *Tests: A comprehensive reference for assessments in psychology, education, and business.* Kansas City, MO: Test Corporation of America.

Sweetland, R. C., & Keyser, D. J. (1991). *Tests: A comprehensive reference for assessments in psychology, education, and business.* Austin, TX: Pro-Ed.

Telzrow, C. F. (1985). [Review of Joseph Pre-School and Primary Self-Concept Screening Test]. In J. V. Mitchell (Ed.), *The ninth mental measurements yearbook* (Vol. 1, pp. 765–767). Lincoln, NE: Buros Institute of Mental Measurements.

Theodorson, G. A., & Theodorson, A. G. (1969). *Modern dictionary of sociology.* New York: Crowell.

Thomas, A., & Pashley, B. (1982). Effects of classroom training on LD students' task persistence and attributions. *Learning Disability Quarterly, 5,* 133–144.

Thomas, C. D., & Freeman, R. J. (1990). The Body Esteem Scale: Construct validity of the female subscales. *Journal of Personality Assessment, 54,* 204–212.

Thorndike, R. L., Hagen, E. P., & Sattler, J.P. (1986). *Technical manual for the Stanford-Binet Intelligence Scale* (4th ed.). Chicago: Riverside.

Thorndike, R. M., Cunningham, G. K., Thorndike, R. L., & Hagen, E. P. (1991). *Measurement and evaluation in education and psychology.* New York: Macmillan.

Tzeng, O. C., Maxey, W. A., Fortier, R., & Landis, D. (1985). Construct evaluation of the Tennessee Self-Concept Scale. *Educational and Psychological Measurement, 45,* 63–78.

Ulrich, D. A., & Collier, D. H. (1990). Perceived physical competence in children with mental retardation: Modifications of a pictorial scale. *Adapted Physical Activity Quarterly, 7,* 338–354.

Van de Vijver, F. J. R. (1995, July). *Topics in cross-cultural assessment.* Paper presented at the IV European Congress of Psychology, Athens, Greece.

Van de Vijver, F. J. R., & Poortinga, Y. H. (1992). Testing culturally heterogeneous populations: When are cultural loadings undesirable? *Bulletin of the International Test Commission, 19,* 37–39.

Vispoel, W. P. (1992). *The Arts Self-Perception Inventory.* Iowa City, IA: Author.

Vispoel, W. P. (1993a). The development and validation of the Arts Self-Perception Inventory for adolescents. *Educational and Psychological Measurement, 53,* 1023–1033.

Vispoel, W. P. (1993b). *The Music Self-Perception Inventory.* Iowa City, IA: Author.

Vispoel, W. P. (1995a). *The development and validation of the Arts Self-Perception Inventory for Adults.* Manuscript submitted for publication.

Vispoel, W. P. (1995b). Integrating self-perceptions of music skill into contemporary models of self-concept. *Quarterly Journal of Music Teaching and Learning, 5,* 42–57.

Vispoel, W. P. (1995c). Self-concept in artistic domains: An extension of the Shavelson, Hubner, and Stanton (1976) model. *Journal of Educational Psychology, 87,* 134–153.

Vispoel, W. P., Forte, E., & Bleiler, T. (1995, April). *The multifaceted, hierarchical structure of early adolescent self-concept.* Paper presented at the American Educational Research Association Annual Meeting, San Francisco.

Vogt, W. P. (1993). *Dictionary of statistics and methodology: A nontechnical guide for the social sciences.* Newbury Park, CA: Sage.

Walker, D. K. (1973). *Socioemotional measures for preschool and kindergarten children.* San Francisco: Jossey-Bass.

Walsh, J. A., Wilson, G. L., & McLellarn, R. W. (1989). A confirmatory factor analysis of the Tennessee Self-Concept Scale. *Criminal Justice and Behavior, 16,* 465–472.

Ward, R. A. (1977). The impact of subjective age and stigma on older persons. *Journal of Gerontology, 32,* 227–232.

Watkins, D. (1988). Components of self-esteem of children from a deprived cross-cultural background. *Social Behavior and Personality, 16,* 1–3.

Watkins, D., & Akande, A. (1992). The internal structure of the Self Description Questionnaire: A Nigerian investigation. *British Journal of Educational Psychology, 62,* 120–125.

Watkins, D., Alabaster, M., & Freemantle, S. (1988). Assessing the self-esteem of New Zealand adolescents. *New Zealand Journal of Psychology, 17,* 32–35.

Watkins, D., & Dhawan, N. (1989). Do we need to distinguish the constructs of self-concept and self-esteem? *Journal of Social Behavior and Personality, 4,* 555–562.

Watkins, D., & Dong, Q. (1994). Assessing the self-esteem of Chinese school children. *Educational Psychology, 14,* 129–137.

Watkins, D., Hattie, J., & Regmi, M. (1994). The structure of self-esteem of Nepalese children. *Psychological Reports, 74,* 832–834.

Watkins, D., Lam, M. K., & Regmi, M. (1991). Cross-cultural assessment of self-esteem: A Nepalese investigation. *Psychologia: An International Journal of Psychology in the Orient, 34,* 98–108.

Watkins, D., & Mpofu, E. (1994). Some Zimbabwean evidence of the internal structure of the Self Description Questionnaire I. *Educational and Psychological Measurement, 54,* 967–972.

Watkins, D., & Regmi, M. (1993). The basis of self-esteem of urban and rural Nepalese children. *Journal of Social Psychology, 2,* 255–257.

Wechsler, D. (1974). *Manual for the Wechsler Intelligence Scale for Children* (rev. ed.). New York: Psychological Corporation.

Wells, L. E., & Marwell, G. (1976). *Self-esteem: Its conceptualization and measurement.* Beverly Hills, CA: Sage.

West, C. K., Fish, J. A., & Stevens, R. J. (1980). General self-concept, self-concept of academic ability and school achievement: Implications for "causes" of self-concept. *Australian Journal of Education, 24,* 194–213.

Wetzler, S., & Marlowe, D. B. (1994). Clinical psychology by computer?: The state of the "art." *European Journal of Psychological Assessment, 10,* 55–61.

Widaman, K. F. (1985). Hierarchically nested covariance structure models for multi-trait-multimethod data. *Applied Psychological Measurement, 2,* 1–26.

Winne, P. H., & Marx, R. W. (1981, April). *Convergent and discriminant validity in self-concept measurement.* Paper presented at the American Educational Research Association Annual Meeting, Los Angeles.

Winne, P. H., Marx, R. W., & Taylor, T. D. (1977). A multitrait–multimethod study of three self-concept inventories. *Child Development, 48,* 893–901.

Woodcock, R. W. (1978). Development and standardization of the Woodcock-Johnson Psycho-Educational Battery. Hingham, MA: Teaching Resources.

Woodcock, R. W. (1990). Theoretical foundations of the W-J-R measures of cognitive ability. *Journal of Psychoeducational Assessment, 8,* 231–258.

Wylie, R. C. (1968). The present status of self theory. In E. A. Borgatta & W. W. Lambert (Eds.), *Handbook of personality theory and research* (pp. 728–787). Chicago: Rand McNally.

Wylie, R. C. (1974). *The self-concept: A review of methodological considerations and measuring instruments.* Lincoln, NE: Buros Institute of Mental Measurements.

Wylie, R. C. (1979). *The self-concept: Vol. 2: Theory and research on selected topics.* Lincoln, NE: Buros Institute of Mental Measurements.

Wylie, R. C. (1989). *Measures of self-concept.* Lincoln, NE: Buros Institute of Mental Measurements.

Yachnick, M. (1986). Self-esteem in deaf adolescents. *American Annals of the Deaf, 131,* 305–310.

Yardley, K. (1987). What do you mean "Who am I?": Exploring the implications of a self-concept measurement with subjects. In K. Yardley & T. Honess (Eds.), *Self and identity: Psychosocial perspectives* (pp. 211–230). Chichester, England: Wiley.

Zimmerman, B. J., Bandura, A., & Martinez-Pons, M. (1992). Self-motivation for academic attainment: The role of self-efficacy beliefs and personal goal setting. *American Educational Research Journal, 29,* 663–676.

Zirkel, P. A. (1971). Self-concept and the "disadvantage" of ethnic group membership and mixture. *Review of Educational Research, 41,* 211–225.

Index

A

About the Author

Barbara M. Byrne holds the rank of Professor in the School of Psychology at the University of Ottawa, where she has been on the faculty since 1987. Subsequent to obtaining her PhD from the University of Ottawa in 1982, she worked as a research associate at the Child Study Centre, University of Ottawa; held a 1-year appointment in the Department of Psychology at Carleton University; held a 2-year postdoctoral fellowship in the Graduate School of Education at the University of California, Los Angeles (UCLA); and recently spent a 6-month sabbatical as visiting scholar in the Department of Psychology at UCLA.

Byrne's research interests focus on construct validation issues related to the structure and measurement of self-concept, burnout, and depression. Author of over 50 journal articles and 5 book chapters, she has also written *A Primer of LISREL Basic Applications and Programming for Confirmatory Factor Analytic Models* (1989) and *Structural Equation Modeling with EQS and EQS/Windows: Basic Concepts, Applications and Programming* (1994), two introductory books on the topic of structural equation modeling.